A Practical Guide to a Big Education

Other titles from Bloomsbury Education

Schools of Thought by David James and Jane Lunnon
Tackling Poverty and Disadvantage in Schools edited by Katrina Morley and Sean Harris
Creating Belonging in the Classroom by Zahara Chowdhury
Representation Matters by Aisha Thomas

A Practical Guide to a Big Education

Balancing Head, Heart and Hand

Edited by Sarah Seleznyov and Robert Lobatto

BLOOMSBURY EDUCATION
LONDON OXFORD NEW YORK NEW DELHI SYDNEY

BLOOMSBURY EDUCATION
Bloomsbury Publishing Plc
50 Bedford Square, London WC1B 3DP, UK
Bloomsbury Publishing Ireland Limited
29 Earlsfort Terrace, Dublin 2, D02 AY28, Ireland

BLOOMSBURY, BLOOMSBURY EDUCATION and the
Diana logo are trademarks of
Bloomsbury Publishing Plc

First published in Great Britain, 2026 by Bloomsbury Publishing Plc
This edition published in Great Britain, 2026 by Bloomsbury Publishing Plc

Text copyright © Sarah Seleznyov and Robert Lobatto and contributors, 2026

Sarah Seleznyov and Robert Lobatto have asserted their rights under the Copyright, Designs and Patents Act, 1988, to be identified as Authors of this work

Bloomsbury Publishing Plc does not have any control over, or responsibility for, any third-party websites referred to or in this book. All internet addresses given in this book were correct at the time of going to press. The author and publisher regret any inconvenience caused if addresses have changed or sites have ceased to exist, but can accept no responsibility for any such changes.

All rights reserved. No part of this publication may be: i) reproduced or transmitted in any form, electronic or mechanical, including photocopying, recording or by means of any information storage or retrieval system without prior permission in writing from the publishers; or ii) used or reproduced in any way for the training, development or operation of artificial intelligence (AI) technologies, including generative AI technologies. The rights holders expressly reserve this publication from the text and data mining exception as per Article 4(3) of the Digital Single Market Directive (EU) 2019/790.

A catalogue record for this book is available from the British Library

ISBN: PB: 978-1-80199-792-8; ePub: 978-1-80199-794-2

2 4 6 8 10 9 7 5 3 1 (paperback)

Cover design by James Fraser

Typeset by Lumina Datamatics Ltd
Printed and bound in Great Britain by TJ Books, Padstow, Cornwall

To find out more about our authors and books visit www.bloomsbury.com and sign up for our newsletters.
For product safety-related questions contact productsafety@bloomsbury.com.

Contents

Introduction 7

Part 1 **Leadership** 11

1. Leading for a Big Education: Building a culture of agency and creativity – Liz Robinson 13
2. Design thinking: School improvement that empowers stakeholders and designs more effective solutions – Matt Morden 21
3. What it means to be evidence-informed: How to engage teachers with evidence and help them to generate their own – Sarah Seleznyov 31
4. Developing teaching and learning: How professional development can build teacher agency and improve learning – Moray Dickson 41
5. Peer review: A better way to 'inspect' schools – Sarah Marriott and Tom Raw 51
6. Behaviour and culture: Exploring non-punitive approaches to relationship and culture building – Helen Gourley 59
7. Collaborative pastoral support: Teamwork to improve learner wellbeing and accelerate learning – Kathryn Puch 67

Part 2 **Curriculum** 75

8. Project-based learning: How interdisciplinary projects support knowledge, skills and competency development – Paddy Russell 77
9. Real-world learning: How preparation for the world of work can be built into the school curriculum – Chris Anders 89
10. Diversity, equity, inclusion and belonging: Ensuring that learners, parents and staff feel a sense of belonging – Andrea Silvain 97
11. Entrepreneurialism: How to construct a curriculum that develops learners' entrepreneurial spirit – Hayley Peacock 105
12. Citizenship education: Preparing young people to shape society – Seb Chapleau 113

13 **Health matters: A curriculum for health and wellbeing**
– Ben Levinson 121

14 **Lunchtimes: How lunchtimes can enable learning experiences for our young people** – Tim Stayner 129

Part 3 **Pedagogy** 137

15 **Play-based learning: Why play matters and how playful pedagogies improve learning** – Sarah Seleznyov 139

16 **Imagination matters: Shaping the conditions for creative learning experiences** – Tom Doust 149

17 **Outdoor learning: How outdoor learning can improve engagement and progression** – Gemma Goldenberg 157

18 **Oracy: Progressively developing learner talk to build confidence and raise attainment** – Daniel Thomas and Emily Thomas 165

19 **Mantle of the Expert: Using drama and role-play to bring learning to life** – Tim Taylor 177

20 **Design thinking as pedagogy: The importance of the Maker{Cycle} in practical subjects** – Alison Buxton 185

Part 4 **Assessment** 193

21 **Competency progression: How can we teach and assess transferable competencies?** – Robert Lobatto 195

22 **Learner profiles: Assessment that evidences the full breadth of learning** – Rosie Clayton and Fran Wilby 205

23 **Interdisciplinary qualifications: New qualifications for future-facing schools** – Bertie Cairns 215

24 **Beyond the curriculum: Qualifications that enable learners to explore their own lines of enquiry** – John Taylor 223

Conclusion 231
Networks supporting schools to develop a Head, Heart and Hand approach 234
Bibliography 236
Index 251

Introduction

What is a 'Big Education'? The authors of this book, who are largely based in the UK, share a vision for what education should and could be. This vision stems from a deep interrogation of the purpose of school: after 14 years of schooling, what do we want young people to be like, and what should they know and be able to do?

For those practising and writing about a Big Education, this vision has clear themes: the need to prepare our young people to live happy and successful lives, to make a positive difference to the people and situations with which they engage, and to be equipped to thrive in the world as it is and as it will become.

Reimagining the purpose of education has implications, of course, on what we then do – implications for every aspect of school life, from curriculum, to pedagogy, to culture, leadership and relationships.

The starting point is that a Big Education – an education of the Head, Heart and Hand – must include but also go beyond the historic view, which emphasises and prioritises Head, or academic learning, and the associated pursuit of academic qualifications. While we all recognise the importance of securing the best possible qualifications for learners in our schools so that they have the necessary passport they need for the next phase of their education or life, we believe that this, as an educational goal in itself, is insufficient.

This means that we cannot simply focus on an education of the Head. We also need to attribute equal value to the Heart and the Hand – offering learners a bigger education.

An education of the Heart considers the importance of learners' physical and emotional wellbeing and their capacity to develop healthy, secure and productive relationships and to have a sense of themselves and their identities, value and purpose. An education of the Hand can be conceptualised as making and doing things; the creative arts and physical pursuits sit here, alongside taking action and doing work that is not just 'for my teacher in my book'. This might include civic action, problem-solving and developing the associated mindsets and skills involved in collaborating with others, presenting ideas and working with different stakeholders.

The recent educational debate in many jurisdictions – and notably in the UK – has centred around a reductive set of dichotomies: traditional versus progressive, knowledge versus skills, direct instruction versus dialogic teaching. We believe that these are false dichotomies. Our model is Head AND Heart AND Hand, not Head OR Heart OR Hand. All are necessary, and none are sufficient without the others. The work, then, is to look in more sophisticated ways at the integration of these aspects: how they are balanced, designed to complement each other and contribute to furthering the broader aims of our school system.

Technological development increases apace, and we enter a time that some have termed the 'artificial intelligence era' (Marr, 2024). 'Truth' has become a contested context, and the rise of 'fake news' and the proliferation of social media become increasingly difficult to navigate (Sismondo, 2017). There are growing political divisions in nations across the world (Carothers and O'Donohue, 2019) and the problems that we need to solve are increasingly complex: the climate crisis, population mobility, wealth inequality and systemic racism (Kawa et al., 2021).

Most of us who work in schools have begun to realise that we are preparing learners for an unknown future, while in the main still using an approach to education that has changed little over the last few centuries. As we move into an increasingly unpredictable future, this book offers educators a pathway with which to reconsider the education that their school offers to its learners, to support them to cope with and tackle the challenges that this may present to them as adults. In practice, this involves considering the Head, Heart, Hand model in four areas: leadership, curriculum, pedagogy and assessment; these four areas represent the four parts of the book.

The chapters provide educators with practical guidance and tools. They include advice from and recount the real-life experiences of serving school leaders, so are credible and pragmatic about what can be achieved, and realistic about the challenges of trying to do this.

Each chapter introduces the author and their context, then describes the problem that they have tried to tackle and the solution that they have tested. Authors are honest about the successes and challenges that they have faced, and give plenty of practical tips that take into account the real-life conditions that we all experience in our schools. Every chapter also includes a short vignette by another school leader, to show that there is no one-size-fits-all solution in education – context matters, and the same aims can be achieved in different contexts using the same underpinning principles but with slightly different approaches. Finally, each chapter ends with some suggestions of further reading and a short series of questions that you might consider if you are thinking about making this change in your own context.

We hope that this book stimulates your thinking, offers you practical advice and can inspire colleagues. We are an outward-facing collaboration of schools and would love you to join us in our mission to offer all learners a Big Education: Head, Heart and Hand.

Sarah Seleznyov and Robert Lobatto
with thanks also to Kezia Lobatto

Rethinking Assessment: https://rethinkingassessment.com
Rethinking Leadership: https://bigeducation.org/rethinking-leadership
Rethinking School: https://bigeducation.org/rethinking-school

PART 1

Leadership

1 Leading for a Big Education: Building a culture of agency and creativity

LIZ ROBINSON

In this chapter, I will explore the role that leadership plays in creating a relational, inclusive culture at the school. Far too often, leadership is seen as being about having all the answers. Leaders feel that they have to be 'superheroes': knowing what to do in all situations, leading from the front and being able to 'help' people by giving them advice and solutions. I refer to this as 'pants-on-the-outside' leadership.

This chapter intends to offer a different mental model of what leaders should 'do' and 'be like', along with four tools that you can consider and apply in your own context to reshape your leadership culture.

The author

I am CEO of Big Education Trust, an organisation I co-founded as a place where those who believe in more radical change in the sector can come together, to collaborate, share, challenge and encourage one another. My time as the head at Surrey Square Primary School in South London developed my belief that schools can play a transformative role in children's lives and shaping whole communities. Social justice and wider change underpin my views that school simply must be about the whole child, the whole family and the whole community.

A different approach to leadership

Big Education's model of leadership is based on the view that we should always have the intention to empower those around us. As leaders, we help to create a vision for the school (Head leadership). It is important to support our staff to act, to think and to decide for themselves, by drawing on and building their own agency (Heart leadership). To bring this to reality, we have a codified set of ideas and tools (Hand leadership) called the Big 8. These are: connecting, contracting, acceptance, catalytic, confronting, advising, feeding back and theory. By developing skills in this way, leaders can intentionally build capacity in others, enabling them to do more and go further on their own in the future. The Big 8 are underpinned by robust evidence drawn from the field of psychology (Lucey et al., 2015).

The benefits of this balanced Head, Heart and Hand approach are significant, for both leaders and those with whom they work. We have found that when leaders use Head, Heart and Hand in balance, team members feel a greater sense of agency, stronger engagement with their work and, importantly, a stronger sense of responsibility for delivering what has been agreed. Leaders often benefit from a shorter queue (literal or metaphorical) at their door. This style of leadership is less directive, more empowering and less reliant on the all-knowing leader – what we might call 'pants-on-the-inside' leadership. This chapter focuses on four of the Big 8 tools, looking at each one in turn and then exploring examples of them in practice.

1. Relationships are key – connecting

The first tool, connecting, is the process of establishing, building, deepening and, at times, repairing relationships. For many, it is a very natural and instinctive thing to do, although some find it challenging. Connecting with others requires us to open up and share something of ourselves and, in the process, create trust. The act of sharing is an act of profound leadership – making ourselves vulnerable as an invitation to others to do the same. Sometimes, we open up and share with an expectation of reciprocation, only to be disappointed when the other person does not share back. While this can feel uncomfortable (I call it a self-disclosure hangover), it is something that we as leaders simply have to handle from time to time.

The technique that underpins connecting is appropriate, inclusive self-disclosure:

- **Appropriate:** Not too *much* information but also not too *little* information. British people can have a tendency to undershare, focusing on safe topics like the weather. So, for many, finding the appropriate level of sharing means opening up more than might be usual or habitual.
- **Inclusive:** This means making space for everyone to share. This can be done informally in conversation, through having an awareness of the flow and actively inviting others to share, as well as modelling that openness oneself. We can also structure this reciprocation in more formal settings, through a turn-taking protocol.

- **Self-disclosure:** This means that we share something meaningful about ourselves, which goes beyond the trivial and superficial and into who we really are. Of course, what we disclose is a personal matter – but the principle is that it is something meaningful and important. For those people who feel uncomfortable with this, it is a powerful point of reflection, which can raise awareness about the impact that it has on others and become something to work on in their own leadership.

My own journey with this is exemplified by the coming together of my more personal and private side ('Lizzie', as I am known to my closest family and friends) and the more public-facing ('Liz'). I developed the confidence to be more open and authentic, including, as an example, feeling that I could dress in ways that were my style rather than having to look 'suited and booted'. Lizzie and Liz became much more integrated and I relaxed into showing more of myself within the context of my work.

This has been impactful on many around me, making me more accessible and human; having the courage to share my vulnerabilities and challenges has opened up so many more authentic conversations and relationships. This includes sharing my experiences of being a mum in a leadership role, and the joys of cold water swimming as part of managing the symptoms of perimenopause. It is much less hard work than 'projecting' a certain image of myself; I show up as my whole self and this allows others to do the same.

Connecting activities and routines can easily be built into any organisation or team. Practical examples of connecting activities include:

- rounds at the start of meetings sharing a highlight of the holiday, something that inspired you that week or a time when you saw someone 'slay' (achieve something incredible!)
- paired activities reflecting on organisational values and how they resonate with you personally
- sharing your 'journey' to this place and time – where have you been and what has brought you here to this moment and this conversation?
- giving space at the start of a one-to-one meeting for a personal check-in
- asking each person to share an emoji in the chat at the start of a short online meeting, as a way of sharing where they are at.

Investing in connecting within teams is an important part of developing a sense of belonging and feeling included. Through enabling each team member to be seen as they are and accepted without judgement, a proactive culture of celebrating diversity and individuality can be fostered.

2. Making agreements – contracting

When I talk about creating relational cultures, where we show up as our whole selves, it can lead many to think that it is a free-for-all where anything goes. Nothing could be further from the truth. The key tool that makes this the case is what we call 'contracting'. This is about making agreements about our expectations of one another. The clearer and more invested we are in this process, the more likely we are to have effective and acceptable ways of working together.

There are many forms that such agreements can take: policies, meeting agendas, targets, action plans, team agreements and codes of conduct. The technique for contracting is based on:

- making sure that there is some authentic connection before you start – there needs to be some trust to allow for an open conversation
- being clear about your own boundaries and expectations before you start – what is OK for you in that situation?
- listening really carefully to each other's expectations and then leaning into any points of disagreement or misalignment
- unpicking the ideas and language to reach shared understanding and clarity about what is really meant – specificity is your friend in this process
- negotiating those points of difference in an open way, compromising where needed or accommodating different expectations where possible
- writing down what is agreed in detail
- returning frequently to the agreement to reflect on where you are – or are not – adhering to what was agreed.

These agreements are powerful in opening up candid conversations about ways of working and giving team members a sense of shared responsibility. By making them explicit and shared, they become 'talk-about-able', enabling all team members to contribute to sustaining and developing a working environment that *works*. Clear expectations help to create environments in which there is greater agency; making parameters clear offers others a clear zone of decision-making within which they can work.

3. Asking questions – being more catalytic

How do you respond when someone asks you a question? Would your default response be to answer it? If we go back to the superhero, 'expert leader' archetype, of course the answer would likely be 'yes'. As you develop a more empowering approach, that is something that will change. Very often, when someone is asking a question, they are really making a suggestion or testing out an idea or some new thinking for them. If we simply answer that question, we close down the opportunity for them to explore their thinking more fully.

A simple shift is to respond to questions with a question. This is the classic Socratic method. So, for example, if someone asks me, 'How can we make sure that the children walk up the stairs more calmly?', I might ask, 'What is your thinking about that?' This is the basis of the catalytic tool: acting to accelerate others' thinking through open questioning. This can then be followed up by summarising their thoughts so that they gain clarity on their own thinking.

As you start to respond to questions with a question, you may notice that they come to you with their own thinking more developed, ready to test ideas with you for your feedback, rather than expecting you to give them the answers – a more empowered culture in action.

4. Managing emotions – being acceptant

Our capacity to notice and process emotions in ourselves varies widely. This is true for different people and also within ourselves, depending on circumstances. There is much work being done in schools to support emotional regulation – and there is much that many adults could learn from the techniques that we teach children. While it is often simpler to suppress or ignore our emotions in the busy course of life, the first necessary stage is to raise our self-awareness and notice how we are feeling.

There are myriad approaches to support this, ranging from meditation techniques and mindfulness to exercise and relaxation techniques. Finding what works for you is key.

Once we have acknowledged the emotions, we can then regulate ourselves and more easily access our rational processing. By integrating the information about our emotional response along with our logical thinking, we can make considered decisions about our next steps and actions.

This process is captured in the powerful model shown in Figure 1.1, adapted from Schein (1999): the considered action model.

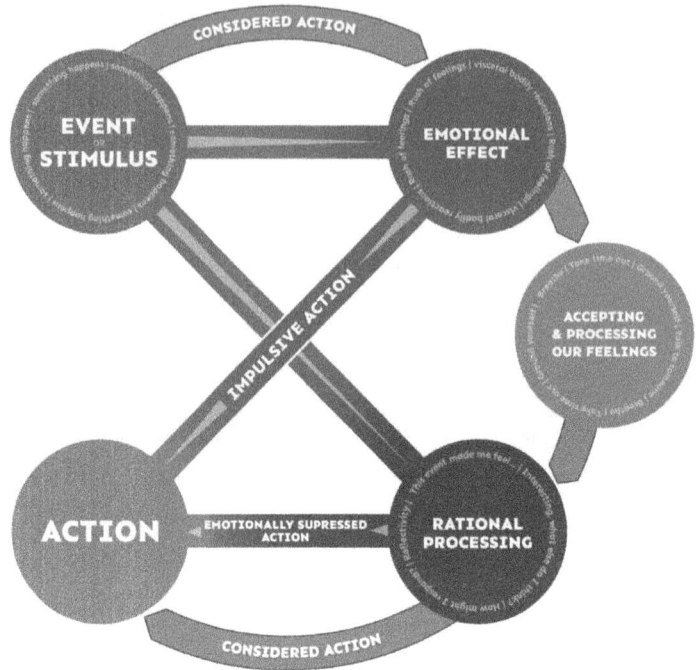

Figure 1.1: The considered action model (adapted from Schein, 1999)

Being able to identify, acknowledge and manage your own emotions is an important precursor to using the acceptant style with others, as is creating a high degree of psychological safety, allowing people the space to feel what they feel. The acceptant style involves simply listening and holding the space without needing to offer solutions. This is something that you may well need to actively practise, interrupting the (very common) instinct to problem-solve.

Challenges and successes

Integrating a new model of leadership can be a daunting task. This work requires individuals to engage in deep, reflective practice and to raise their awareness of the impact that their approaches have on others around them. The process of shifting towards a relational culture can take time and will require constant explanations of the why. In reality, many leaders have some of these tools already integrated into their work, but it is helpful to begin to use the language from this chapter to describe strategies that you are using, so that others are aware and can begin to build these same skills into their own practice.

We believe that this deep and slow change process is worthwhile. Making small changes over time can have a significant impact, building capacity across the whole school community. Making the changes detailed here will help you to be reflective and to notice the impact that your approaches have on those around you. These tools invite us each into an authentic dialogue with ourselves and others about the leader that we are and the leader that we might be. As Tolstoy (1900) wrote, everyone thinks of changing the world, but no one thinks of changing themselves. An education of the Head, Heart and Hand is only possible when leaders lead with Head, Heart and Hand. These tools from the Big 8 toolkit show us the way in which to achieve that.

Building a powerful leadership culture

Laura Ciftci, Headteacher, Jerounds Primary School

Since I have begun to use the transformative Big 8 coaching toolkit to empower our leaders with the skills and strategies needed to cultivate a relational and highly focused work culture, promoting innovation and fostering new thinking, we have created a workplace atmosphere that values collaboration, encourages new ideas and supports professional risk-taking.

We have used the approach to create a supportive environment where professional relationships are built, maintained and deepened. Central to this approach has been the principle of giving feedback effectively. Our ethos now ensures that feedback is constructive, compassionate and focused on growth, enabling staff to embrace opportunities for development without fear or defensiveness.

One of the most impactful elements of the toolkit has been its focus on professional accountability. We have coached leaders to hold others to account in a manner that is both firm and fair, balancing high expectations with empathy and understanding. As a result, leaders now navigate challenging conversations with confidence, ensuring that performance standards are upheld while maintaining trust and respect within teams – all highly effective for driving school standards and aspirations.

Similarly, the toolkit has promoted reflective practices at all levels at Jerounds – from teaching staff through to our cleaning staff. Through the use of structured coaching techniques, leaders and line managers now

> ask powerful questions, actively listen and guide their teams towards solutions that are both innovative and effective.
>
> Moreover, we have designed and implemented professional development to support our leaders to manage emotions – both their own and those of their colleagues – and this has helped to nurture a harmonious and productive work environment. This emotional intelligence has been pivotal in sustaining resilience, fostering wellbeing across the school community and retaining staff.
>
> These tools have been a game-changer for our school: enhancing the professional capabilities of our leadership team; transforming the culture and climate of our school; and building a place where staff and learners alike can thrive. We are grateful for this powerful development opportunity and look forward to continuing to embed its principles in our daily practice.

Questions to consider

- Where might there be more space for others to step up and take more ownership within your school?
- How intentional are your school about building trust and relationships? How might you increase this? Does everyone feel included, safe and 'seen'?
- How clear are our expectations? To what extent do you have agreements in place that are mutually agreed? How effective are they in shaping the conversations about quality and effectiveness?
- How likely are you to give answers rather than ask questions? How might you interrupt that pattern?

Further reading

Berger's dissertation 'Exploring the connection between teacher education practice and adult development theory' (2002)

Edmondson's article 'The role of psychological safety' (2019)

Rogers' book *On Becoming a Person: A therapist's view of psychotherapy* (1967)

Thomas and Kilmann's book *The Thomas-Kilmann Conflict Mode Instrument* (2002)

2 Design thinking: School improvement that empowers stakeholders and designs more effective solutions

MATT MORDEN

In this chapter, I explain the importance of empowering staff to be authentically involved in school improvement using the design thinking approach. I will share what design thinking is and how we have used it at Surrey Square to find effective solutions to problems.

> **The author**
>
> I have been working in primary education for over 20 years in schools in both Essex and London. I have taught across the primary phase and am currently headteacher of Surrey Square Primary School in South East London. Surrey Square serves a vibrant and diverse community, with 84 per cent of families in the lowest band on the IDACI deprivation index and 25 per cent living in temporary accommodation. The school is deeply committed to the wellbeing of the whole community, equipping learners to thrive and build a better world through its core values of responsibility, respect, enjoyment, community, perseverance and compassion.

The pressure of time

Schools are fast-paced environments where daily challenges often lead to leaders feeling pressured to solve problems quickly. This can result in less-effective solutions and leave staff feeling like decisions are imposed on them. Involving staff in the process offers an opportunity to build greater ownership and commitment. However, this approach is not without challenges. Time is the most precious resource in schools and, with competing demands such as lesson planning, assessment and professional development, finding opportunities to engage teachers in meaningful problem-solving is complex.

What is design thinking?

For us, design thinking is both a process (Hand) and a mindset (Heart). It encourages us to approach problems differently and use intentional strategies to develop new solutions. By spending more time with a problem and incorporating diverse perspectives, design thinking helps us to move beyond predictable and tired responses to the challenges that we often face.

A critical aspect of design thinking is its human-centred approach. It puts people at the heart of problem-solving and ensures that solutions are rooted in their experiences and needs. In summary, design thinking emphasises:

- **user-centricity and empathy:** listening to those affected by the problem in order to design meaningful solutions
- **collaboration:** bringing people together to generate diverse perspectives and ideas
- **experimentation and iteration:** testing solutions and refining them based on feedback
- **patience:** sitting with a problem longer than feels comfortable to uncover deeper insights.

We use the Double Diamond model (Design Council, 2019; Figure 2.1) to visualise and guide our design thinking process. The key stages include:

1 **Challenge – define the problem:** Clearly identify the challenge and formulate a concise problem statement.
2 **Discover – understand the problem and connect with people affected:** Gain deep insight into the problem by:
    - using tools like the root cause model

- empathising through conducting interviews with those affected
- horizon scanning to learn from other schools and organisations, to gain broader perspectives.

3 **Define – frame the challenge clearly:** Based on findings from the discovery phase, share the understandings gleaned with your team to ensure that decisions are based on strong, evidence-based insights. Collaborating during this phase helps to foster ownership and buy-in from key stakeholders. Use the 'How might we… ?' framework to refine the challenge into a more specific question. Facilitate a democratic discussion and vote on the most relevant question to pursue.

4 **Develop – generate solutions through inspiration and co-design:** The goal here is to ideate and generate as many solutions as possible: use ideation activities to encourage diverse thinking and remove barriers to creativity. Share all ideas, no matter how outside-the-box, and vote on the one with the most potential. Remember, the aim is to help people to freely generate as many ideas as possible, without criticism, no matter how crazy they may seem (Taylor et al., 1958).

5 **Deliver – test, refine and improve:** Prototyping and testing are crucial; build a prototype and test it with a small sample, such as one or two classes or year groups. Evaluate the impact of the solution, reject what doesn't work and refine what does. This cyclical approach ensures continuous learning and improvement while addressing the challenge effectively.

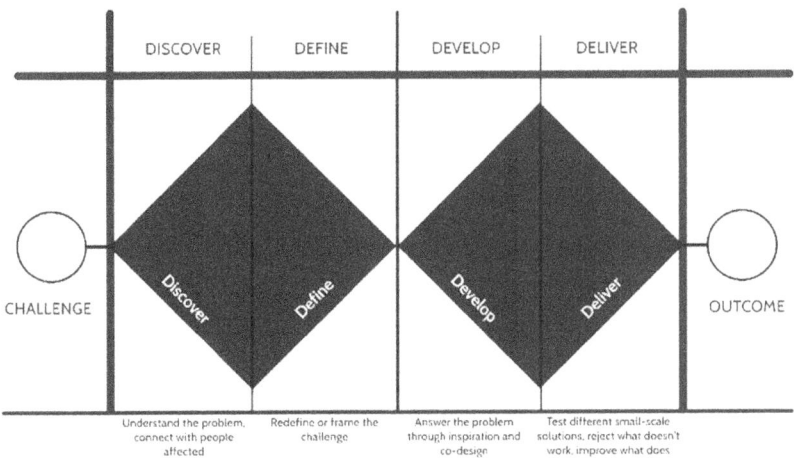

Figure 2.1: Double Diamond model (based on Design Council, 2019)

How we use design thinking

At Surrey Square, we mapped the design thinking process against our six core values to guide our approach. This has given us our six principles for school improvement:

- **respect:** truly listening to those affected by the problem
- **community:** bringing people along on the journey and empowering them
- **responsibility:** ensuring inclusivity in problem-solving
- **perseverance:** spending sufficient time with the problem
- **compassion:** designing empathetic solutions with those whom they impact
- **enjoyment:** finding joy in testing and iterating before scaling solutions.

We were focusing on developing our curriculum through the lens of inclusivity and decided to explore this more deeply through the design thinking process. We established five working groups, each aligned with an area of our school development plan related to creating a more inclusive curriculum.

Each group's work was framed by a problem statement, and staff were invited to select the group working on the statement about which they felt passionate. To ensure consistency, we embedded working group time into our weekly staff meeting cycle, structuring the sessions around the design thinking process.

Here is an example:

1. **Challenge:** We knew that not every child leaves Year 6 (10 to 11 years old) having had the same social and cultural experiences.
2. **Discover:** We identified barriers such as budget constraints, staff expertise and inconsistent prioritisation. Interviews with children, staff and parents highlighted varied experiences and expectations. We also explored external resources, including the National Trust's '50 things to do before you're 11¾' (www.nationaltrust.org.uk/visit/50-things).
3. **Define:** Key insights included the importance of trips in enhancing learning, creating lasting memories, reducing teacher workload through systemic planning and the need for equality in our offer. This led to questions such as: How might we ensure that there is an equal offer of essential enriching experiences for all children?

4. **Develop:** The working group generated multiple ideas and ultimately chose to create a progression booklet for children to complete, inspired by the National Trust resource.

5. **Deliver:** Initially, a prototype booklet for children was trialled with Year 1 (five to six years old) and Year 4 (eight to nine years old). Feedback revealed that it was overly complex, so the concept was adapted into a more practical teacher guide (Figure 2.2), mapping out key experiences for each year group. This guide is now successfully embedded across the school, supported by a commitment to dedicated planning time. During start-of-year inset days, an entire afternoon is allocated for teachers to use the guide to plan and book trips and experiences for the year. This time is highly valued and has led to a significant increase in the number of opportunities offered to children. This reflects the iterative nature of design thinking, with solutions refined through feedback to maximise their impact.

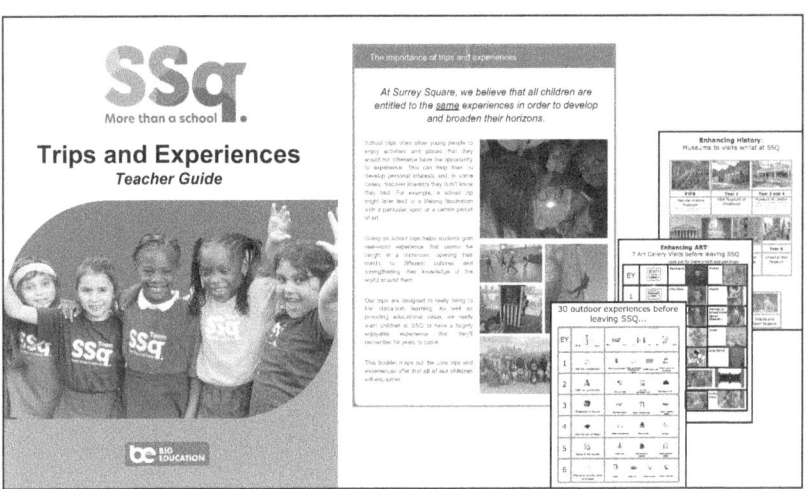

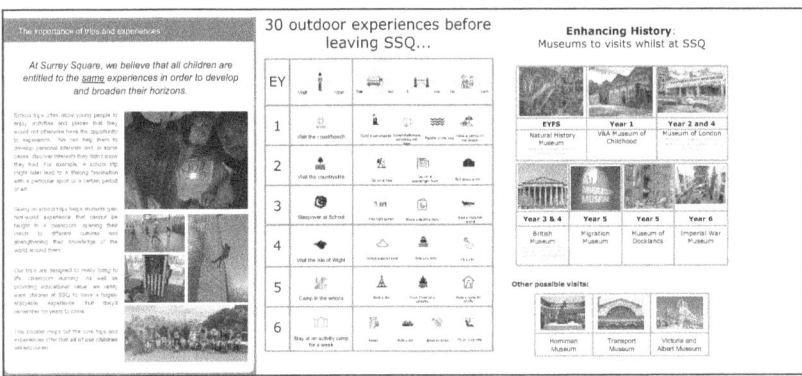

Figure 2.2: Surrey Square's *Trips and Experiences Teacher Guide*

The design thinking process is now embedded in our annual school development plan. Each leadership team member leads a working group dedicated to a specific aspect of the plan, with the senior leadership team (SLT) identifying areas where staff input would be most valuable and impactful. At the start of the year, SLT members pitch their groups and teachers sign up for the one that appeals to them most, ensuring motivation and ownership from the outset. The groups span a range of themes, such as EAL (English as an additional language) provision, sports equity and our Eco programme. One 90-minute staff meeting per half-term (six times a year) is dedicated to this work, and regular feedback and collaborative tuning in SLT meetings ensure alignment and progress across all groups.

Challenges and successes

One challenge with this process is balancing it alongside other areas of professional development so that it integrates smoothly into the school's broader priorities – something that we have addressed by embedding it into the school development plan and staff meeting cycle. It also requires staff to embrace the idea that this is not about quick fixes, but about taking time to understand and address problems in depth. Sitting with a problem for an extended period can feel uncomfortable, and sustaining momentum over the long term demands focus, energy and commitment. To address this, we use the Double Diamond model to help staff to embrace the slower pace, offering clarity on where we are in the journey and reassurance that they're on track. Regular progress updates from each group are shared in meetings, helping staff to see the bigger picture, celebrate achievements and feel the collective impact of their work.

Ensuring that all staff feel engaged is also critical. Some may find the collaborative approach daunting or struggle to see their role in the broader framework. Overcoming this requires clear communication, regular check-ins and confidence-building support. The iterative nature of design thinking means that there can be uncertainty or setbacks when prototypes fail, so we test ideas with one or two year groups before scaling up. This targeted approach allows staff to see solutions in action and recognise that refining or discarding ideas is valuable learning. Successful trials build confidence in full implementation, while less effective ones still strengthen professional curiosity and resilience.

At Surrey Square, we continuously refine and evolve our processes, incorporating feedback and reflecting on the impact of our actions. This ensures that our approach remains dynamic and responsive to the needs of our community. While our model is not fixed, we have already observed many significant benefits from working in this way.

One of the key advantages is a deeper understanding and stronger commitment to the areas that we are developing. By engaging with the process, our team gains valuable insights that lead to more thoughtful and effective solutions. Additionally, this approach has fostered a willingness to take risks, as a variety of outcomes are prototyped and explored.

We have also noticed a significant shift in mindset among our staff. By prioritising a slower, more people-centred approach that digs deeper into challenges and looks outwards for inspiration, we have cultivated a culture of curiosity and intentionality. This has transformed staff from being more passive participants to becoming actively engaged stakeholders, taking greater ownership of various aspects of school life. This has led to innovative solutions that may not have emerged through more traditional approaches. For example, the 'Diversity of Books' working group went beyond curating a list, instead rethinking how books are experienced in the classroom. Each class now displays a Top 100 Diverse Books on picture shelves, with covers facing outwards so that they are highly visible. This not only allows children to see themselves and their families reflected visually in the stories in their classroom environment every day, but it also sparks motivation to explore new books and recommend them to peers. The 100 books are carefully curated and form the year's class texts and novels.

Staff members feel empowered to contribute their unique perspectives, which enriches the problem-solving process. The collaborative nature of design thinking has also strengthened relationships among staff, fostering a greater sense of teamwork and shared purpose. Finally, the iterative process ensures that solutions are more thoroughly tested and refined, increasing their effectiveness and sustainability.

This iterative, reflective Head, Heart and Hand model empowers our community and strengthens our collective efforts towards meaningful and sustainable improvement.

Tackling teacher workload

Katy Rosser, Assistant Headteacher, Redriff Primary School

Our school had been in a two-year period of significant development in teaching and learning. Staff had worked tirelessly to research, innovate and drive improvement in teaching and learning, and by January 2024, learners, parents, staff and Ofsted concluded that the offer for our children was outstanding. We were at a point of reflection and celebration: we were taking a breath.

During this period of reflection, we conducted a staff survey to gain a deeper understanding of how staff were feeling. The survey revealed a strong feeling of togetherness, shared vision and unity among staff, but only 58 per cent of staff had positive feelings about workload.

We were not surprised by this finding. After a period of significant change, staff were finding the workload overwhelming. As a school passionate about supporting staff and thinking innovatively, we knew that we could not ignore this issue. As a recurring, deep-rooted issue that appeared impossible to resolve, we classified workload as a 'wicked problem' (Rittel and Webber, 1973).

What we did

To tackle this wicked problem, we used the design thinking model. During a training day, we led teaching staff through the Double Diamond design thinking process.

1 Our first stage was to *discover* the workload problem. For this phase, staff engaged in a talk task. In groups of four, they discussed what the workload problem meant to them. The *discover* stage encouraged honest sharing of personal experiences of workload. This gave us data about the workload problem and what it meant for our community.
2 After opening up the problem, next we used the *define* phase to converge ideas and refine our understanding. Staff were asked what contributed to workload and were encouraged to give honest, detailed answers. Staff then used critical and collaborative thinking to analyse which factors contributed most to workload.
3 At this stage, staff were encouraged to *develop* ideas to solve the workload problem. They were asked how they would solve the problem given unlimited resources and how things could be done differently. It was essential that staff were inspired to think innovatively at this stage. At the end of this ideation stage, staff were asked to vote for the ideas about which they were most excited.

4 The final stage was to *deliver* selected solutions. We recruited staff for a working group, ensuring that they could meet in their normal working hours. This group piloted, evaluated and implemented many solutions to help to solve the workload problem. These included: streamlining meetings; introducing 'golden week', with the final week of each term having no meetings so that teachers had more time for end-of-term assessments and to prepare for the next term; slide planning with notes, rather than completing additional planning pro formas; and updating the PPA (planning, preparation and assessment) space (including a coffee machine!) so that teachers could plan collaboratively in a peaceful and productive space.

Because the changes that the working group implemented came from the staff, they had a strong positive impact on staff feelings around workload. After nine months, 72 per cent of staff reported feeling more positive about workload. Perhaps most importantly, the design thinking process led to a shift towards greater staff empowerment. Staff now know that their voices are valued, understand that we should not shy away from wicked problems and the difficult feelings that come with these, and feel motivated to continue to find their own solutions.

Questions to consider

- How are stakeholders currently included in school improvement planning in your context?
- Do staff feel that they can influence and create change in your school?
- How can you shift the focus in your school from quick fixes to careful problem-solving processes?
- How can you build time into your school's schedule for authentic collaboration?
- What difference could collaborative problem-solving approaches make to the achievement of your school improvement goals?

Further reading

Brown and Katz's book *Change by Design: How design thinking transforms organizations and inspires innovation* (2019)

Hill's book *Dark Matter and Trojan Horses: A strategic design vocabulary* (2012)

IDEO's resource 'The field guide to human-centred design' (2015)

3 What it means to be evidence-informed: How to engage teachers with evidence and help them to generate their own
SARAH SELEZNYOV

In this chapter, I explain what it means to be evidence-informed through a Head, Heart and Hand lens, why and how we can enable teachers to engage in and with research, and how to value their own school-level data so that they can design changes to practice that really work.

> ### The author
> I have been working in inner-city schools for over 30 years as a teacher, headteacher, school improvement consultant, professional development lead and researcher. I currently work as Associate Headteacher at School 360, part of the Big Education Trust, while also finishing my PhD and working on a multitude of interesting education projects around the world.

Understanding and using data and evidence

Inside schools, we can sometimes have a very narrow 'Head' understanding of what 'evidence' and, specifically, 'data' mean. For many school staff, evidence is findings from research conducted by university academics, while data is numbers: assessment, attendance, behaviour tracking and test results. This narrow perspective on evidence means that we undervalue the much broader and often much more meaningful sets of data and evidence available to us.

Engaging with academic research is a good thing. Thanks to many calls for a closer relationship between research and practice, organisations like the UK's Education Endowment Foundation (EEF) have worked to make research material more accessible and digestible to teachers, through easy-to-read practice guides and research summaries, all freely available online. However, we still struggle to engage teachers with research evidence in ways that improve practice. All too often, I work with teachers who don't know or use the evidence, and either waste their time reinventing the wheel or implement changes that are not right for their learners.

Godfrey (2017) talks about 'evidence-based practice', where teachers are told to implement ideas that come from 'what works' evidence produced by academics, with little account taken of whether this new practice matches the needs of their community and their children. Instead, Godfrey advocates for 'research-informed practice', when teachers engage in and with both academic and practitioner forms of research, using evidence from both to make changes to their practice. In my experience, it is this kind of practice that has the biggest impact on teachers, since it gives them agency both to explore what works for them in their context and to generate new learning for other teachers to use.

If we are to do research-informed practice well, we need to expand our understanding of what 'evidence' is and could be. Over the last few decades, the EEF has promoted the idea that randomised control trials (RCTs) are the 'gold standard' of educational research (e.g. EEF, 2016). Biesta (2007), however, believes that this focus on RCTs and externally generated evidence is actually damaging, because of the importance of developing in teachers the skill and confidence to make professional judgements about whether an approach will work for them and their learners. Teachers are actually better placed than academics to conduct research because they are at the chalkface, seeing, hearing from and sensing the impact of any changes to practice on the people that matter: the learners.

Similarly, if we really want teachers to be data-informed, then we need to help them to rethink what 'data' is and how to gather it and use it to inform their work. Learners are more than their test scores. Teachers need to understand the value of the day-to-day, moment-to-moment anecdotal data that they gather: the things that people say, do and feel, and their opinions on what and how they are learning. They alone can make sense of the complex and sometimes contradictory data that they gather about learners and their learning.

So what does this look like on a practical level and how can we enable teachers to get involved?

Strategies to engage teachers with the evidence

Really reading the research

Teachers cannot easily access educational research and do not have time to read multiple journal articles to develop a deep understanding of an issue. However, only reading research overviews and blogs does not provide an in-depth understanding of a research field.

One way in which to tackle this is to turn journal articles into an engaging professional development activity. Drawn from Stoll and Brown's work on research engagement (2015), the 'strips activity' technique successfully enables teachers to engage with a large body of research and reflect on which of it has relevance or meaning for them. In our school, a keen reader (usually me!) selects 20 to 30 significant sentences or short paragraphs from journal articles. We print out these chunks of text on strips of paper, and teachers collaboratively discuss and cluster them into themes, comparing their classifications with other groups of teachers. This process can take between 60 and 90 minutes in a professional development session, depending on the number of strips, and makes sure that teachers fully understand and consider the importance of each strip.

Teachers are then asked which of the strips resonate with them. This helps them to develop their own lines of enquiry. When they are then provided with access to the underlying articles, they will often decide voluntarily to read the journal article from which it was drawn. In this way, teachers willingly engage with quite challenging and lengthy academic material.

Teachers are busy people, so professional development time needs to be allocated for reading. Leaders need to support teachers to read research collaboratively and encourage them to ask critical questions.

Of course, as any school leader knows, fully reading the evidence is only the first step. What really matters is using that evidence in the classroom.

Becoming a teacher-researcher

One of the best ways in which to make this happen is to engage teachers in cycles of iterative enquiry in their own classrooms. Hargreaves calls this 'tinkering' (1999), a process of 'haphazard trial and error' in the classroom. Timperley et al.'s model is of 'spirals of enquiry' (2014), involving repeated cycles of identifying and exploring problems, taking action and checking impact. Lesson study (Seleznyov, 2018) uses live classroom practice to engage teachers in collaborative cycles of research and reflection.

What do all these professional development approaches have in common? They encourage teachers to:

1. Engage with the evidence.
2. Have a group of learners in mind.
3. Generate a research question.
4. Gather baseline data to reveal the current situation.
5. Design a change to practice, based on this data and the evidence.
6. Implement the change with expert support, adapting it as it embeds.
7. Gather impact data to reveal what difference the change made.
8. Assess success and share with colleagues.
9. Plan for next steps.

Using the rich data available

When working on stages 4 and 7 of teacher research, it's important that teachers understand that 'data' is not just numbers. It's actually a much richer set of information that tells you the full story about what's happening for those learners. I love the work of Wenger et al. (2011), who argue that stories bring numbers to life and make them meaningful, while numbers act as a short-hand for sets of stories, and they are both stronger together:

> 'Many indicators without stories reflect too many assumptions. Many stories without indicators fail to cross-reference and reveal key… elements… It is the combination of data… with… stories that yields an integrated picture.' (pp. 37–38)

When I ask teachers to gather data, I help them to gain confidence in the value of their observations of learners. If they do want to formalise the gathering of

Table 3.1: The Leuven Scale for Wellbeing

Level	Wellbeing	Signals
1	Extremely low	The child clearly shows signs of discomfort such as crying or screaming. They may look dejected, sad, frightened or angry. The child does not respond to the environment, avoids contact and is withdrawn. The child may behave aggressively, hurting themselves or others.
2	Low	The posture, facial expression and actions indicate that the child does not feel at ease. However, the signals are less explicit than under level 1 or the sense of discomfort is not expressed the whole time.
3	Moderate	The child has a neutral posture. Facial expression and posture show little or no emotion. There are no signs indicating sadness or pleasure, comfort or discomfort.
4	High	The child shows obvious signs of satisfaction (as listed under level 5). However, these signals are not constantly present with the same intensity.
5	Extremely high	The child looks happy and cheerful, smiles, cries out with pleasure. They may be lively and full of energy. Actions can be spontaneous and expressive. The child may talk to themselves, play with sounds, hum, sing. The child appears relaxed and does not show any signs of stress or tension. They are open and accessible to the environment. The child expresses self-confidence and self-assurance.

such data, I support them to design their own tools, such as questionnaires and interviews, and to write good questions for each. If relevant, I show them how to code classroom transcripts so that they provide meaningful, measurable data. I teach them how to turn qualitative observations into numbers using tools like the Leuven Scale (Laevers, 1999) or how to design their own simple observation tools (see Table 3.1 and Figure 3.1).

Finally, I help them to triangulate the data: not valuing one piece more than another, not dismissing discrepancies, but considering the full rich picture of learners and their learning. Collecting and analysing data before designing and implementing any change, and then repeating the process as the change is implemented, helps to ensure that any change is well thought-through and can flex and improve over time. This rich and ongoing use of data is key to developing a researcher mindset in teachers.

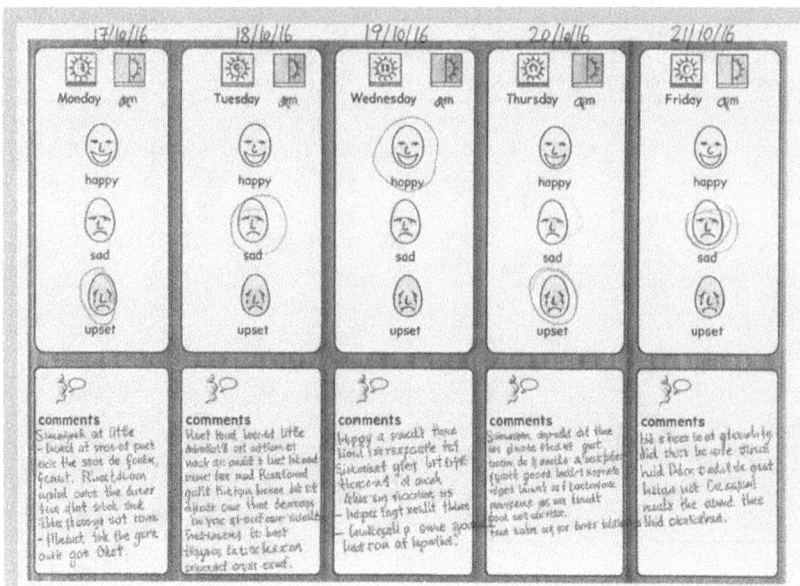

Figure 3.1: Example of a teacher-designed observation tool

Challenges and successes

Real professional development for teachers takes time, and that must be given during working hours. Critically, most professional development time does not contribute to teacher learning, since it is used for admin and compliance: rework this time and reallocate it to make space for teacher research, which really does support teacher learning. Research engagement needs to be led by someone who is passionate about it, someone who reads widely and has a curious mind. There is usually someone like this in every school: find them, give them a leadership role and provide them with the time and space in which to make it happen. As leaders, we need to have the courage to let teachers take risks. Any change to practice can cause a natural dip before it starts improving learning. Research is not a quick fix. You will not see a difference in attainment over a term or even a year, but if you are taking account of the richer dataset, you will see the roots of change; believe in their promise and you will see impact over time.

If you can hold your nerve and invest people and time, you will see a huge growth in teacher agency, motivation and confidence. Teachers who generate their own evidence through participating in collaborative enquiry projects are more likely to use research evidence to change their practice. These enquiry projects help teachers to own their problems, gain a deep understanding of potential solutions and develop their own evidence-informed solutions. They provide teachers with a better understanding of classroom learning and leaders with a richer dataset with which to support strategic planning and quality assurance of practice across the school.

Lesson study for whole school professional development

Tanya Roberts and Katie Bowles, Sandringham Primary

Lesson study (LS) has been used for several years as an approach to professional development at Sandringham Primary School. While looking for a model of professional learning that would give agency to members of staff, the school discovered LS and it soon became the perfect vehicle with which for teachers to successfully engage in research through classroom practice.

Previously, members of staff had engaged in research through study sessions. However, we found that LS made the research come alive by bringing it into the classroom. As Stigler and Hiebert write, 'If you want to improve teaching, the most effective place to do so is in the context of a classroom lesson.' (2009, p. 111) For us, LS does that job. Figure 3.2 explains our LS cycle.

We begin our cycle by identifying our focus. Our foci have varied over the years, depending on the needs of the school at that time. Relevant research is provided to our teacher teams, including extracts from chapters, relevant podcasts and activities/tasks to try with the focus learners. Time is given to all members of staff to complete their reading. Teams then come together and discuss their reflections, focusing both on what they agree with and on the challenges to their current thinking.

Once this has been completed, our teams produce baseline data, thinking about how things look in the classroom at the start of the process and about what learners and teachers hear, say, feel and do in their classrooms. They envision what they hope the impact will be at the end of the process. Each team produces a research question based

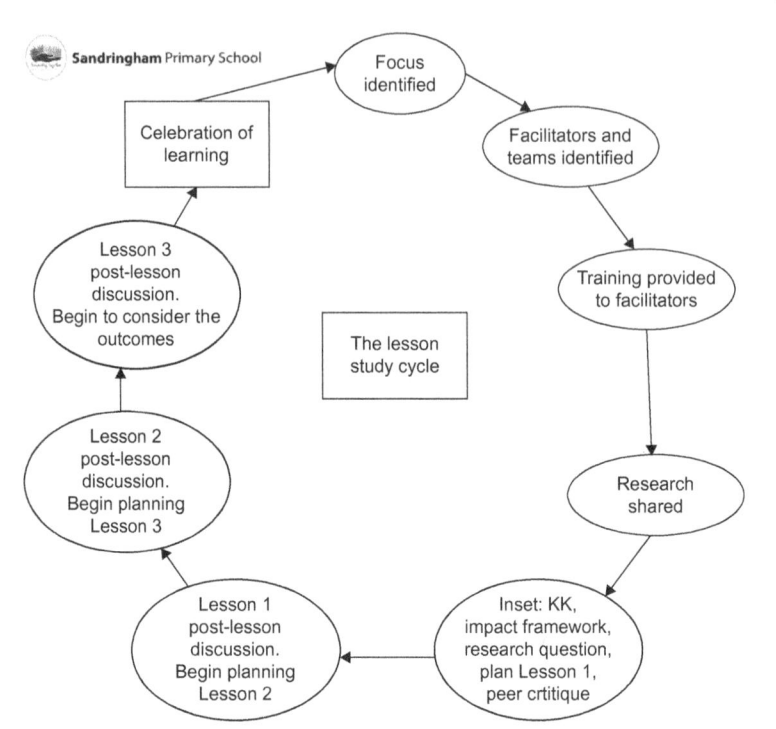

Figure 3.2: The lesson study cycle

on the needs of the learners in relation to the research focus, and each of the three research lessons is built around the research question. This allows our teams to centre their thinking on the initial question, to collect data and to draw informed conclusions in order to make changes to their practice beyond the LS cycle.

Following each of the three research lessons, time is given for in-depth post-lesson discussions. The teams discuss their observations, as well as the comments and reflections made by the children during their short post-lesson survey. The professional conversation helps to frame planning for the next lesson in the cycle. At the end of the third lesson, the teams look back at their initial focus and begin to draw a conclusion. This is recorded in our LS reflection pro forma and shared with the whole teaching staff in a celebration event. The whole LS cycle and findings are drawn together and a book is produced each year.

Here are two examples of research questions and changes implemented from this year's lesson study, which had a focus on reading for pleasure:

- **Year 3: What can we do to stimulate talk in a comfortable, social setting?** Teachers encouraged children to discuss familiar class books and books from home with friends, revealing that social dynamics greatly influenced the depth of these conversations. The team now intentionally creates relaxed, open-ended opportunities for book talk, giving children choice and time in which to explore and ask questions.
- **Year 6: Can the introduction of informal book talk in a classroom setting help reluctant readers to build a more positive reading identity?** Children were given opportunities to pitch books that they have read and enjoyed to their peers. Alongside this, teachers also shared books that they had read and suggested them to individuals based on their knowledge of them as a reader. Year 6 continued to provide opportunities for this informal book talk and recommendation-sharing during the summer term. The teachers noticed positive changes in the learners' confidence in articulating their likes and dislikes regarding a book that they had read.

As our LS project has developed, our teachers have become more confident risk-takers. Teachers can see the benefits of LS, and enjoy the opportunity to engage in research and plan collaboratively. It has become an integral part of our professional learning.

Questions to consider

- How do leaders in your school use and understand the word 'data'? Is it being used in its fullest sense to capture everything that is important for stakeholders?
- To what extent do your staff have a research mindset and how are you promoting this in your school? Look for curiosity, willingness to take risks and an appetite for innovation.
- Does your professional development model encourage teachers to both use external evidence and generate their own, by applying research to designing context-specific solutions?

Further reading

Sebba and colleagues' resource 'Powerful professional learning: a school leader's guide to joint practice development' (2012)

Seleznyov's article 'Lesson study: An exploration of its translation beyond Japan' (2018)

Seleznyov's chapter 'Helping teachers to embed learning from research' (2020a)

4 Developing teaching and learning: How professional development can build teacher agency and improve learning

MORAY DICKSON

In this chapter, I explain how a group of school leaders developed principles with which to improve the design of professional learning in their schools, and then present one practical example of how these principles were applied in the schools.

> **The author**
> I am headteacher at School 21, an all-through school (ages 4 to 18) in Newham, London, part of the Big Education Trust and birthplace of the Voice 21 oracy charity. Before joining School 21, I worked in schools across East London and in the Middle East, where I led a British international school.

Professional development matters

We know that teacher quality is perhaps the greatest predictor of learner outcomes, but we are often less aware of the fact that in-school variability in teachers is far greater than inter-school variability (Sartain et al., 2011). This means that, as school leaders, we should prioritise enabling all our teachers to teach as well as the best of our teachers, and professional development (PD) is key to making this happen. However, regular research shows that teachers often find in-school PD irrelevant, saying that it focuses on school improvement rather than teachers' own needs (DfE, 2023a; Pedder et al., 2008), lacks continuity and often consists of a series of one-off sessions, with no time allocated for testing new ideas in the classroom or reflecting on changes (Pedder et al., 2008).

As a group of school leaders considering how we might improve teacher PD, we wanted to tackle the disconnect between PD sessions and their impact in classrooms. We felt that even when teachers found PD sessions stimulating and relevant, not all were able to translate these ideas and new knowledge into actionable changes in their teaching. This gap between research and practice is often referred to as the 'knowing–doing gap' (Knight, 2007).

Shaping teacher professional development

We decided to produce a set of guiding principles that would drive the design of professional learning in all our schools. We considered the framing of three aspects in our principles:

- **Head:** The intellectual aspect of professional development – what content and knowledge should be included and how should teachers incorporate this into their practice?
- **Heart:** The relational aspect of professional development – how could teachers be motivated to engage and how could we learn together as teams?
- **Hand:** The skills aspect of professional development – what skills development should be included and how could we enable teachers to try these new skills out in the classroom?

Our principles are unpacked in Figure 4.1, followed by an example of how the principles were used to shape PD in our schools.

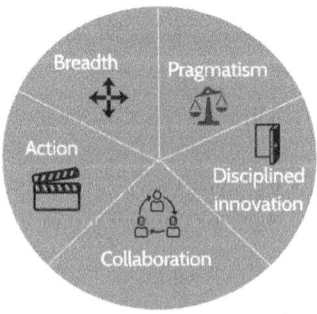

Figure 4.1: Big Education's principles of powerful PD

1. Breadth: Beyond subjects and key stages

Professional development needs to go beyond the confines of a specific subject or key stage and engage with broader educational themes, perspectives, methodologies and philosophies. This breadth is important if we want teachers to gain fresh insights and adapt innovative strategies from a range of disciplines within their own teaching practice.

We identified four key areas within which one might consider breadth, and developed guiding questions for school leaders to use as prompts when designing their offer.

2. Pragmatism: Balancing priorities to achieve meaningful application

In order to tackle the pervasive knowledge–practice gap, we wanted to consider a pragmatic approach to PD, focused on the ability to translate theoretical knowledge into practical applications within the classroom. As educators, our time is precious, and we felt that PD should offer solutions that are not only innovative but also immediately applicable. To this end, we

Table 4.1: Guiding questions incorporating breadth

Leadership	Does our professional learning develop a wide range of leadership skills? Do we look beyond education for leadership inspiration?
Curriculum	Does professional development consider the full breadth of curriculum, beyond the National Curriculum? Do teachers get the opportunity to see innovative curriculum approaches from the UK and beyond?
Assessment	Are there opportunities for teachers to rethink their approaches to assessment and develop a wider conception of what and how we assess? Do we support teachers to move beyond being fixated on tests as our main assessment method?
Pedagogy	Are staff sharing the strongest aspects of their craft and codifying these practices to share with others? Have we explored pedagogical approaches through research and practical application?

needed to make sure that actionable strategies, teaching tools and resources that could be readily implemented in daily teaching practice were included in PD sessions.

Professional learning in today's high-pressured educational context also needed to consider staff wellbeing and do so through a lens of compassionate accountability (Cruddas, 2024). There is no question that teachers and schools should be held to account but, in order to be most effective, accountability needs to be conducted through partnerships between leaders and teachers, and with compassion as a compass. If teachers primarily tend towards having a performance rather than a learning mindset, they are less likely to develop their practice (Watkins, 2010). Professional development therefore needs to support rather than coerce teachers to change their practice. If practice change does not happen, then perhaps that teacher needs some tailored support beyond the session – for example, a coaching conversation or team teaching. Similarly, as leaders, we need to be understanding about dips in quality when teachers are working to change their practice – it often gets worse before it gets better!

Finally, being pragmatic involves balancing the internal and external factors shaping PD: whole-school priorities matter, but so do the needs and passions of individual professionals. Some PD time and budget need to be allocated to enable teachers to work in small groups on issues that matter to them, and we must always consider requests from teachers to attend specialist PD outside the school.

3. Disciplined innovation: Balancing tradition and progress

Innovation is the lifeblood of education, but it must be approached with a disciplined mindset; striking the right balance between traditional pedagogies and cutting-edge innovations is crucial. Disciplined innovation therefore involves critically assessing new ideas and approaches to determine their practical applicability and impact on learning.

This means that our teachers are required to become research-informed (Godfrey, 2017), through both using evidence from research and researching its real-world application in the classroom. Schools might consider implementing PD models that help to structure teachers' own research and connect it with research and good practice evidence, such as lesson study, action research or teacher inquiry projects.

4. Collaboration: The power of collective wisdom

As a group of school leaders, we were firmly committed to the power of teacher collaboration and felt that it was crucial to design PD in a way that maximised opportunities for collaboration. Collaboration extends beyond sharing lesson plans; it involves engaging in meaningful discussions, exchanging ideas and collectively solving challenges (Hallgarten at al., 2014). When educators come together to share their experiences, expertise and challenges, the collective wisdom of the group becomes a powerful resource for professional growth. To this end, we considered powerful collaborative PD models like lesson study (Seleznyov, 2020b), professional learning communities (Stoll and Louis, 2007) and communities of practice (Lave and Wenger, 1991).

The exchange of ideas not only enriches individual PD but also contributes to the overall improvement of a school's teaching practices. For us, collaboration in the realm of professional learning involved creating and sustaining a culture of mutual support and challenge, plus sharing learning both within the structure of the PD of the school and beyond. To this end, we considered the guiding questions around collaboration below:

- What does collaboration look like in your school?
- What opportunities do colleagues get to collaborate in, across or beyond their year group or phase?
- Does your school collaborate with other schools?
- Are opportunities for collaboration prioritised by school leaders?
- Have you established protocols for purposeful collaboration?
- Is there structured and protected time for collaboration?

5. Action: Implementing change in the classroom

The ultimate measure of effective PD is its impact on learning (Guskey, 2002), and yet much of the PD that teachers experience never makes it into the classroom, for reasons including time and workload pressure, misalignment with school policy and the need to simply move on to the content of the next PD session. PD needs to be longer than a single session so that teachers have the time to apply their learning in the classroom and then come back together to reflect on the impact on learning. Sometimes, additional PD time needs to be given, to enable teachers to amend their plans or make relevant resources that will support the implementation of the new practice. Practice change is a process and it will take time, in terms of both PD sessions and duration, before it really makes a difference. Giving teachers opportunities to support each other through practice change can be powerful – for example, peer lesson observations, video reflection, lesson study or team teaching.

Challenges and successes

Aligning individual PD goals with whole-school priorities while respecting teacher autonomy can be a delicate balancing act. This requires careful planning to ensure that both personal and institutional objectives are met.

As do all schools, we constantly face the pressures of time, money and workload. No change can lead to stagnation, but too much change can lead to stress. We have found that it is all about redeploying PD time and budgets, rather than finding more. So often, the precious time that we have is given over entirely to compliance training and business matters. If we can find creative ways in which to do these things – for example, through bulletins or online sessions – then this can free up the important face-to-face time for real learning.

Finally, there will always be teachers who struggle to engage, take on board change or implement practice change with quality. We must recognise that some teachers will need personalised coaching and support to really change their practice.

We have seen in our schools that it is possible to overcome these challenges. The PD models that we have implemented, based on the five principles, have given our staff agency, motivation and engagement. We believe that our approaches to PD support recruitment and retention, because teachers are, at their heart, learners and they want to work in schools that support their learning journeys. We also believe that our models support teacher wellbeing, by enabling choice, making sure that there is time to engage and personalising the offer to meet teacher need.

Building a culture of growth at Wapping High School

Serra Sanders, Assistant Headteacher

In recent years, we have prioritised creating a professional environment where growth, development and collaboration are at the forefront. We recognised the need to align three processes to ensure that staff development and support lead to meaningful outcomes:

1. **performance management:** an essential process that showcases teacher progress throughout the year, linked to specific targets
2. **coaching:** training our staff to become coaches, practising active listening and enabling those that they coach to seek out their own solutions
3. **PD:** ensuring that staff stay current with the most effective pedagogy and strategies to support learning.

It was from this space that our Professional Development and Coaching (PDC) programme was born. The PDC programme aims to provide passionate teachers with development opportunities that support learning through coaching. Research consistently shows that effective practitioner development occurs through observations that offer critical feedback. While quality-assurance-based lesson observations have a role in schools, they are often infrequent and focused on evaluation rather than on the development of pedagogy and practice. We also believe that learning and teaching should not revolve solely around accountability. Instead, feedback should be precise, actionable and designed to foster improvement, reduce stress and enhance job satisfaction and wellbeing.

By placing staff in triads that include at least one experienced coach, we created an avenue for more frequent, low-stakes observations. Each triad consists of colleagues with varying levels of expertise, ensuring a balanced exchange of perspectives and fostering collaboration. Coaches guide discussions and provide actionable feedback, while other members contribute by reflecting on shared practices and identifying growth opportunities. For example, a triad might include an early career teacher (ECT), a mid-career teacher and a senior coach, working together to explore strategies for differentiated instruction. This structure not only facilitates professional growth but also builds trust and a shared commitment to improving learner outcomes, with a focus on development rather than evaluation and fostering a culture of growth and collaboration.

Our approach to enhancing learning is informed by the Great Teaching Toolkit (Coe et al., 2020). It emphasises that effective teaching involves a strong understanding of subject content and how learners learn it. Teachers should foster a supportive learning environment, manage the classroom effectively to maximise learning opportunities, and design activities that engage and stimulate learners' thinking.

Staff members are trained to focus on one domain at a time, selecting a specific area of focus for learning walks, conducted three times a year during 'Open Door Fortnight'. These observations prioritise providing precise feedback, offering one 'glow' (a strength) and one 'grow' (an area for improvement). Crucially, the feedback includes a bite-sized action step – a single, high-leverage change likely to have the most significant impact on practice.

After receiving feedback, staff members continue working within their triads, with coaching sessions feeding into the next cycle of learning walks. This iterative process ensures continuous improvement and fosters a sense of autonomy and ownership over professional growth.

We then designed a system that integrates coaching, observations and goal-setting into a live performance development document. This document allows staff to record and reflect on their learning and growth throughout the year, creating a cohesive thread of development that runs through the school.

By intertwining coaching, PD sessions and performance management, we have moved away from viewing these elements as isolated activities. Instead, they now overlap and inform one another, fostering a culture of sustained growth.

This model addressed all five principles:

1 **breadth:** giving teachers choices in terms of the domain that they want to explore
2 **pragmatism:** through the allocation of PD time to the process
3 **disciplined innovation:** through the focus on the Great Teaching Toolkit and its domains
4 **collaboration:** with peers in triads
5 **action:** through the classroom observations.

The challenges

Despite the progress that we have made, implementing this integrated approach has not been without its challenges. One key difficulty has been ensuring consistency across triads, particularly in maintaining a shared understanding of what effective feedback looks like. While experienced coaches play a vital role, the variability in their approaches sometimes creates discrepancies in feedback quality.

Another challenge lies in securing sufficient time for triads to meet and conduct meaningful discussions. Balancing these sessions with existing workloads can be demanding, and ensuring staff commitment to the process requires ongoing encouragement and reinforcement of its value.

Additionally, creating a truly safe space for open-door observations has occasionally met with resistance, particularly from staff who may feel vulnerable or apprehensive about being observed. Building trust and shifting mindsets towards development rather than evaluation is a continuous process.

The successes

We have seen that the psychological safety established through Open Door Fortnight encourages staff to observe, reflect and engage in meaningful dialogue. This supportive environment fosters the exchange of precise, actionable feedback, empowering colleagues to take ownership of their professional development.

Furthermore, the opportunity to experience lessons beyond one's subject area encourages cross-curricular collaboration. Teachers draw inspiration from diverse pedagogical approaches, leading to cross-fertilisation of ideas. For example, literacy techniques observed in an English lesson may inspire more effective communication in science, while interactive questioning methods from humanities might strengthen engagement in mathematics.

It's important to emphasise that Open Door Fortnight is not about accountability but about fostering intrinsic motivation within our teaching community. While participation is voluntary, it is embedded within our professional development meeting cycle to ensure access for all. There are no formal follow-ups for those who choose not to take part. We celebrate the positive experiences shared in triad coaching sessions, highlighting the professional growth that it fosters.

As Peps Mccrea (2018) says, developing teacher expertise is the biggest lever that we have for improving the experiences, outcomes and life chances of the learners in our care. By prioritising teacher growth over evaluation, we aim to achieve this outcome. The PDC programme represents an investment in our staff, recognising that enhancing teacher practice directly translates to better outcomes for learners.

Questions to consider

- How does your current PD programme support teachers in bridging the 'knowing–doing gap'?
- What structures or practices could you implement to ensure that PD sessions translate into actionable classroom changes?
- How can you rework the time that is already available to make sure that it is committed to structured collaborative learning opportunities?
- How can choice and personalisation be built into your PD model?
- How do you bring external evidence into PD sessions, in ways that empower and engage teachers without devaluing their own expertise?

Further reading

Hall's article 'Evaluating change processes: Assessing extent of implementation (constructs, methods and implications)' (2013)

Hargreaves and Fullan's book *Professional Capital: Transforming teaching in every school* (2015)

O'Leary's book *Classroom Observation: A guide to the effective observation of teaching and learning* (2020)

5 Peer review: A better way to 'inspect' schools
SARAH MARRIOTT AND TOM RAW

In this chapter, we explain peer review, a different approach to reviewing practice in schools, and consider how it can help to foster collaboration and drive school improvement.

> **The authors**
>
> Sarah Marriott is the headteacher of Pinner Wood, a large primary school in Harrow. Tom Raw, formerly an English teacher and head of department, is now the headteacher of Wapping High, an inner-city school in East London. United by a shared goal of meaningful school improvement, we advocate for a collaborative approach to supporting schools.

Shifting the focus

All schools in England have experienced the current high-stakes inspection system, with its sharp focus on accountability. We can all recall being classroom teachers when an inspector entered the room, sat silently at the back and scribbled away on their clipboard. The pressure to 'tick the right boxes' and 'get it right' was overwhelming. As senior leaders, we have experienced this system in its entirety: the need to put on a performance, ensuring that every detail is carefully curated to secure the grade that we need. Even in the most successful inspections, can we really say that the inspectors got under the skin of the school?

Of course, as committed educators, it is our duty to be accountable and to learn what we can do to improve the life chances of the young people in our care. It is a privilege and a calling. However, the purpose of inspection in its current form has shifted from that of a 'critical friend' to that of a 'critic'. Rather than empowering leaders, it often leaves them feeling inappropriately scrutinised and unsupported. In 2018, the NAHT Accountability Commission reported that the way in which schools were being held to account for standards was doing more harm than good, and since that time it does not feel that anything has significantly changed. In The Schools, Students and Teachers Network report 'Labouring to love headship' (SSAT, 2024), 51 per cent of the 236 senior leaders surveyed identified accountability systems as the most common pressure that they faced.

Most school leaders can already identify their areas for development and do not need a high-stakes inspection to reaffirm what they already know; many feel that this system is no longer fit for purpose.

As part of Big Education, we sought to develop an alternative model that fosters collaboration and improvement, one that removes the fear factor that we feel is driving leaders away from the profession in record numbers. We wanted a system that would allow school leaders to be open and reflective, moving away from the pressure to 'showcase' and instead providing space for meaningful reflection and constructive discussions.

Our vision was to offer leaders a lens through which to truly understand their practice: to step back, observe and consider how their school is currently doing and can grow. With this in mind, we developed a Big Education peer review model, designed to support and not scrutinise, to guide and not grade.

Developing a peer review model

Three schools collaborated to design a peer review process and handbook. Peer review is not a new concept; various models exist, each with a unique focus and process. Our starting point, therefore, was thorough research to identify best practices. We explored various existing models in detail, many of which we could have used. However, we were keen to develop a cost-effective model that did not depend on an external team. Instead, we chose to create a model that could be developed by current school staff, ensuring a sense of ownership.

Our framework emphasises honesty, reflection and support, working collaboratively with schools on their chosen areas for development. We aimed to create a meaningful professional development opportunity for both the reviewed schools and the reviewers involved in the process.

Our reviews focus on the bigger picture: exploring what truly makes schools great. Schools have autonomy to draw their area of focus from the Big Education Diagnostic Tool (Figure 5.1), which offers a much broader framework

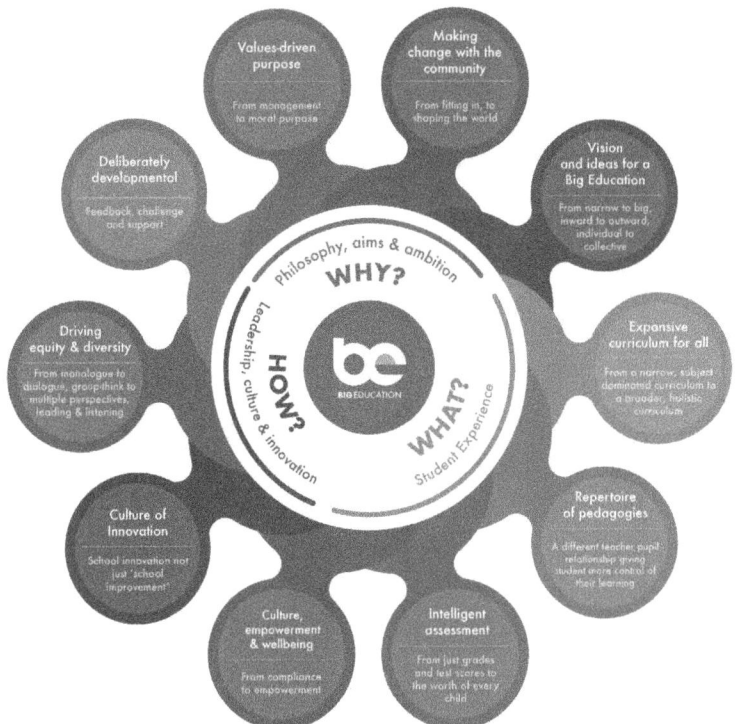

Figure 5.1: Big Education Diagnostic Tool

for self-assessment than the current inspection framework, allowing for a broader and more expansive view of education.

For the actual reviews, the first step was for the school to choose their focus. Before each review, the lead reviewer (usually a headteacher) met with the school leaders who were hosting the review to understand their goals, and together they framed a guiding question and developed a half-day schedule to see everyday practice.

For example, one school had been developing the use of oracy across the curriculum. The headteacher's goal was to understand whether this was having an impact and whether it was being used consistently across the school. After meeting to discuss this theme, leaders agreed on the following guiding question for the review: Is oracy practice consistent and valued across the school?

On the review day, the team arrived early to introduce themselves, engage with staff and ensure a welcoming environment. Working in pairs, they conducted observations, spoke with stakeholders – including learners, staff, leaders, parents and governors – and attended relevant activities. The aim was to gather a wealth of information with which to shape meaningful feedback.

At the end of the day, the team met alone to consolidate their findings. They then fed back to school leaders, using phrases such as 'We saw, we heard, we wondered' and 'Have you considered?'. This framing took away the judgemental language often associated with any review. Instant feedback eliminated the long wait for a report and fostered a collaborative discussion. Schools retained full autonomy over how to use the feedback. It was important that the reviewers served only as a reflective lens; we did not use this process to draw conclusions or to share practices from our own settings unless specifically requested by the school.

Following the review, schools received a written summary of the observations of the review team and had the option of follow-up workshops to help to implement findings. However, during our trial phase, most schools felt equipped to take action independently.

The final stage was to conduct an evaluation and a follow-up call with both the reviewed school and the lead reviewer, to ensure consistency of approach and gather any feedback in order to model the open practice that we were aiming to achieve.

Challenges and successes

We knew that this type of review would rely on high levels of trust between schools. Schools often see themselves as competitors, and the current assessment system, with its one-word descriptors, reinforces this competitive mindset. In our trial, three schools collaborated, already familiar with and supportive of each other's values. This early trust was crucial. As we expanded the project in our second year, to include schools unfamiliar with one another, we remained mindful of this challenge. It was important for the lead reviewer to take time beforehand to understand each school and its goals for the review.

The yearly review cycle begins with thorough professional development for all reviewers to ensure consistency. Unlike traditional inspections, which can feel inconsistent depending on the team, we strive for fairness and equity in every review.

Our team of reviewers was drawn from the participating schools and came from a range of sectors, from Early Years to sixth form, spanning inner-city state schools to rural independents. Initially, we questioned whether reviewers should be matched by their specific experience. For example, could a secondary colleague effectively review an Early Years setting? Did independent school expertise matter for reviewing similar schools? Ultimately, we found that reviewers adapted well to any setting and, in fact, working in contrasting environments often proved to be valuable professional development for the individual partaking in the review, offering interesting new insights to the reviewed school.

Timing was another key consideration. How long should a review last in order to be truly effective? To everyone's surprise, half a day proved sufficient to gather a wealth of valuable information. This duration felt just right: long enough to gain meaningful insights, while respecting the busy schedules of those involved. We understand the demands of daily school life and aim to minimise disruption. The chosen time-frame allows us to examine the focus area from multiple perspectives and to provide insightful, actionable feedback.

Recognising that every school is unique, our reviewers remained openminded, seeking to understand each school's ethos and context. A review can fail if a reviewer is too fixed in their perspective or relies solely on their own school's experiences and values. To prevent this, our training ensured that all reviewers approached schools with fresh eyes and an appreciation for their individual practices. Documentation sent prior to each review ensured that the reviewing team could research and understand the school's context before arrival at the door.

All schools in our initial trial found the review process both successful and highly valuable. Feedback across all schools highlighted several key themes:

- Schools felt that they could be open and honest.
- They had control over what was reviewed.
- The process aligned with their development plans.
- The review team was supportive and they appreciated the reflective approach.
- The external perspective provided deeper insights than an internal review.
- Feedback was constructive, non-threatening and non-judgemental.
- Probing questions helped to shape the next stages of school development.
- Staff felt supported and comfortable being themselves.
- The model is beneficial both for the schools being reviewed and for the reviewers, who gain valuable insights into different educational settings, enriching their own professional growth.

During the trial, the team conducted reviews into oracy practice, formative assessment and play-based learning, each an area chosen by the school itself. In most cases, the schools had already dedicated significant time and effort towards refining and embedding these practices. The review process served as a reflective exercise, allowing schools to assess the impact of their work and plan next steps.

Each school had a strong understanding of the progress that they had made, but the peer review process enabled them to uncover insights that they might not have previously considered. A clear example of this was the oracy review. Having invested substantial resources into oracy across the school, the review helped the school to understand the level of consistency in practice and challenged staff to think more deeply. It encouraged them to refine their approach and, most importantly, to articulate a clear and shared vision for oracy across the school.

Interestingly, all three participating schools also underwent Ofsted inspections during the trial. Comparing the two experiences, schools overwhelmingly found peer reviews to be more supportive to school improvement. The process allowed them to dive deeper into areas that they wanted to develop and to identify next steps, neither of which are enabled by an inspection visit.

Next steps

Given the success of the trial, Big Education has expanded the model. We are now working with more schools across the country to implement peer review.

Moving from judgement to support: Peer review at King Alfred School

Takako Yeung, Assistant Head

As a senior leadership team, we discussed what we wanted the focus of the review to be and settled on the question 'To what extent are higher-attaining learners challenged and stretched in maths across the school?'. This aligned with our school priorities and was an area on which we were keen to get an external perspective.

Our preparatory meeting with the lead reviewer enabled us to share our aims for the review and to explain our context and experience. It was useful in building trust and a positive relationship before the review had begun. In collaboration, we agreed a timetable for the day, and we were able to draw on the experience of previous peer reviews to shape the day effectively.

Reviews in the education sector can often be seen as judgemental and about uncovering what is going wrong. It was therefore important to clearly articulate to our staff what the purpose of the review was and how this was going to be different. It was not easy to convince staff of this at first, but it was helped by the review team reconfirming the supportive nature of the process to relevant staff on the morning of the review. Afterwards, all the staff involved expressed what a positive experience it had been.

By setting out the collaborative and non-judgemental nature of the peer review, staff felt able to be open and honest in their discussions. There was no need to simply show off our best selves; instead, staff felt able to share their whole experience, confident that this would enable useful feedback.

We received verbal feedback at the end of the review morning, which allowed for discussion and immediate reflections. The team shared successful examples of what they saw and then possible thoughts or questions to take forward. Receiving feedback in this format meant that it didn't feel judgemental or instructional; rather, they were things for us to consider based on an external perspective. Some of the thoughts reflected our own thinking and others provided a fresh perspective. Both were useful and led to constructive discussions with staff about current practice and next steps.

We were free to decide how we wanted to share the feedback more widely, and this allowed us to do it in a way that supported our aims for the review. The peer review has helped us to focus and clarify our actions in a key priority area. The collaborative nature of the process means that staff have felt supported and listened to, and that we are therefore taking the next steps forward together.

Questions to consider

- What do you hope to gain from the peer review process?
- How can you build a trusting relationship between schools that fosters openness and reflection?
- When visiting another school, how will you ensure that you remain true to the process without being influenced by your own preconceptions or practices?
- How will you maintain a consistent approach across schools, ensuring that objectives, protocols and processes are clearly defined?
- How will you structure your write-up to be non-judgemental while still encouraging reflection and deeper consideration of current practice?

Further reading

Godfrey's book *School Peer Review for Educational Improvement and Accountability: Theory, practice and policy implications* (2020)

NAHT's report 'The principles of effective school-to-school peer review' (2019)

6 Behaviour and culture: Exploring non-punitive approaches to relationship and culture building
HELEN GOURLEY

In this chapter, I explain how using non-punitive approaches to relationships and culture-building in schools reduces the need for sanctions, creating a more inclusive environment.

> **The author**
> I am an experienced teacher and school leader. I became the founding teacher of Big Education's new primary school, School 360, in September 2021, and later became the assistant headteacher and SENDCo.

The problem

In September 2021, School 360 opened its doors to its first cohort of Reception (four- to five-year-old) learners. Emerging from the COVID-19 pandemic and multiple lockdowns, we recognised the need for a behaviour and culture policy that had the wellbeing of the children at its heart. We wanted to focus on positive relationships, with the hope of reducing exclusionary sanctions, such as time spent out of class, which would result in more learning time lost. We hoped to work against the growing number of exclusions in the UK post-pandemic (Gill et al., 2024).

The impact of all types of exclusion can be huge: lower attainment, especially in more disadvantaged groups (EPI, 2023); rising levels of mental ill health; long-term impact on economic activity and employment (Gill et al., 2024); and a greater likelihood of or vulnerability to criminal exploitation (Ofsted et al., 2018).

Children with a mental health condition or a special educational need, those who grew up in poverty and those who come from some ethnic minorities are disproportionately affected by more punitive approaches. This link has been long established (Gill et al., 2017).

At School 360, we wanted to create a Heart-focused behaviour system that promoted inclusion rather than exclusion. We had read about the importance of values-based leadership (Copeland, 2014) and decided to commit to a core set of values that would shape the school, including our behaviour and culture. We considered them through three lenses: the individual, relationships with others and relationships with the wider community (Table 6.1).

Table 6.1: School 360's values considered through three lenses

	Self	Others	Community
Courage	Don't give up when things are tough; learn how to say no when it's the right thing to do.	Look after your friends and family, standing up for them even when it's not easy.	Be bold about what we can achieve if we work together, and work bravely to make it happen.
Joy	Be joyful in the present moment, knowing what to be grateful for and how to improve and maintain your own wellbeing.	Develop meaningful, productive, joyful relationships that are beneficial for both people.	Look for opportunities to be of service and make the world a more joyful place.
Responsibility	Take responsibility for your own behaviour and actions, act as you want to be treated.	Act with honesty and integrity towards others in your peer group, the school community, and the wider world.	Aspire to effect social change — the world is my responsibility.
Kindness	Look after your body and your mind, be kind to yourself.	Assume positive intent, balance the needs of others against your own, knowing that treating others well improves your own wellbeing.	Ascribe equal value to each person in the human race, be compassionate and see the humanity in everyone.
Curiosity	Be constantly curious, ask questions, see things from different angles, see mistakes as learning opportunities.	Be curious about what others experience and believe, form your own opinions and challenge stereotypes.	Work in a disciplined way as part of a community of innovators to implement important innovations.

There are numerous case studies of the positive impact of a values-based education on learners and adults in the school community (e.g. Hawkes, 2010). This chapter hopes to give practical examples of ways in which we use a values-based approach to behaviour and culture to promote inclusion at School 360.

Introducing a values-led relational approach

We recognised the problematic nature of extrinsic motivation (Niemiec and Ryan, 2009), so we decided not to use rewards and sanctions but to use the values to shape behaviour and culture expectations. We created a system based on building intrinsic motivation, which reflects humans' inherent tendencies to learn and develop (Flavell, 1999).

Teaching staff are proactive in naming the values that they want to see, and the learners learn to acknowledge the same in themselves and others. Learners' names are displayed in classrooms when they actively demonstrate the values, but never for a negative reason. Learners do not expect nor receive extrinsic rewards, such as stickers. This creates a culture where verbal recognition and pride in one's own behaviour keeps learners motivated. For example, children who have gone 'above and beyond' to show the values will receive a phone call home to their family, get their picture displayed in their classroom and be celebrated in assemblies.

We hold restorative conversations when learner behaviours are not as they should be: learners work with an adult to consider how they will repair any harm caused and to plan how they might behave in the future. This does not fix a situation quickly, but it has led to learners being better able to self-manage.

Key to the success of this approach is a deep understanding of the values themselves. Reception spend their first term studying the values through stories and role-play. Around the building, floor-to-ceiling displays of inspirational people that represent each of the values are displayed, and staff encourage children to be curious about these role models. Each new Reception class spends a term exploring some of these individuals, culminating in them voting for whom they would like their class named after and why. In subsequent year groups, learners are taught about each value through the lens of the nine protected characteristics, via a carefully sequenced progression of skills.

Oracy assemblies are linked to the discrete values sessions taught in class: learners sit in a circle and have opportunities not only to listen but also to discuss values-based themes and contribute their ideas and reflections. This means that children learn from us but also from each other.

Our project-based learning approach (Berger, 2003) focuses on social and environmental justice, enabling learners to take action on issues that matter to them, using community-organising approaches (Jameson and Chapleau, 2011). Project-based learning pedagogies build curiosity and responsibility: children follow their own lines of enquiry, learning independence and choice, which has resulted in high levels of wellbeing for learners.

Learning to give and receive feedback with kindness encourages learners to be courageous and take responsibility for their own learning. This feedback culture (Drago-Severson and Blum-DeStefano, 2018) means that children seek feedback, give helpful peer feedback and use feedback to improve work iteratively.

A focus on play-based learning with continuous provision from Reception to Year 2, and playful learning beyond (Mardell et al., 2016), means that learners and staff experience joy on a daily basis. Learners with special educational needs and disabilities (SEND) are included, not excluded, benefiting from the same rich curriculum experience and receiving extra adult input from staff.

None of this could be achieved without consistency across the community. Both our staff and parent codes of conduct are framed around the values to ensure consistency of expectation. The recruitment process provides opportunities for candidates to talk about their own relationship to each value and to demonstrate them through interview tasks. Fortnightly coaching conversations with a development coach encourage staff to reflect on how they are experiencing and demonstrating the values at School 360 and to explore other opportunities to do so in their role.

Challenges and successes

One particular area that remains a challenge is measuring the impact of our approach. Currently, we ask staff to track behaviour incidents that involve SLT intervention and incidents where learners have lost learning. We also ask staff to track when there has been a positive intervention. This enables us to monitor who is losing learning time. This data is presented at learner progress meetings with the class teacher and SLT each term. However, the quality of this data relies on several different factors: how consistently staff track behaviour incidents; individual staff members' interpretations of the behaviour and culture policy; and the adaptation of consequences for different year groups, e.g. the severity of a reflection time consequence might differ from Reception to Year 6. These challenges are compounded through being a new school – taking on new staff each year – and require constant professional development and coaching to ensure consistency.

Another area of challenge is how we measure the impact on the wellbeing of our learners. We are in the early stages of using ImpactEd, an online survey platform for schools to measure learners' wellbeing through age-appropriate surveys. However, this is not appropriate for our youngest learners in Reception and Year 1. Work is ongoing to ascertain the best method for measuring their wellbeing.

So what successes have we seen? We have very few behaviour incidents involving SLT intervention, and school visitors – including those involved in formal reviews of practice – remark on our high learner wellbeing, positive relationships and independence. Families seek us out, having heard about our innovative approach to behaviour and culture, and this has helped us to recruit new learners at a time when many local schools are closing classes. Staff responses to the teacher engagement survey from ImpactEd put our teacher Net Promoter Score in the top 25 per cent of all schools in the benchmark, meaning that our staff believe in the school and would encourage others to join.

Building a positive, inclusive behaviour and culture policy requires hard work and consistency. However, what we have learned so far is that this work matters: for learners, families, staff and the community. It is important because if we are to raise the attainment and life chances of our most vulnerable learners, then we must reduce exclusions of all kinds: learners must be in lessons and enjoy them in order to have a chance at an excellent education.

Developing coaching for belonging, trust and connection

Tom Shaw, Director of Research and Development,
Carr Manor Community School

Why?

Carr Manor Community School is a through school (2 to 19) in Leeds, UK. Relationships are at the heart of everything that we do. We believe that knowing our children well is fundamental to their success, fostering belonging, trust and connection. Our approach to inclusion is grounded in restorative and relational practices, ensuring that every learner and family has a trusted adult who supports their learning and wellbeing.

Our school is guided by four core values:

- know our children well
- partners in learning
- character for learning
- enjoy and achieve.

These values are embedded through a small-group pastoral structure. Hibbin (2023) describes this as a 'whole school ethos of care' and a 'Distributed Network of Relational Accountability'.

What?

Every member of staff – teaching and non-teaching – leads a small coaching group of eight to ten learners from mixed year groups: Reception to Year 5 and Years 6 to 11. These coaching groups meet three times a week on the following timetable:

- **Monday check-in:** sharing goals, concerns and achievements
- **Wednesday check-up:** engaging with careers, values, wellbeing and citizenship
- **Friday check-out:** reflection, celebration and problem-solving.

To strengthen home–school relationships, we hold a termly 'Meet Your Coach Day', where coaches meet individually with each child and their parents for 30-minute conversations about challenges, wellbeing and progress. This aligns with Axford et al.'s (2019) finding that authentic partnerships must be embedded in a school's culture.

Alongside learner coaching, staff coaching circles provide space for professional reflection and peer learning (Rohrbasser et al., 2022). Our Inclusion, Safeguarding and SEND team supports this framework, ensuring that children get the right response from the right person at the right time.

The challenges

Shifting from a form tutor system to coaching required cultural and structural change. Careful attention to group dynamics and how learners related to their coach was essential. Training staff to take on coaching roles meant developing new skills, knowledge and beliefs. We made sure that we had enough coaches by using all staff – teaching staff and support staff. This meant that all staff would be connected to the lived experience of learners and families and could see how their work impacted on learner outcomes.

Ensuring that Meet Your Coach Days became meaningful rather than a formality required a shift in home–school communication, moving from transactional updates to genuine, supportive dialogue (Axford et al., 2019).

The impact

The coaching programme continues to transform our school culture. Learners describe their groups as 'school families', a space where they feel safe, supported and valued. Staff report knowing learners on a deeper level, allowing for earlier intervention. When people do not meet expectations, staff look for the right response with the right person. This can mean appropriate sanctions, but they 'became a qualitatively different experience for both learners and staff' (Warin and Hibbin, 2020, p. 36) as a result of the quality of relationships. In addition, non-teaching staff feel more connected, gaining a new perspective on their roles.

This approach has led to:

- well-above-average Progress 8 scores
- no permanent exclusions in 20 years
- low staff absence and high retention rates.

Most importantly, our success isn't just measured at 16 or 18 but by whom our learners become at 25 or 35 – critical citizens navigating careers, building families and shaping communities. By prioritising authentic relationships, we create a space where everyone feels seen, supported and empowered to flourish – in body, mind, heart and soul.

Questions to consider

- Do you have a system with which to track behaviour in your school?
- Which learners in your school have behaviour incidents recorded?
- What underlying system will you implement to ensure consistency across staff, learners, curriculum and pedagogy?
- What systems do you have to collect family views?
- How will you ensure that children with SEND in your school are supported within the behaviour and culture system?
- How will you track the impact of any changes? Do you have a method of tracking the wellbeing of learners in your school?

Further reading

Kohn's book *Beyond Discipline: From compliance to community* (2006)

Niemiec and Ryan's article 'Autonomy, competence, and relatedness in the classroom: Applying self-determination theory to educational practice' (2009)

Rogers' book *Classroom Behaviour: A practical guide to effective teaching, behaviour management and colleague support* (2015)

7 Collaborative pastoral support: Teamwork to improve learner wellbeing and accelerate learning
KATHRYN PUCH

In this chapter, I explain why pastoral support and the provision-mapping process can ensure that no child slips through the net, considering how it enables children to holistically make progress and achieve their potential.

> **The author**
>
> I have been working in inner-city schools for over 30 years, as a teacher, deputy headteacher and SENDCo. I have supported other schools to successfully implement the provision-mapping process and am currently SENDCo and wellbeing lead at Surrey Square Primary in Southwark, London.

Developing a deep understanding of the child

Many schools have both pupil progress meetings and meetings that identify how best to meet the needs of children with SEND. Why have separate meetings when a single Head, Heart and Hand meeting with the whole team working with the child could look at all relevant data: attendance, academic achievement, behaviour, wellbeing and social skills? In truth, many factors impact a child's progress, and in order to ensure that every child achieves their potential, these need to be analysed holistically by the whole team.

A child who is consistently late to school will see minimal (if any) benefit from an intervention designed to support their reading at the start of the school day. A child who lives in poor housing, with damp and mould, will have greater barriers to learning. We need to try to find out as much information as we can about the child, and use it to inform planned support and provisions.

At Surrey Square Primary, 10 per cent of families have no recourse to public funds (NRPF), 84 per cent of families fall within the lowest IDACI (Income Deprivation Affecting Children Index) bracket, 20 per cent of children are identified has having SEND, 46 per cent have English as an additional language (EAL), 25 per cent live in temporary accommodation and 59 per cent are classified as disadvantaged. This data has equal value to the stories that children and families tell about their lives. Both are vital to help us to understand each child's pastoral needs and what is required for them to flourish and achieve their potential.

Introducing provision mapping

Rather than a series of termly meetings with separate teams, we practise something that we call 'provision mapping'. This involves a more frequent, continuous cycle of gathering information, analysis and action planning. Rather than a one-off meeting that happens termly, provision mapping is a process of gathering information, analysing it and planning next steps. Preparation is key to the actual meeting being purposeful, but it is the processes that are in-built on an ongoing basis that enable it to have such a positive impact.

Firstly, we timetable a weekly pastoral team meeting, attended by the headteacher, deputy headteachers, family wellbeing coordinator, Place2Be project manager (counselling) and safeguarding lead. Information about our children and their families is shared, actions are identified and minutes are taken. Key points are then shared with relevant staff so that support strategies can be put into action.

Having this shared responsibility, with a team to offer advice and think about possible ways in which to help and support, has been critical over the years. Because they are focused on ensuring that the best support and way forward are identified, the team is confident to challenge decisions. This could mean challenging a decision made by an external professional, seeking clarification or escalating a situation to an external professional in a higher position. Previous minutes are reviewed at the next week's meeting and any progress is noted.

We also timetable what we call Provision Mapping Meetings (PMMs) for every year group at the beginning of each term. These meetings are attended by the curriculum and assessment lead, SENDCo, class teachers, support staff and learning mentor. All staff are released from class for the whole day for this meeting.

Preparation for the PMM is key. The year group lead teacher prepares academic data, identifying children who are working above, at or below age-related expectations, as well as those who have not made expected progress.

The attendance lead prepares to highlight children whose punctuality and attendance are a concern, as well as where there has been significant progress. The pastoral team prepares an overview of relevant information and any medical information that needs to be highlighted. The SENDCo prepares data on behaviour incidents and wellbeing and anxiety, usually drawn from surveys carried out as part of our assessment week. The class teachers carry out observations during weekly taught social skills sessions and other classroom sessions, identifying children who need support. Support staff analyse the previous term's data in order to understand the impact of interventions that they carried out.

The meeting has an agenda and starts by sharing successes from the previous term. For those children who made excellent progress in showing our core values, demonstrated an improvement with punctuality or had fewer behaviour incidents, positive postcards are sent home. It is important to recognise and celebrate progress that has been made.

The year group lead then shares an overview of the headline data and their views on the child's academic learning, highlighting progress and attainment against predictions and previous outcomes. We intentionally go through personal outcomes before the academic outcomes, as the personal outcomes often have an impact on the academic learning. For example, a child who has been on a holiday abroad, missing a significant amount of school, will probably experience a dip in academic progress.

It is vital that the whole team is present, unpicking data and planning provisions and actions. Everyone is a valued part of the process, making decisions and planning next steps to support the children. Provisions are varied: it could be time planned with Teddy, our school dog, for an anxious child; a staff member supporting a particular child who struggles to successfully interact with their peers; or additional reading support to accelerate academic progress. The PMM takes place over a morning, and the whole team is out of class all day, allowing next steps to be planned and resources to be gathered so that everything can start the following day.

To enable a holistic approach to supporting children's progress, it is vital that this is modelled and embedded throughout school systems and practices. Throughout the year, we ensure that professional development is balanced, focusing on wellbeing (for staff and children), relationships and behaviour, as well as reading, writing and academic learning. To support staff wellbeing, we plan a Golden Week every term, during which there are no planned meetings before or after school, and staff are encouraged to leave work early or come in later than usual. We provide a staff breakfast before school in that week, encouraging staff to connect and take time out with each other. In addition, every Friday after school, staff who want to can meet for tea and cake, taking time out to reflect on the week and connect with each other before the weekend.

It is also important that we value and celebrate the holistic progress that the children make throughout the year. As a school, we have six core values that we proactively teach and use to talk to the children about choices that they make. We intentionally report on progress towards the values on the children's end-of-year reports. We comment on their ability to interact socially, as well as their behaviours for learning. At the end of Year 6 (10 to 11 years old), children leave with an eportfolio, as opposed to a traditional end-of-year report with SATs results and academic progress. The eportfolio is created by the children themselves and showcases a variety of successes and achievements throughout their years at primary school, including progress towards living our core values, social skills and talents, as well as test results. Parents and carers are invited into school so that the children can present their portfolios to an audience.

Challenges and successes

Other schools often ask how we manage to release so many staff from the classroom for the whole day. We make it happen because we value it and can evidence the impact that it has. When there are PMMs across the school, we use our sports coaches to do an extra session of PE, we use our non-class-based staff to help cover and we split the affected classes across the other classes throughout the school. We make it work and it happens.

The time taken to prepare and analyse the data beforehand can be lengthy. We dedicate an after school professional development session to this, so that teachers have the time to do it. Year group staff discuss data and ideas for groupings and provisions prior to provision mapping. Preparation, pre-thought and ownership of the data and planned provision are key.

We are continually developing and fine-tuning the process, but some of the key successes so far are:

- All staff feel empowered and part of the decision-making and planning process.
- All staff know key information about children, helping everyone to understand different needs and how to support them.
- No child slips through the net: every child's data is analysed and provisions are identified both academically and personally.
- Learners' anxiety at the latest data point is 6.5 per cent lower than the national average, which is very positive. Wellbeing is 6.8 per cent higher than the national average (ImpactEd surveys from December 2024 can be bought at www.impactedgroup.uk/services/evaluation).
- Progress data in reading, writing and maths is in the above-average banding (school performance data 2023–24).
- Our staffing is stable; staff retention is high. In our senior leadership team, there are six members of staff, with combined school service years of over 100.

We know our families and children very well and are continually able to refine and develop our systems to make them more efficient and to maximise impact.

Learning and pastoral pathways: Always show compassion

Mr R. McFeeters, Principal, Ardnashee School and College (ASC)

ASC provides education for children and young people aged 3 to 19 with moderate, severe and complex needs. Our Learning and Pastoral Pathways model (see Figure 7.1) promotes a child-centred approach to education, enabling staff to plan creative, differentiated, personalised and engaging lessons with learners' pastoral needs at the heart of the curriculum. There are three learning pathways (Achieve, Succeed and Conquer), supported by three pastoral pathways (Advocate, Support and Champion), and the latter enable the former. The pastoral pathways ensure that teachers can refer learners for support from the pathways support team of school-based nurture teachers and classroom assistants. This specialist team is skilled in therapeutic intervention programmes and behaviour support programmes.

ASC across the school!

	Who we are!	How we educate!	How we support!
A	Always	Achieve	Advocate
S	Stay	Succeed	Support
C	Curious	Conquer	Champion

Figure 7.1: ASC's Learning and Pastoral Pathways model

Learners at ASC experience significant barriers to learning as a result of their special educational needs, but the COVID-19 pandemic created additional barriers to learning and, in some cases, learners found the return to education extremely challenging and distressing. In 2020, staff engaged in an inquiry-led study to prepare for a recovery curriculum post-pandemic. The outcomes of the study led to a whole-school initiative called the Good Morning Programme (GMP), focusing on learner wellbeing and supporting learners to feel ready to learn before accessing their daily timetable.

The GMP ensured that learners' nurture needs were addressed, and a toolkit was produced to enable staff to plan for improved engagement in learning. All learners begin their day with GMP, which replaced a busy, fast-paced form time. The programme is designed to prepare learners to access their timetable in an alert, organised and calm manner. Teachers plan from a toolkit of activities and the structure is based on a sensory circuit. The activities are organised to support learners with self-regulation and to help them to feel calm as they transition into the daily timetable. Staff outline that this is an important time for pastoral care.

Resources and strategies were developed by staff and a GMP toolkit forms part of the school policy. The creative toolkit is used by staff to design a personalised GMP in response to the needs of all learners in their care. The programme is structured around alerting, organising and relaxing activities. A typical GMP structure includes:

- individual greeting from staff
- a sensory circuit to alert and organise learners
- sensology session to relax learners (a therapeutic intervention used to support regulation)
- sharing the visual schedule for the day ahead.

Prior to the introduction of GMP, learners were entering lessons after spending a long period of time on school transport and being expected to quickly focus on learning. By protecting time for supporting learners with regulation and routine, we have recorded improved engagement in learning and have far fewer referrals to our school-based nurture team.

Questions to consider

- What do the systems for monitoring pupil progress look like in your setting? Are they proactive or reactive?
- How is the personal progress of children monitored, e.g. social skills, attendance or behaviour incidents? Is this looked at alongside academic progress? Does it hold equal weight?
- Are support staff involved in decision-making and data analyses? What benefits could there be to involving them more thoroughly?
- How do you ensure that all staff in the year group team feel involved, informed and empowered to support all children and families' needs?
- What approaches can you use to find information and to build relationships with families to better support their needs and the needs of their children?

Further reading

Cullen et al.'s report 'Special educational needs in mainstream schools: Evidence review' (2020)
van Poortvliet et al.'s report 'Improving social and emotional learning in primary schools: Guidance report' (2019)

PART 2

Curriculum

8 Project-based learning: How interdisciplinary projects support knowledge, skills and competency development
PADDY RUSSELL

In this chapter, I explain how project-based learning (PBL) can be used to provide rich, deep and impactful educational experiences that increase intrinsic motivation to learn, develop both knowledge and skills and promote changemaker attitudes and abilities in young people.

> **The author**
>
> Since April 2019, I have been headteacher at Ladybridge High School in Bolton, which has a distinctive 'Trivium' educational philosophy and an inclusive ethos. Before working at Ladybridge, I worked in a variety of leadership roles in schools in Rochdale, Manchester and Bolton, and ran a teacher training programme across schools in a South African township.

A broader vision of education

At the time of writing, more and more young people are voting with their feet and rejecting the current school system. This is evidenced by reduced school attendance (according to the Centre for Social Justice (2025), 1.3 million children were persistently absent in the autumn term 2024) and rising numbers of children educated at home (Department for Education (DfE, 2024) figures show an increase of 21 per cent in 2023/24 from 2022/23). Alongside this, we have rising levels of disengagement and internal truancy and increases in suspensions and permanent exclusions across the country (government figures (DfE, 2025) show a 21 per cent increase in suspensions and a 16 per cent increase in permanent exclusions in 2023/24 compared to 2022/23). While there are multiple factors at play here, it is clear on the ground that the current curriculum and teaching and assessment methods championed by so-called 'traditionalists' are not helping.

The mission statements of schools around the world reflect a broad consensus of opinion that education is about more than developing the narrow band of knowledge that is required for success in examinations. A true education should enable a young person to develop a range and depth of knowledge, skills and competencies that empower them to thrive throughout their lives. This is powerfully articulated by Mick Waters in his chapter in *Education Forward* (2017), where he examines the many purposes of education. While they include being ready and able to pass exams, they also encompass showing a young person the world of work, giving them a voice and equipping every individual with the necessary knowledge and skills to manage their own life.

Despite this ambition, in reality, the teaching and assessment of academic knowledge dominates in many schools. This is particularly prevalent in the UK, where the high-pressure accountability system typically leads to teaching and assessment practices that are limited to academic knowledge alone.

We have also seen the reinforcement in recent years of a false dichotomy between education as knowledge acquisition *or* skills development. A great education involves both. Great teachers have always had the ability to skilfully move across the continuum of teacher- and learner-led approaches (see Figure 8.1), both directing the learning *and* knowing when and how to build independence and agency.

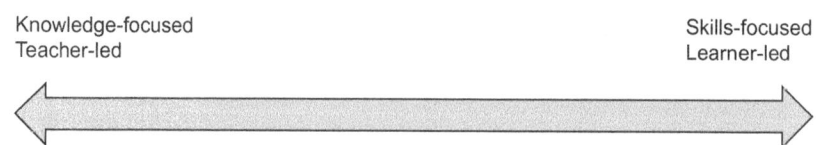

Figure 8.1: The continuum of learning approaches

Project-based learning (PBL)

To embrace this broader vision, we have developed our approach to PBL at Ladybridge. This is an instructional approach, where learners actively explore real-world challenges and problems through extended, hands-on projects that foster deep understanding and critical thinking. Done well, it is an excellent way to move across this continuum, leading to the development of both knowledge and independent learning skills and, importantly, the agency to thrive in life.

Many educators have unfortunately seen progressive educational approaches implemented poorly and, through this, lost their belief that these approaches can be effective. Just like any pedagogical approach, without thoughtful, deliberate planning, PBL will fail (the same, of course, could be said for traditional teacher-led approaches). One of the challenges for PBL is that teachers have greater training and experience in more traditional teaching methods. Hopefully, this chapter can provide practical guidance to schools and educators who are prepared to increase the scope of their pedagogical approach and introduce an element of PBL within their wider curriculum.

PBL at Ladybridge

Based in Bolton, Ladybridge High School is a large and diverse school with a 'Trivium' philosophy of education (see our school website for more details). This is made up of three pillars, which PBL enables us to bring to life:

1 **Knowledge:** Learn something new from an expert – this includes experts beyond school.
2 **Exploration:** Debate, discuss, form your own ideas and gain authentic, real-world experiences.
3 **Communication:** Communicate your ideas to others and perform publicly in different ways to a variety of audiences.

We approach the Trivium in two ways:

- **Project Trivium:** Our learners from Year 7 to Year 10 (11 to 16 years old) engage in at least one interdisciplinary project each year. These projects connect with the local community and all teachers complete the project themselves during the project planning phase. Examples of projects are given later in the chapter (p. 82).

- **Everyday Trivium:** The majority of our pedagogical approach is not fully project-based but involves the everyday use of 'signature practices' related to the Trivium. Some of these practices are essential elements of PBL, such as connecting with experts, real-world connection, public showcase and presentational talk. These practices can be used in everyday teaching as well as in PBL. Other practices form the backbone of great everyday teaching and are not specific to PBL, such as responsive teaching, modelling, critical thinking and exploratory talk.

Getting staff on board and skilled up

In the early stages of our journey towards the vision of the Ladybridge Trivium, we arranged for all our staff to visit our local cinema to watch a special showing of the documentary film *Most Likely to Succeed* (2015). This documents PBL at High Tech High School in San Diego in the United States, and demonstrates the life-changing impact of interdisciplinary PBL. Closer to home, we have arranged for large numbers of our staff team to visit XP School in Doncaster. XP's work on enquiry-based learning, with its strong focus on community engagement, is phenomenal. Our visits have also witnessed the strength of the XP culture, created in large part through the 'Crew' time at the start of each day. Building a genuine sense of stewardship and a belief that it is the responsibility of everyone in the group to help each other to achieve their goals, Crew drives learner investment and engagement in each project. The work of High Tech High and XP have been deeply influenced by Ron Berger's work, summarised in his book *An Ethic of Excellence* (2003).

Many of our staff also saw the value of connecting learning to the real world through working on Comino projects, such as Poet in Residence, Environmentalist in Residence and School Life to Public Life, and work experience at the McCann advertising agency. These raised expectations of what young people can achieve when provided with authentic, rich and challenging experiences, and formed the foundation and inspiration for our ideas on how we could create real-world learning projects for our learners.

Having motivated hearts and minds, our approach to introducing the practicalities of PBL to staff follows an 'I do, we do, you do' sequence:

- **I do:** The SLT completed a project on the history of Manchester, which culminated in the creation of a piece of poetry to be displayed in the Manchester Poetry Library. As part of the project, the team worked with Mike Garry, a well-known and widely published Manchester poet, and Andrew Davies, author of *The Gangs of Manchester: The Story of the Scuttlers, Britain's First Youth Cult* (2009).
- **We do:** All members of staff completed a project on migration, which culminated in the creation of a public service announcement to raise awareness about the issues around migration to the UK. As part of the project, the staff worked with local residents who have migrated to Bolton and BRASS, a local Bolton charity that supports asylum seekers.
- **You do:** Heads of department worked together to plan projects that teachers completed on a training day, in preparation for the launch of the projects with learners later in the academic year.

Through the process summarised above, teachers experienced first-hand the joy (and challenges) of experiencing PBL. This was vital in order for staff to see the value in this style of learning and to build the knowledge and expertise required to plan and lead projects.

Partnerships

Building connections locally has enabled us to create meaningful projects with links to the local community. In addition to BRASS, we have worked with the Bolton Business Club, Bolton Council and the Greater Manchester Combined Authority (GMCA). The support of external national partners, such as the Comino Foundation and Big Education, has also made a difference. Over the years, the Comino Foundation has provided a multitude of incredible opportunities for our learners, including working with MPs, senior business executives, postgraduate learners, museum curators and climate change experts. These relationships also allow our learners to see these people in their own context, whether that is touring the Houses of Parliament or working on a project inside an advertising agency. Being part of the Rethinking Schools network with Big Education has also made a significant difference to us. The network has provided opportunities for us to connect with and share practice with schools who are working in similar ways in other parts of the country.

PBL examples

Some of the projects that our learners have experienced or are currently working on are listed in Table 8.1. All have a driving question, an immersive experience and a clear final outcome.

Table 8.1: Examples of PBL at Ladybridge

Subjects, year group and title	Driving question	Immersive experience	Final outcome
Science and physical education, Year 8 (12–13 years old): Health and longevity – Blue Zones	Can Bolton become a 'Blue Zone', where people lead long and happy lives?	• Talks from Bolton Public Health Team and professional fitness coaches • Fitness testing at a local leisure centre • Creation of personalised health and fitness cards	Learners made a lifestyle pledge, which has been displayed publicly in school. The learners explained the project to parents, staff and governors during a launch event, where the pledge wall was unveiled.
English and drama, Year 9 (13–14 years old): Power and protests	What is worth fighting for?	• People's History Museum, Manchester	All Year 9 learners gave a 'pop-up' speech on an issue about which they are passionate at different locations around the school site. The audiences included younger learners, staff, governors and community partners.
Technology and art, Year 9 (13–14 years old): Ladybridge Recipe Book	How can we celebrate cultural diversity through food?	• Working with food photographers and visiting specialist supermarkets	This project is ongoing, creating a Ladybridge Recipe Book that will be available for sale.

Subjects, year group and title	Driving question	Immersive experience	Final outcome
Computing and music, Year 8 (12–13 years old): Creating music through programming	Can we create music without instruments?	• Session with Sonic Pi musician	Original compositions were created and shared with other learners.
Languages, Year 9 (13–14 years old): Spanish exchange	And you, who are you?	• Online collaboration with schools in Spain – Google Meets and a visit to Spain for GCSE learners in Year 10	Learners produced work on their identity that was shared with the partner school in Spain. All learners also had a viva with a community partner to communicate what they had learned through the project.
Mathematics, Year 10 (14–15 years old): Applied eco-maths	How can we use maths to create an accurate map without technology?	• Fieldwork and measurements at Martin Mere Nature Reserve	In a presentation to peers, former learners, governors and staff, learners shared their methodology and results.
English, Year 7 (11–12 years old): This Is Us II	What amazing stories are there in our local community?	• Inspiring stories from a professional athlete and local community members	The This Is Us website was created and a book published.
Humanities, Year 7 (11–12 years old): Bolton Rewind – Regenerate	Bolton – what can the past tell us about the future?	• Walks around key areas of Bolton • Work with museum curators	There was an exhibition of learning in the school and in a local shopping centre, which was attended by Bolton council staff and councillors.

Challenges and successes

This work has led to many successes. One particular highlight was a learner presenting his ideas on housing policy to members of the council, who were in the process of making important decisions related to new housing developments. The extensive opportunities that we have given our learners to present their ideas to external audiences has helped them to be comfortable and confident in such situations, which we hope empowers them for the future.

However, this work has also not been without its challenges. A key issue has been to incorporate sufficient training time to equip teachers with the skills to plan, organise and assess projects, while also training staff in other areas and having sufficient department time to manage everything else that schools do. Building these projects fully into the curriculum, rather than as a 'bolt-on' on top of the curriculum, was also essential to ensure that this training time is worth it. We created a simple curriculum map with heads of department to identify opportunities for interdisciplinary projects. This exercise is valuable regardless of a school's desire to engage in PBL, and is now available for our parents and carers on our website. We looked for opportunities to combine the projects with learning and assessment activities that needed to happen anyway – for example, when our learners made their pop-up protest speeches, we assessed them using the GCSE English language speaking and listening criteria.

Another challenge has been organising for all learners in a large year group to take part in the immersive experiences. As part of the Bolton Rewind – Regenerate project, we had 210 learners visiting the Smithills Estate, Bolton Museum and the Aldi distribution park, all on the same day. The logistical obstacles of organising this event were not easy to overcome! However, it was these experiences that provided the fuel to energise the later stages of the project and led to some deeply impressive learning demonstrated at the final exhibition. Providing administrative support for teaching staff is vital to help with these organisational challenges. A team effort is required from staff; this is aided by all staff understanding the purpose of the projects.

Balancing the need for high standards and expectations while remembering that imperfections are inevitable is vital. On the one hand, you must have a high bar for what you expect to be produced through the project, particularly at the final exhibition. On the other hand, it is important to recognise that 'mistakes' will help to drive future improvements, for both learners and staff. As is often quoted at High Tech High and by Ron Berger (2003), kind, specific and helpful feedback will lead to improvement in the long term. Aiming for high-quality, beautiful work, while having the patience to know that this will not happen overnight, is the ultimate goal.

A human approach to project-based learning

Kath Bransby, Education Coordinator, Waldorf UK

What we do

The Waldorf curriculum is developmental – it responds to and prompts children and young people's social, emotional, physical and cognitive development through both its content and its pedagogy.

In Class 3, we focus on learning to work with others, recognising that this requires cooperation, teamwork, rules, roles and tools. The curriculum is centred around how human beings have worked together over time and in specific places to meet their basic needs. One of these fundamental needs is food, so the children engage in an immersive, cross-curricular block of learning on farming and food production.

How we do it

The children visit a farm, either on a residential trip or through regular visits to a local farm. They learn about the history of farming, particularly in the local area, developing historical concepts of continuity and change, historical perspectives and understanding of how people's lives have shaped Great Britain. The children find out about which livestock thrive locally and what raw materials and products come from those livestock, exploring how the geographical environment influences what breeds of sheep can be kept locally, for example, and what kind of wool they produce. They then process that wool – washing, sorting, carding, felting – and design and make practical items, using design technology principles and finding out about the potential and limitations of the material. History, geography and careers education combine, exploring different local trades, including farming, shepherding, shearing and weaving. They also compare the locally produced wool and its products to other materials, such as cotton, linen and silk, understanding some of the ways in which their local area is linked to the rest of the world.

Over the course of the year, the class grows a crop, often something culturally and historically significant such as wheat. Their science learning includes seasons and weather conditions, soil types and pH, the plant's life cycle and what it needs to grow successfully. The children care for the wheat, harvest it, process the grain, learn how to use a primitive bread oven and eat or sell their own bread.

Another project might be to keep chickens. The children are expected to research the rules and regulations for keeping chickens, create a budget and raise the money to buy the animals and their feed. Having previously learned about measurement in maths and the history of measurement, they put this into practice when planning out and clearing a space. They spend time and effort caring for the chickens – feeding them, moving the coop, using the manure as compost and collecting the eggs. Finally, they sell the eggs or use them to cook.

Threaded through each block or project is a focus on the ethical implications of their work: sustainability, environmental responsibility, stewardship of the land, working conditions and wages. There is learning about economics – buying and selling, supply and demand. The children record their work in a beautifully presented 'main lesson book'; they create pictures, maps and plans; they sing work songs and play games about digging and ploughing. Each block or project is celebrated with a festival, a celebration of work or a market, where the children can share their learning with peers, family and friends.

The challenges

Planning and delivering a complex, cross-curricular block, while still ensuring that the key curriculum is covered in sufficient depth, is a core challenge for teachers. It requires subject knowledge, practical expertise, skill and the creation of links and connections with the local community. In Waldorf education, the class teacher remains with the class for up to eight years, so although schemes of work can be shared from one year to the next, planning has to be adapted to the particular group of children, to the learning opportunities available locally and to the confidence of the teacher.

The successes

Experiential projects such as this provide children and young people with a deep appreciation for the interconnectedness of the subjects of the curriculum – history, geography, design technology, maths and literacy –

> but also for the significance of the relationships between human beings, their labour, their communities and their impact on and connection with the environment. Learning is deep, embodied and long-lasting. Most importantly, children and young people develop an understanding of themselves as competent, capable people who can make a tangible, concrete contribution to their community and to wider society.

Questions to consider

- What training experiences do your staff need in order to create, manage, deliver and assess PBL?
- What local connections do you have – or could you develop – to enable you to create some interesting projects that have an authentic impact on the local community?
- To what extent are your heads of department on board with this mission? How could you help them to understand this work better?
- Do the young people understand the purpose of PBL? Is your WHY clear enough?
- What are the specific qualities that you are looking to develop in young people? How could you assess these qualities, alongside academic knowledge, through these projects?

Further reading

Berger's book *An Ethic of Excellence: Building a culture of craftsmanship with students* (2003)
Price's book *Education Forward: Moving Schools into the Future* (2017)
Sprakes and ap Hari's book *How We XP* (2019)
The feature-length documentary *Most Likely to Succeed* (2015)

9 Real-world learning: How preparation for the world of work can be built into the school curriculum

CHRIS ANDERS

In this chapter, I explain the challenges that a narrow exam-focused view of education can cause, and how we can respond to this by building opportunities for young people to develop real-world skills that will enable them to thrive, both at and beyond school.

> **The author**
>
> I have been the headteacher at Park Community School in Havant, Hampshire, for over 15 years. The school is focused on developing a broad, useful curriculum. A long-term vision guides curriculum developments that reflect local employment opportunities and are inclusive, meeting a wide range of learners' interests and needs.

Educational purpose

In many schools, educators have reduced learning for children aged 4 to 16 to acquiring and applying facts, often abstractly and rarely in real-world contexts – a purely Head curriculum. Some children love the abstract and thrive when solving mental problems, but many do not. The current frameworks and accountability mechanisms offer little opportunity or incentive to tailor education to individual children and different communities. As a headteacher, a strong sense that successive government expectations of leadership achievements are not right drove me to reflect on what we do and why we do it. At Park, we now have our own philosophy and approach to best educate our learners. It is grounded in the school's community and not in what others can imagine or measure in a league table.

The Department for Education describes its mission as creating 'opportunities for children and learners to achieve and thrive today, so they have the freedom to succeed and flourish tomorrow' (DfE, n.d.). Yet rather than promoting innovation, the DfE rewards conformity to the system. The shift away from practical subjects and coursework to written terminal exams has created an accessibility problem and lacks relevance to the world of work. Employers say that they want young people who are confident and able to communicate and work in a team. Yet terminal written exams and their associated benchmarks do little to promote these employment skills or measure school leavers in more relevant ways. Attitudes to learning and demonstrating hard work – one's best – matter in life much more than small differences between arbitrary exam grades. Young people should leave our schools showing more of what they can do that would interest employers; we need more creative metrics to demonstrate wider learning and competencies.

Real-world learning

Thinking differently: Engaging education

We have a 60-year school plan based on continual curriculum development and delivery. We aspire to achieve success for all in our community by fostering attainment, resilience and autonomy. English and maths are foundations for learners, but we also need to embrace a real breadth of courses and educational opportunities to prepare learners to succeed in life – and not just a narrow academic best at age 16. Children who are proud of their education and who have found things that they love to do are motivated and become adults who push their own children. Real-world learning is an important aspect of learners and parents' support for Park; seeing the opportunities that the school provides, they especially value our investment in each learner's long-term future.

Philosophical foundations

Our approach draws on the insights of thinkers who promoted education as a transformative force:

- Plutarch likened the mind to a fire to be kindled and not a vessel to be filled. Education should spark curiosity and self-improvement.

- Søren Kierkegaard (1992) emphasised freedom of choice and the responsibility that it entails, arguing that education must nurture individuality and prepare learners to face life's anxieties.
- Paulo Freire (2018) critiqued 'banking education', advocating instead for a dialogic approach that respects learners as active participants. He believed that education should empower learners to write their own lives and challenge societal norms.
- bell hooks (1994) expanded on Freire's ideas, promoting engaged pedagogy, a practice that integrates intellectual, emotional and spiritual growth to foster critical consciousness and social change.

Putting it into practice

Horticulture was our first venture into real-world alternatives. While the school is in an urban setting – once Europe's largest public housing estate – it is near the countryside. There are local careers outdoors, and we needed to show that it was a feasible and exciting route to take after school. We began by teaching horticulture informally. To then take it forwards, a history teacher retrained to deliver the Royal Horticultural Society courses. We identified areas of the school grounds that could do with improving, and then growing and planting began.

Different courses need different facilities. I wanted real-world learning not in poorly converted classrooms but in places of work. I dreamed about a shop, buying and selling goods directly from China – a new Silk Road. Our enterprise manager and I shared the aspiration to create a print business offering apprenticeship training opportunities for post-16 learners and high-quality products for local businesses and our school. Our business manager, facilities manager, enterprise manager and I went searching for premises for a shop and a print business. However, our search for a shop failed, as all were too expensive or too small.

Our crumbling buildings meant that the local authority, Hampshire County Council, had to rebuild Park. We needed storage space for school equipment during the rebuild and somewhere dust-free for reprographics. We thought bigger and looked at an industrial unit. Since it offered greater flexibility and better value for the space, we settled on one about a mile from the school. Many years later, it is still home to our print business, where learners and other young people work alongside professionals. It is also home to an additional provision, Inspired Learning, where certain Key Stage 4 (14- to 16-year-old) learners study in smaller groups.

The building work also pushed development in the horticulture curriculum. For lessons to continue, we required outside space away from school. The search by the chair of the governors and myself led to the rental of a horse field. Over time, with the support of a local farmer, it has become our smallholding. Most learners go there at least once each year. After Year 11 (age 16), some learners now study horticulture and animal-based subjects at college.

Our construction skills centre came to be based in a further education college that had ceased to be viable. One of our school governors, a former local councillor, suggested it as being ideal for us. In the spirit of never saying no, it took a year to negotiate the lease. A year or two seems to be normal when setting up a new facility; leases and readiness for school children, as well as staffing requirements, all take time. Today, we run construction courses for learners from Park and half a dozen other schools, making rental and staffing affordable.

The need for skilled staff in subjects not offered as teacher training courses can be a barrier. We employ skilled builders to work alongside the head of technology, who oversees the City and Guilds course. Our site manager teaches younger learners some basic skills – in plastering, for example. In horticulture, a science teacher was happy to retrain. Time away from school is a cost but also an investment in curriculum development.

Today we have a successful programme of real-world learning experiences in our Key Stage 3 (11 to 14 years old) 'much more than just a school' rotation. Wonderful experiences, efficiently timetabled, help children to find something that they might love to do. The small groups try careers working alongside adults who do the job each day. It is the epitome of practical learning: cooking with the chefs in the school kitchen; making a film in our TV studio; visiting our smallholding; or working in our print shop.

This year we have developed hair and beauty with City and Guilds accreditation. Many schools used to run such courses, but education funding and accountability measures meant that most stopped. We are also in the first year of a health and social care course, which links to opportunities in our on-site nursery.

All Year 7 (11- to 12-year-old) learners now have a horticulture lesson each week. One child excitedly told the head of school that this was the first plant that they had owned. We are now searching for more firsts – significant landmarks, often in places that we might not look, and not as big or expensive as being the first in the family to go to university. Taster sessions in welding, utilising local charitable-trust-purchased equipment, have just begun. Other firsts include training as a barista, using a commercial wind tunnel, breeding chickens, building a brick arch, printing a book and racing a go-kart.

Learner recruitment gives an early opportunity to apply for a job, go through an interview, experience success or disappointment, earn an income and set up a bank account. Our business manager began Park's learner recruitment agency, and work includes site support, community reception and chicken-keeper. The school community manager oversees the employment of current and recent learners. A summer work crew employs learners to refresh and decorate classrooms as a holiday activity.

Challenges and successes

Making this happen has required drive and determination – and it has undoubtedly been worth it. During school, many learners appreciate the breadth, having a break from academic lessons and getting to know other school staff. It has also helped the transition beyond school. Not only has it resulted in industry-recognised qualifications, but a lot of learning is what happens during a day of work, through conversations with supervising adults.

Many of our young people are better prepared for college courses. To help to improve retention rates at college – and hence reduce NEETs (not in education or employment) among 16- to 24-year-olds – a pilot programme has run for two years that offers mentoring support for individuals. Health Foundation funding through Havant Borough Council led to the appointment of a mentor at South Downs College; based for part of the year in school, they are able to get to know learners before supporting them through their first term at college and beyond.

Drawing from Thomas More's concept of Utopia (1516), we aim to create 'much more than just a school' – a curriculum rich with opportunities and meaningful choices. Through our wide-ranging provision, we are inclusive and we expand horizons. Real-world learning opportunities teach common sense and problem-solving, and nurture cultural capital to help in navigating life's uncertainties. By embedding values of attainment, resilience and autonomy, we prepare learners to shape their futures with purpose and agency. We foster belonging through engaging learning experiences that inspire and challenge. We create a positive culture, where learners increasingly model pride in their achievements and share their successes with peers and younger learners.

We are almost 30 years into our 60-year plan for our school and community. The journey requires patience, persistence and many enthusiasts in school and beyond – a large group of people who trust one another, sharing our vision of the vital role that a rounded education plays in a powerful community. As we continue to push our learners until they can push themselves, we reaffirm our commitment to making a lasting difference – not just in test scores, but in lives lived well. Being an educator at Park is like a quest – a journey to better prepare young people for the challenges of today and possibilities of tomorrow. Some colleagues have committed their entire career to this quest. Others, such as our bursar, have forgone the benefits of the commercial world for the excitement of doing things that maintained secondary schools just do not do. Forty staff members were learners at the school and have returned to help the next generation. Together, we kindle fires of curiosity, ensuring that every learner's journey can be both purposeful and transformative for the individual and our community.

Engaging learners through alternatives to GCSEs

Will Goldsmith, Headteacher, Bedales School

Bedales School, founded in 1893, has the confidence and freedom to explore better alternatives to the educational status quo. We strive to put children at the heart of everything that we do. We were early adopters of co-education and pupil voice (our student council was founded in 1913) and we do not require learners to wear uniform.

Bedales Assessed Courses (BACs)

After 20 years of GCSEs (statutory exams at age 16), we explored alternative curriculum and assessment approaches. Centrally controlled curriculum and GCSE exams stifled the potential of our learners, particularly in the arts. Reliance on GCSEs narrowed our learners' educational horizons and were not always relevant to learners' interests and needs. Learners now study a limited number of GCSEs (English language, maths, sciences – double or triple – and a foreign language) and then choose up to five Bedales Assessed Courses (BACs). These are two-year courses with continuous assessment and often a final exam. There is more collaboration, research, creative thought and problem-solving, and a natural progression to A level study. Teachers can shape the syllabus according to current real-life events or their learners' interests and go way beyond the confines of the GCSE syllabus (for more on BACs, see Chapter 23).

BACs stretch and challenge learners through a curriculum that is more than purely academic. Learners work on real-world projects, such as building barns, devising theatre, organising and presenting at public events, supporting charities and creating garments or furniture. These projects involve greater responsibility than is normally given.

For example, our English literature course looks superficially like a very traditional offering: Shakespeare, nineteenth-century novels, poetry. However, the freedom to choose texts and how to assess has a dramatic impact on learners: English literature is one of the most popular A levels in the school, bucking the national trend of declining numbers in England (Roberts, 2024).

The department uses a combination of controlled assessment, coursework, exams, vivas and a self-reflection diary to assess. It is currently experimenting with the inclusion of a blog or diary for each piece of work submitted, in order to bypass learners using AI. Drama texts are often chosen to reflect a local theatre production and learners are given choices of texts.

The challenges

The breadth of the curriculum at Bedales and 'rough equivalence' between BACs and GCSEs can cause challenges. This is, as Lucas and Spencer note, 'difficult given the very different nature of, say, outdoor work and ancient civilisations... trying to ensure comparability of grading with dissimilar GCSEs is another [challenge]' (2020, p. 175).

We anchor BAC practice and standards by consulting outside bodies. For example, the Independent Schools Inspectorate reviewed BAC content, assessment and pedagogy. Holding moderator meetings across subjects to analyse BAC and GCSE data confirmed our confidence in BAC standards and processes.

The impact

Bedales partnered with Research Schools International and affiliated with Harvard's Graduate School of Education in a project about motivation. A mixed-methods study found that learners at Bedales report being 'a good amount' or 'very' motivated in academic courses. Learners describe how the school culture supports their independence as curious learners with a genuine love of learning. We also saw a marked improvement in standards at A level following their introduction. Learners applying to university add BACs to their list of qualifications as easily as their GCSEs and IGCSEs. We provide information about BACs to the university application system, which universities can view.

The future

Having reviewed BACs as part of a ten-year strategy for the school, we are now preparing new BACs in sciences and modern languages, so that from 2029, learners will only take English language and maths GCSEs, with all other subjects being BACs.

Questions to consider

- What should schools educate young people to be able to achieve?
- What does your local employment market need?
- How can your curriculum be reshaped to offer learners opportunities to engage in real and meaningful experiences?
- How can you match learners' interests and develop the skills that employers seek for both those who find that the current system suits them well and those who do not?
- Are there ways in which you could monetise school resources and/or activities so that learners experience moving into the world of work?

Further reading

Freire's book *Pedagogy of the Oppressed* (2018, 50th anniversary edition)
bell hooks' book *Teaching to Transgress: Education as the practice of freedom* (1994)
Kierkegaard's book *A Fragment of Life* (1992)

10 Diversity, equity, inclusion and belonging: Ensuring that learners, parents and staff feel a sense of belonging
ANDREA SILVAIN

In this chapter, I explain why diversity, equity, inclusion and belonging (DEIB) is important at a strategic level in order to actively promote a sense of belonging for all in our school communities, including those with protected characteristics.

> **The author**
> I trained as a primary school teacher in 2008 and have spent my career working in schools across East London, the community where I was born and raised. I was a senior leader at an all-through school before starting my current role as a founding headteacher at School 360.

Making it a strategic priority

The DfE (2023b) found that 15 per cent of UK headteachers and senior leaders in schools in England were not from a White ethnic background, whereas 38 per cent of learners are from ethnically diverse backgrounds (GOV.UK, 2025). This can create a gap in personal experience and understanding of the challenges faced by underrepresented groups, including ethnic minorities, working-class learners and LGBTQ+ communities. While these leaders may have a genuine desire to create more inclusive environments, a lack of lived experience can make them hesitant to engage with DEIB work, as they might fear saying the wrong thing or making well-meaning but problematic decisions.

Even when there is a clear desire from school leaders to engage with DEIB initiatives, a combination of issues often complicates the process. These may include personal discomfort, lack of clear guidance, fear of making mistakes and resistance from the wider team. Furthermore, without strong systems in place to hold school leaders accountable for DEIB outcomes, there is less incentive for them to invest heavily in the work. Many school leaders feel the pressure to balance a range of priorities, and DEIB work may sometimes feel like an idealistic extra instead of a core part of the school's mission.

Our approach to DEIB

At School 360, our mission statement is: *Think differently, learn together, change the world*. As leaders, we recognise that in order to fulfil this mission to empower our children to change the world, we need to be active and deliberate in our approach to DEIB. For this work to be authentic, it should run as a golden thread through everything that we do at the school, and not be an add-on.

We have produced a set of values that underpin everything that happens in the school – leadership, behaviour, culture, curriculum and pedagogies – in a deliberate attempt to be values-led (Hawkes, 2005). See Chapter 6 and Table 6.1 (p. 60) for more on this.

From these values, we have developed a values curriculum, which teaches children about the nine protected characteristics from the UK 2010 Equality Act in an age-appropriate way:

- age
- disability
- gender reassignment
- marriage and civil partnership
- pregnancy and maternity
- race
- religion or belief
- sex
- sexual orientation.

This curriculum is delivered through a weekly taught session for all classes. Children learn about a diverse range of inspirational people who experience some of the protected characteristics and who also represent our school values. In order to create a sense of belonging, challenge stereotypes and ensure that children are always seeing a diverse and inclusive range of positive representations, including those that may look like themselves, these inspirational people are displayed around the school alongside the values.

This commitment to DEIB also shapes the broader curriculum, making it anti-racist and anti-discriminatory in all ways. A key part of this is giving the children a degree of agency with which to explore problems that are important to them, their communities and the world around them, and we facilitate this through a project-based learning approach (Berger, 2003). They explore these problems with the support of outside experts from diverse disciplines, ranging from builders to archaeologists, athletes to chefs and artists. What is important to us is that learners feel included and that their voice is valued within the world of which they are a part now, and not just in preparation for the future.

Teachers also consider the social justice lens when planning these projects. For example, to encourage thinking about underrepresented or marginalised voices throughout history, when the children in Year 1 study the Great Fire of London, they consider the perspectives of the Dutch and French immigrants who were blamed for the fire at the time.

Our focus on oracy as a pedagogy simultaneously creates not only a dialogic but also a more democratic learning environment. This supports children to learn to tell their own stories, have their own voices and listen to the stories and voices of others, in order to really understand and be inclusive in their approaches to the world (Golder at al., 2019).

At School 360, we prioritise DEIB when considering our approach to attainment groups. Based on research into the potentially negative impact of splitting children by achievement level (Marks, 2016), as leaders we set an expectation that all lessons are low-threshold and high-ceiling (Boaler et al., 2000). Children who find the learning more difficult are never taken out of whole-class teaching sessions to experience a different curriculum offer, as this would just mean them taking a different and less challenging trajectory, from which they may never return. If these children need extra help, then they receive it in the form of increased and carefully planned adult interactions and interventions. We found that this put school policy at odds with the expectations of, for example, synthetic phonics programme providers, and yet the children's outcomes show that this works. Fewer children fall behind, and both progress and attainment are strong across the board. Children who find learning easier are challenged through the feedback opportunities that the teachers have carefully built in.

This focus on DEIB issues also supports the growth of our community panel, a voluntary body where a number of parents are active participants, along with members of our local community. This panel of members works with Citizens UK to listen to the needs of the community and then organise meetings with decision-makers. They have tackled issues from street lighting to local parks, and from recycling to food banks. As an example, they supported parents to address some of the disparities between how privately renting tenants and housing association tenants were being treated on a local housing development. Both the panel and the school leaders are committed to hearing and including all the voices of the diverse parent community.

We know that our focus on curriculum for learners, parents and the community through a DEIB lens is only implemented, embedded and successfully maintained when the right staff team is in place. We focused on recruiting a diverse staff team, representative of the diverse community that the school serves. With the support of HR (human resources), applications for roles were both anonymised and anonymously scored. Questions such as 'what does a school committed to social justice mean to you?' and 'where might you experience tension between two of our school values?' are designed to encourage diversity of thought among the candidates. We understand the benefits of cognitive diversity in creating a collectively intelligent team, with which we can build and grow the school (Syed, 2019).

Teachers and teaching support staff are offered the same staff professional development each week so that everyone has the opportunity to learn and develop, irrespective of their role. We aim to take an inclusive approach with staff, just as we do with the children. Every member of staff is offered a coaching conversation every two to three weeks, which aims to provide a psychologically safe space in which to reflect on what is going well and discuss any support that staff may need in their role.

The DEIB diagnostic tool

In 2022, we worked with a wider group of schools to share our experiences of DEIB in our settings and to explore the extent to which we felt that it was on the agenda at a strategic level. We looked at this across each of the nine protected characteristics. Our collaboration led to the creation of a DEIB diagnostic tool (https://bigeducation.org/next-big-10-outputs/28294) with key questions designed to support school leaders to think deeply about their approach to DEIB through the lenses of curriculum, staffing and culture.

Each of the nine protected characteristics is explored through these lenses, and prompt questions are provided to support the leadership team with self-assessment. The aim is to shift organisational mindset from not simply needing to meet the requirements of the law but going beyond this to promote a sense of belonging and to positively shape experiences for learners, their families and the wider community.

The diagnostic tool includes some broad questions, such as:

Are your school policies inclusive of this protected characteristic to protect learners and staff from prejudice? For example, the behaviour policy?

It also includes more specific questions regarding each protected characteristic, such as:

Has an assessment been carried out to determine the need for a multi-faith/ prayer room/space?

The leadership team look at each protected characteristic in order to reflect on the following:

- What is the effect of our current approach?
- How do we know – what evidence do we have?
- What is next?

Once school leaders have gathered their data and evidence through surveys, learning walks, observations and interviews, they can then evaluate themselves using one of the best-fit options:

- This is new thinking for us.
- We are exploring ideas and trying some of them.
- We have a range of practices in place and are beginning to see the effects of these.
- We have effective practices in place and can clearly evidence the difference that they make.
- We can articulate our practices and their effectiveness so that others can learn from us about them.

This work is long-term and needs to be strategically planned. The DEIB diagnostic tool provides the opportunity to think not only about how an organisation is currently doing across each area of the protected characteristics, but also about what needs to be done next in terms of curriculum, staffing and culture.

As challenging as it may be to get it right, DEIB in school leadership is essential for creating an environment where every member of the school community feels the sense of belonging that they need in order to truly thrive.

Valuing diversity and hearing all voices

Emma Lee, Assistant Headteacher, Ladybridge High School

At Ladybridge, diversity is a much-celebrated part of our school identity and our culture. We have over 36 languages spoken by our learners, all protected characteristics are represented in our community and our catchment area covers a wide range of families in Bolton.

What we do

Our school has a vision that is embedded in every area of the school and which is the driving force in decisions about changes to policies and all aspects of curriculum development. The beliefs that form this vision outline the responsibility of educators to strive for equity and inclusion for all learners:

- Learning is for all.
- Learning changes lives.
- Honesty promotes learning.

In short, we want our learners to see themselves represented in the texts that they read and the people whom they study. We want them to feel able to express their true selves in their original work. A key part of this is our oracy work, which nurtures 'competent, confident speakers who are comfortable in their own skin' and who are therefore able to confidently express their opinions and celebrate their identity.

We have already had huge success with our Human Library, where our learners booked a 'real live person' to hear the story of their life and passions. We also published a *This Is Us* book, in which learners and staff told their own life stories and shared what is important to them and their families. Our Year 7 learners have been collaborating to publish a second book, which narrates and celebrates stories from our wider community.

Our next steps

The Big Education DEIB diagnostic tool has been instrumental in supporting heads of department in evaluating their curriculum areas, particularly at Key Stage 3, where there are fewer restrictions or guidelines on subject content compared to Key Stage 4/GCSE curricula. Through our continuing work on curriculum development, we actively seek opportunities to ensure that the curriculum represents our learners.

This year, for example, we are planning our Key Stage 3 project-based learning curriculum to include concepts such as 'How can we explore our cultural identity through food?' (combining food and nutrition, art and photography) and 'What is worth fighting for?' (combining English and performing arts), which explores the works and words of marginalised historical figures such as Alan Turing and Emmeline Pankhurst.

These projects will encourage our learners to use their own lenses to critically view the world around them, looking at local, national and international issues that affect everyone and understanding the importance of considering a multitude of perspectives.

Questions to consider

- What is the collective understanding of DEIB in your organisation?
- What are the views of those in your organisation, including staff that experience the nine protected characteristics, and how do you know?
- What are the barriers to hearing underrepresented voices within your organisation and how do you overcome these?
- How inclusive is your curriculum approach?
- How do you keep DEIB on the agenda at a strategic level within your organisation?

Further reading

Syed's book *Rebel Ideas: The power of diverse thinking* (2019)
Wilson and Kara's book *Diverse Educators: A manifesto* (2022)

11 Entrepreneurialism: How to construct a curriculum that develops learners' entrepreneurial spirit
HAYLEY PEACOCK

In this chapter, I explain the urgent need for education to evolve and foster an entrepreneurial spirit in young people. In today's rapidly changing world, learners need the knowledge, skills and confidence with which to navigate an unpredictable future. The traditional education model, rooted in outdated methods, no longer meets the needs of today's learners (World Economic Forum, 2025). To address this, we introduce the founder's mindset: a transformative approach that encourages adaptability, resilience and agency.

> **The author**
>
> An education entrepreneur, I founded the Little Barn Owls group of Reggio Emilia-inspired nurseries and then Atelier 21, a pioneering future school for four- to 16-year-olds located in West Sussex. Atelier 21 has an innovative, emergent curriculum, which evolves and develops with the learners as they move through the school.

The founder's mindset

None of us can predict what's coming next. Technology is advancing at an unprecedented pace, and the world that our children and grandchildren inherit will be very different to the one to which we have been used.

As we step into the second quarter of the twenty-first century, the gap between what our education system does and what it needs to do is widening.

Graduate training programmes have long highlighted the disconnect between what education provides and what employers need. Rather than equipping learners with the skills to learn, live and work in today's world, schools still prioritise test results and, in England, a highly 'knowledge-based' curriculum.

Atelier 21 challenges the traditional education model by creating a founder's mindset and an entrepreneurial spirit. These are not just for business owners; they are essential for 'intrapreneurs' too – those who think and work with agility within organisations. Whether starting a company or entering employment, learners need the same core skills that conventional education often stifles.

By prioritising the skills and mindsets essential for life beyond school, we equip learners to navigate an unpredictable world, focusing in particular on:

- fostering confidence through experience and not external validation
- encouraging learners to embrace failure as an essential part of learning
- empowering learners to take ownership, overcome barriers and embrace calculated risks
- cultivating an entrepreneurial attitude so that learners remain curious and consider opportunities where others see obstacles.

Success today demands more than knowledge; it requires adaptability, agency and a dynamic mindset of possibility. The founder's mindset isn't just about business; it is a way of thinking, feeling and acting that defines innovators, leaders and changemakers.

Putting this into practice

Our founder's mindset is embedded into every aspect of learning. We have created an educational framework that enables our learners to be resourceful, adaptable and unafraid to take calculated risks, and hence flourish in any context. They start their own ventures, develop financial literacy and cultivate that all-important entrepreneurial spirit.

The four keystones of the founder's mindset at Atelier 21 are:

1 self-directed learning (SDL)
2 the democratic approach
3 project-based learning (PBL)
4 'learnish' (the classroom routines for strengthening metacognition).

Self-directed learning (SDL)

Learners have protected time each week to decide what to learn and improve at. This supports them in making meaningful choices and pursuing skills, subjects, projects and questions that excite them. This approach builds critical thinking, independence and the confidence to navigate an ever-changing world.

For example, Year 5 and 6 learners (ages 9 to 11) led World Book Day for the younger learners. They worked together to design six activities, planned a schedule for each year group, from Reception to Year 4 (four to nine years old), and communicated with parents and school staff about the event, considering a range of adjustments to meet the needs of the different-aged learners. The class was supported by their teacher, who adopted a curious mindset around their unfolding decisions but resisted controlling any part of the day, so that the learners could authentically take responsibility for the event themselves (no matter how successful it may have turned out to be). Some elements went very smoothly and others were learning opportunities on which learners could reflect.

The democratic approach

Entrepreneurial mindsets are about agency, innovation and risk-taking. All learners have a voice and are encouraged to use it to make proposals for anything that they consider the school should stop, start, do more of or do less of, including rule changes (known as school agreements). This approach nurtures agency and accountability, vital life skills.

For example, the school is not governed by rules but instead is founded on school-wide and class-based agreements, which the learners help to define and iterate over time. Coupled with the comprehensive peer mediation training that self-elected learners take on, this replaces a school behaviour policy. Learners ask themselves three questions to resolve issues: 1. Can I deal with this by myself? 2. Do I need a peer mediator? (If so, one is called from another class from Years 5 to 11 (ages nine to 16).) 3. Do I need to take this to a class meeting? This is an open discussion with class peers and teachers, for the whole class to decide whether a sanction is appropriate and what this might be. In addition, learners submit proposals on these agreements to the school's pupil ambassadors every Friday; these elected learners vote on behalf of the proposal, feed back to the learner and staff community, and take ownership of decision-making.

Project-based learning (PBL)

Learners of all ages work on projects. They are named Big Studies in the primary years (four to 11), and are provided via the International Baccalaureate Middle Years Programme (IB MYP) interdisciplinary approach in the senior school. The projects integrate various subjects and disciplines, including maths, English, science and the arts, and are formed around big questions spanning nature and the natural world, rights and responsibilities, time and space, events that changed the way we live, and money and enterprise. PBL offers opportunities for self-managed research and decision-making, while engaging learners with real-world issues in a collaborative and hands-on approach to learning.

For example, when our Year 2 and 3 learners (aged six to eight) came across a giant nest in the local forest, they became immersed in the possibility of an imaginary creature that could have inhabited it. Studying and researching aspects of geography, religion, science, art, maths and literature, the creature project was a daily immersive and emergent class project spanning the school year in 2023. The learners were so captivated by the creature project that the class pitched for seed money from the school's founder to write and publish a book about their project to sell at the annual school business fair. The class wrote, illustrated, edited and graphically designed their book. They liaised with the printers, chose the colour, shape and density of paper and set the prices (including extra for signed copies). They made a profit, which added to the Children's Business Fund. This fund represents profits made by the learners in their various enterprising activities throughout the year, and which they can choose how to spend. The finances and the bank account are controlled by the pupil ambassadors.

Learnish

'Learnish' is the fluency to navigate and understand the learning process itself. It's about knowing how to learn, unlearn and relearn critical traits for successful entrepreneurs. Underpinned by metacognitive concepts, it describes the role that an individual takes in learning and how that impacts them and the rest of their class.

For example, we consciously adopt and switch between 'Learning Mode' and 'Performance Mode'. Learning Mode is when a new topic has been introduced, learners are researching, discovering, exploring the topic, and 'mistakes' are encouraged. This creates opportunities for intellectual exploration without attachment to outcome or presentation until there has been proper space for thinking. When our Year 2 and 3 learners returned from lunch to find that their classroom had been transformed into an immersive rainforest for them to explore, for example, they were in Learning Mode. They gathered geographical information, facts and wonderings and wrote them on leaves to be hung from the cardboard tree that they created together, without focus on the neatness of their handwriting or the accuracy of spelling and grammar. In this way, there was less attachment to outcome and more involvement in the processes of learning, exploring and iterating.

Then, a conscious switch to Performance Mode focused the young learners' minds on how they wanted to present themselves and their learning. Our rainforest explorers progressed to collating and summarising their work into more extended pieces. This Performance Mode involved writing clearly, with correct spelling and grammar, and drawing pictures from their initial sketches. While the specific example given here has a literacy focus, Learning Mode and Performance Mode are applicable in all disciplines and across all ages, within the school and beyond into adult life, where fear of failing or judgement of self and others can significantly inhibit mental growth and prevent progression.

The two modalities reflect how the brain works by giving a learner permission to focus on one modality at a time. This leads to more efficient learning, a more expansive mindset, a greater depth of understanding and, ultimately, a more complete, polished presentation and a deeper connection to their work.

Our young learners embrace failure and iterate quickly. They are well versed at getting themselves out of the learning pit and readily celebrate their mistakes as a natural and embracing way of learning and getting better at something.

The challenges and successes

One of the biggest challenges in weaving entrepreneurial spirit into the school environment is overcoming the conditioning and experiences of the staff who work there. We are all shaped by our past beliefs and values, and to become a pioneering educator, one must be ready to challenge these ingrained views. Educators need to look beyond what brought them here and reimagine what is needed for today's children in tomorrow's world.

To create an education that is fit for the future, we must shift from the language of teaching to the language of learning. Louis Malaguzzi (1998), the founder of the Reggio Emilia educational philosophy, wrote about teaching and learning not being separate banks of a river, where learners watch the learning flow by them. Instead, teachers and learners need to be in the flow of the learning together, on the same journey, to strengthen the learning itself and the metacognitive understanding of how to learn well.

This shift is foundational: staff must engage in continual self-reflection and unlearning to model the growth mindset that we promote in our learners. For this reason, we are in the unusual and fortunate position to set aside 14 inset days a year for reflective professional dialogue.

Another challenge is overcoming deeply ingrained societal narratives about success and security. We invest considerable time and resources in supporting parents to understand and champion this approach. To be an Atelier 21 parent means being open-minded and willing to embrace a growth mindset, even if the education that their child is receiving differs from their own experiences.

The school succeeds by becoming a living example of the educational philosophy that it espouses. One of the key reasons for our success in cultivating a founder's mindset and entrepreneurial spirit is that we don't just teach these concepts in theory; we live them. The school itself is a dynamic, evolving entrepreneurial venture, teaching learners the skills that they need in order to thrive in an ever-changing world.

For any pioneering approach to be effective, it must be tested and compared to traditional models. The success of the founder's mindset is evident in measurable outcomes: learners demonstrate greater self-belief and reduced fear of failure, thriving in a culture of curiosity and empowerment. Four years after opening its doors, our first Year 11 cohort will graduate with the International Baccalaureate MYP in July 2025, poised to pursue diverse educational and career paths with confidence in their adaptability and problem-solving abilities.

Developing an entrepreneurial mindset in the secondary curriculum

Michelle Billington, Assistant Principal, Darwen Aldridge Community Academy

As assistant principal responsible for entrepreneurship, my role was to support the development of an entrepreneurial spirit within the local and school community, enhance skills, dismantle perceived barriers to success and promote entrepreneurship.

What we did

Leading a team of teaching and non-teaching staff, I developed an entrepreneurship curriculum, taught as a standalone subject, focusing on equipping learners with entrepreneurial skills and encouraging them to become active citizens.

We involved the local community through innovative events like fashion shows, talent shows and community fairs at the Academy, which were a collaboration of learners and members of the local community. We housed a business incubation centre and learners led their own entrepreneurial initiatives, developing learner-run stores, charity fundraising events and social enterprises.

After visiting Finland and completing the Team Mastery programme with Akatemia CIC, I integrated the principles of Team Academy into our curriculum for Year 7 learners, focusing on a coaching model to support young people in developing enterprises and fostering resilience, creativity and collaboration.

How we did it

Classes were timetabled for larger groups, with two team coaches facilitating sessions. Learners underwent Belbin testing and were organised into teams of eight, with each member assigned a specific role.

Project-based learning was introduced following a structured format, in which learners tackled challenges, developing social or commercial enterprises. Supported by masterclass sessions with guest speakers, learners learned by doing and were coached by their Team Coach throughout the process.

The challenges

Teachers had to shift from being knowledge imparters to coaches, who created a safe space in which for learners to experience failure and learn from it. In addition, we had to manage external perceptions of the unconventional lesson format, which was challenging.

The impact

Learners developed self-assessment and reflection skills by maintaining individual learning logs, tracking their progress in knowledge, skills and attitude development.

They were also encouraged to step out of their comfort zones by thinking independently and taking a proactive approach to their learning. They learned to collaborate effectively, becoming creative problem-solvers and resilient individuals. Learners worked well independently and were enthusiastic about their achievements, with many taking their ideas further by turning them into reality.

This proactive learning approach was applied to other subjects, with many learners continuing to run their own small enterprises into Key Stage 4 and beyond. By engaging with stakeholders and participating in real-world events, learners enhanced their understanding of the world of work and gained valuable experience for their CVs.

This work enabled us to develop relationships with local businesses and stakeholders, creating a network of employers who supported the curriculum and bolstered the broader careers agenda. Parents supported their children's achievements and attended school events, such as charity fundraisers.

Questions to consider

- How can you create daily opportunities for learners to feel powerful and capable?
- What strategies will you use to normalise failure as a part of the learning process?
- How will you support educators in adopting and modelling entrepreneurial mindsets?
- What systems can you implement to measure the development of resilience, adaptability and self-belief in learners?
- How can you help learners and families to shift from fear-based decision-making to intrinsic confidence and risk-taking?
- How can you engage your local community to support learning for learners?

Further reading

Cagliari's book *Loris Malaguzzi and the Schools of Reggio Emilia: A selection of his writings and speeches, 1945–1993* (2016)
Claxton's book *What's the Point of School? Rediscovering the heart of education* (2008)
Covey's book *The 7 Habits Of Highly Effective People* (2020)
Kiyosaki's book *Rich Dad Poor Dad* (2017)
Sinek's book *Start With Why: How great leaders inspire everyone to take action* (2011)

12 Citizenship education: Preparing young people to shape society
SEB CHAPLEAU

In this chapter, I explain how schools can embrace the challenge that our society faces in terms of the increasing mistrust that people feel towards democratic processes. I also reflect on the unique role that educational institutions can play in strengthening communities.

The author

I am a community organiser and headteacher-in-residence with Citizens UK. Having founded La Fontaine Academy, I was its headteacher between 2013 and 2020, establishing what quickly became a thriving community school, focused on learner leadership and ensuring that parents, teachers, learners and neighbours worked together to take responsibility for the wellbeing of their neighbourhood. Until recently, I was also the executive headteacher of an all-through special school in North London.

Anchor institutions

As we enter the second quarter of the twenty-first-century, reading the headlines makes it clear – if it ever needed to be clearer – that the role of educational leadership extends far beyond issues of academic achievement. It is also, I believe, about preparing young people to actively engage with and shape the world in which they live. At a time when global trust in democracy is waning, citizenship education that focuses on practical engagement is more crucial than ever. Schools, as foundational civic institutions that can build communities and a sense of what society could – or should – be about, bear the responsibility of equipping learners not only with knowledge but also with the skills and tools needed to participate in and improve society and its democratic systems.

I am a believer in the importance of anchor institutions. These institutions are there to serve a purpose that often transcends their immediate outcomes: a nursery isn't just about looking after children and providing them with the skills and knowledge that will enable them to thrive in the future; a school isn't simply there to teach our children to read or count or use maps and recorders; a local football club isn't simply there to entertain us for 90 minutes a week. As anchor institutions, these places intrinsically serve a purpose that is greater than what it actually says on the tin: they are there to create links between people, to develop and sustain the social capital that makes life more than a utilitarian journey. In many ways, it gives meaning to whom we are as humans.

Very few institutions can play as significant a role – a civic role – in young people's lives as schools. American political scientist Robert Putnam (2000), interested in the notion of 'social capital', repeatedly notes how civic life beyond schools has been eroding since the beginning of the second half of the twentieth century: faith institutions, community organisations and neighbourhood groups are losing the difficult battle against the marketisation and individualisation of our lives. Community life isn't a norm any longer; it's become an exception.

Schools can shape a more human view of what the world we live in ought to look and feel like, and school curricula can be a great tool with which to reassess what it is that we think should happen in our society. As Ganz says 'many are out of practice at coming together, committing to one another in pursuit of a shared purpose, deliberating together, deciding together, and acting together – the essential practices of democracy in its most everyday form' (2024, p. 11).

Citizenship education

If we accept this premise, citizenship education can be seen as the process that enables young people to engage with democracy, while also – and very importantly – understanding that democracy itself is about coming together, standing together, deciding together and acting together. In other words, democracy is about living together.

Citizenship education, therefore, is a matter of the Head, Heart and Hand. It invites us to imagine what community life is about: what it means to live together in harmony (Heart) and shape what happens around us accordingly (Head and Hand).

Considering the need to prepare young people to exercise their agency, schools must take a proactive role in shaping informed, engaged citizens who have both the confidence and the competence with which to act. This entails moving beyond teaching learners *about* democracy towards empowering them to *practise* it in meaningful ways.

To foster trust in democracy, young people must experience its mechanisms and see their own potential to influence change. Talking about democracy or civic responsibility is insufficient. Instead, learners need structured opportunities to engage with real-world issues, debate solutions and implement actions within their communities. Practical citizenship education turns abstract ideals into lived experiences, anchoring democratic values in tangible outcomes.

Moreover, citizenship education must focus on teaching young people to be powerful. Power is the essential ingredient for shaping the world for the better. When young people are taught to challenge the injustices that they face, they can move beyond hope towards meaningful action. As leaders in schools, we must emphasise that it is not hope that leads to action; it is action that inspires hope. At a time when power is concentrated in the hands of too few, schools can play a role in reviving democracy by bringing power back to the public square.

As I argued in *Education – Power – Change* (Chapleau, 2022), schools have a mission not just to educate but also to actively shape the world for the better. This requires a cultural shift within education systems to prioritise civic engagement as a core function of schooling.

Putting it into practice

Schools must first recognise their role as civic anchor institutions – not only because democracy needs it, but also because healthy human interactions depend on our collective ability to come together, commit to one another in pursuit of a shared purpose, deliberate together, decide together and act together.

Next, this means building partnerships. Being an anchor institution requires fostering strong relationships within and between local communities, businesses and governments to create a supportive ecosystem for citizenship education.

With this in place, schools need to model democratic principles within their curricula, and not tokenistically or superficially. Democracy isn't only a matter of the Head. It needs to be rooted in the Heart and the Hand too. Encouraging learner participation in what goes on beyond the school gates, enabling them to experience what it's like to be powerful and, crucially, what it's like to win, is of fundamental importance. As a community organiser working with hundreds of schools, I often put to them that every child, by the time they leave school, should have worked with others to craft and win a campaign that has made their life – and those of their community – better. As much as we enable our young people to *win* at reading, writing, mathematics, etc., we owe it to them to teach them how to *win* at democracy too.

The process of equipping learners with practical citizenship skills should be as deliberate and systematic as teaching them to read. Literacy is developed through structured and sequenced instruction, progressing from phonics to comprehension. Similarly, citizenship education should be scaffolded to ensure that learners acquire foundational skills before advancing to complex civic engagement.

- **Foundational knowledge:** Learners need a strong understanding of democratic principles, rights and responsibilities. This includes studying historical and contemporary examples of civic engagement and the impact of collective action.

- **Skill development:** Practical citizenship education must prioritise the development of key skills, such as critical thinking, collaboration, communication and problem-solving. For instance, teaching learners to analyse political issues critically, evaluate evidence and articulate reasoned arguments prepares them for informed decision-making.

- **Real-world applications:** Classroom learning should translate into action. Schools can facilitate projects that address local issues, such as organising recycling programmes, advocating for pedestrian safety or collaborating with local governments to improve community resources. These activities not only build civic skills but also demonstrate the effectiveness of democratic processes.

- **Support for teachers:** For practical citizenship education to succeed, teachers must feel confident in their ability to guide learners through these processes. Professional development opportunities, collaborative planning time and access to resources are essential to empower educators.

Challenges and successes

It can be a challenge to push against the tide. What I've argued for isn't the norm – yet. As such, we need leaders who embrace this challenge while accepting that it won't be an easy journey.

In our school system, things are very prescribed: there are frameworks (Ofsted, the National Curriculum, assessment frameworks and their connected progress measures, etc.) and there are structures, and these are often resting on rules set by people whose self-interest is not to question the world as it is. Many schools, in my experience, talk about their role in equipping children to become leaders who can flourish in life. And to flourish in life, one has to truly understand how to shape what happens in one's life. While not underestimating the challenge of achieving this goal, what we teach in terms of knowledge and skills should revolve around the achievement of human flourishing, rather than working within prescribed frameworks and antiquated structures.

And this is where leadership becomes a political act: it is politics that makes the world go round. Politics means people getting involved and taking ownership of what they want society to look like, so that their lives become more meaningful. The choice to be a shaper of society – as opposed to a receiver – is exactly that: a choice. And making a choice is a political act.

I fiercely believe that school leaders must champion the vision of education as a transformative force, prioritising initiatives that align with this mission. They should continually assess whether their schools are fulfilling their civic mission.

This vision requires systematic planning, from equipping teachers to designing learner-centred initiatives that yield tangible results. Schools must embrace their identity as civic anchor institutions, committed to shaping a better world. This is not just an educational imperative but a democratic necessity. The future of our societies depends on the ability of today's learners to engage with the world practically, thoughtfully and confidently.

Fair Fares campaign

St Thomas More Catholic High School, North Shields

As described in *Hungry for Change* (Chapleau, 2022), learners at St Thomas More Catholic High School in North Shields were deeply affected by the rising cost of public transport, which made it difficult for many of them to travel to and from school, as well as attend extra-curricular activities or part-time jobs. Recognising this as an equity issue, and supported by Tyne and Wear Citizens, they launched the 'Fair Fares' campaign. Guided by their teachers, the learners conducted surveys, collected data and presented their findings to local transport authorities. They created persuasive presentations and reached out to the media to amplify their voices.

What made this campaign particularly impactful was the persistence of the learners and their strategic approach. They didn't merely highlight a problem; they provided evidence-based solutions. Over several months, the learners engaged in discussions with council members, organised petitions and mobilised support from local community groups. Their organising efforts culminated in a public hearing, where they presented their findings alongside testimonies from affected families.

The campaign's success – securing reduced fares for learners, thus saving tens of thousands of pounds for their community – demonstrated the transformative potential of organised action. Through this project, learners gained first-hand experience in public policy, negotiation and the importance of collective effort. It showed them that inequity can be challenged effectively, reinforcing the idea that power, when wielded strategically, can reshape systems for the better.

'Your actions have shamed us today'

Radford Primary Academy, Nottingham

A group of Year 6 learners from Radford Primary Academy in inner-city Nottingham, supported by Nottingham Citizens, confronted their local authority about the dire state of their local park. The learners had conducted thorough research into the conditions of nearby play areas, gathering surveys from families, documenting visits and engaging in conversations with their peers. Their findings were troubling: broken equipment, overflowing bins and a pervasive sense of feeling unsafe. Just weeks before their public presentation, they had photographed a broken bottle on a baby swing and reported it to the council, demanding urgent action.

Determined to bring about change, the learners invited local decision-makers, including councillors, housing managers, police community support officers and environmental officers, to a public forum held in the very park that they sought to improve. As the learners presented their case, sharing stories of anti-social behaviour and safety concerns, a councillor was moved to declare, 'Your actions have shamed us.'

The immediate aftermath of the learners' organising work was tangible. The council initiated a clean-up of the park, increased patrols by the anti-social behaviour unit and committed to using the learners' findings to support future funding applications for better security and maintenance. The learners had successfully held local leaders accountable, demonstrating the power of organised, informed civic action.

The initiative did not end there. As the Year 6 learners transitioned to secondary school, they passed the responsibility to the incoming cohort, who continued to monitor progress and prepared to call local councillors back to account for any unmet promises. This ongoing project exemplified the learners' belief in their ability to effect change, reinforcing the school's ethos of developing active, responsible citizens who challenge injustice and take pride in their community.

Questions to consider

- Are your learners being equipped with the skills that they need to shape their world for the better?
- How can the curriculum be reworked to enable them to learn and use these skills?
- Are your teachers supported in delivering impactful citizenship education?
- What professional development might your staff need?
- Is your school contributing positively to the strengthening of your local community?
- How can you find out what your community needs and the best ways in which to achieve these changes?

Further reading

Chapleau's book *Schools in their Communities: Taking action and developing civic life* (2020)

Chapleau's book *Hungry for Change* (2023)

Chapleau's chapter 'Schools as anchor institutions – a community organiser's perspective' (2024)

Cortés's book *Rebuilding Our Institutions* (2010)

The Crick Report, 'Education for citizenship and the teaching of democracy in schools: Final report' (1998)

Foa et al.'s report 'Global satisfaction with democracy 2020'

Gecan's book *People's Institutions in Decline* (2018)

13 Health matters: A curriculum for health and wellbeing
BEN LEVINSON

In this chapter, I explain the fundamental importance of physical health. When we are making difficult decisions about what to prioritise in our curricula, I explore why physical health must be at the top of the list, and then share how we have done that.

> **The author**
>
> Kensington Primary School is a three-form-entry school in Newham, East London, statistically one of the least healthy places in the country. I am the executive headteacher and have developed a curriculum and culture that prioritises health and wellbeing over the past ten years. As a result, we have contributed to national discussions and policy around the centrality of health and wellbeing in education, and how to turn this into reality.

The importance of health

When it comes down to it, nothing is more important than our health. In the here and now, children who are healthy – physically and mentally – attend school, engage with learning, retain information more effectively, build more positive relationships and are happier (Public Health England, 2024). But we are also creating the foundations for – hopefully – long, healthy, happy lives.

We know the impact of early experiences on lifelong health (Center on the Developing Child, 2025). This is true for both actual health (diabetes, cancer, depression, stress) and everything associated with this, such as the ability to create meaningful, lasting relationships or having the resilience and perseverance to deal with challenges in life.

If our role as schools is to help children to flourish, then surely a crucial element of this is their health? When we applied that question to our curriculum (and the National Curriculum), we found it wanting. As we began to unpick this, we realised the fundamental importance of health for our children. Like so many schools, we had a whole extra curriculum outside of our actual curriculum, and often this was where all the best learning happened. Why? Surely the best bits should be the bits that are actually timetabled, from 8.45 am to 3.15 pm, Monday to Friday?

Putting health at the heart of the school

Through the careful management of resources, we freed up a member of staff to spend a year researching different curriculum approaches. Although this was a significant commitment, we knew that it was essential to later success, and it meant engaging with our children, team and community and speaking to a wide range of partners, businesses, the local authority, our multi-academy trust, Ofsted… really, anyone who would talk to us! We continued to prioritise time and resources, and it took another year to create Curriculum K (for Kensington), in partnership with both our team and external experts.

We rolled it out in stages, with significant professional development support for our team along the way and lots of opportunities for feedback and iteration. Our curriculum was reshaped and redefined into four key areas of equal importance: health, communication, academic and culture. Within 'health', there are multiple strands that cover both physical and emotional health.

Physical health

When we looked at PE, given the challenges that our children faced and the underpinning purpose of what we were doing, the focus on sport seemed disproportionate. We restructured our PE curriculum (and renamed it physical health) so that the focus was on precisely that – physical health.

The physical health curriculum comprises both fitness and skills for life lessons. Fitness lessons are 30-minute, high-energy sessions to raise heart rate and build cardiovascular fitness. These take varied forms, from simple playground games to circuits and adapted sports matches. In Years 5 and Year 6, children use Myzone heart rate trackers to better understand the intensity of the work that they are doing and create a better connection with their body, rate of work and output. Ultimately, as long as the children are moving, then this is what is important. Skills for life lessons are based on a gymnastic progression to build strength, flexibility and balance, attributes that are integrated into other sports throughout the year.

Children spend two and half hours a week doing physical health lessons. They also have active learning breaks (both for health and also because of the proven links to focus and concentration), active learning lessons and a focus on activity at lunch and playtimes.

Emotional health

We started with the PSHE (persona, social, health and economic education) and RSE (relationships and sex education) curricula. Again, we felt that these did not go far enough in giving our children a fundamental understanding of their emotional health. We expanded this to give them a greater depth of knowledge and the tools that they needed to effectively manage their emotional health.

Children have emotional health journals and complete short activities through the week to develop and reflect on their emotional health, as well as a timetabled lesson.

In order to create sufficient time for all of this and the rest of the curriculum, children have four hours of maths a week and six hours of English, including reading, writing, grammar, spelling and handwriting.

Health science

These different initiatives connect to our science curriculum. Teachers look to draw links so that children understand the chemical and biological processes that sit behind their physical and emotional health, as well as the wider impacts of factors such as sleep and diet.

Beyond the curriculum

While the changes to the curriculum were key, we needed to go further.

Uniform

Children come in activewear every day: trainers and tracksuits. Research (Ryan et al., 2024) shows that children, particularly girls, are more incidentally active during the day as a result of this. It also reduces time spent changing and makes it more affordable for parents.

Clubs and boosters

We have always made sure that there is a range of after-school clubs that all children can access, including those aimed at health. Our boosters are also targeted across the curriculum to support children in all areas, from reading to health.

Relationships and regulation

Our behaviour policy had focused on extrinsic rewards and sanctions, but this did not match our approach to emotional health. We now have a Regulation and Relationships Policy that is built around children being safe, secure, seen and soothed. All staff have been trained in emotion coaching and we use this across the school to support children to understand their emotional responses and the impact on their behaviour. We work to teach them methods for early identification when their feelings escalate, how to interrupt this cycle and strategies for self-management.

Wider community

From Workout Wednesdays – families and children dancing for 15 minutes before school – to our role as the Beacon Well Trust, in partnership with Youth Sport Trust as part of Well Schools (www.well-school.org), we look for ways in which to put health at the heart of what we do. As a trust, we have created a Sports Hub that delivers both professional development and support to our team, as well as running sports competitions for our children and those from other schools. We have partnered with London Marathon to run a series of inspiring events for our children. We are also the delivery partner for Major League Baseball, with a baseball diamond at one of our schools and a burgeoning baseball team.

Whole school

To make this a transformation and not just a tweak, it had to permeate all aspects of our school. Our starting point is always building the relationships that allow our children to be healthy and happy and to love learning. We have therefore focused on the health and happiness of our team, because if they are not healthy and happy, then they will not be able to support children to be healthy and happy. This has included removing tasks that have less impact – marking, specific planning formats, summative data collection and analysis – and looking at the key elements of wellbeing and how best to support these. This has included physical health. We will often have walking meetings around the local park and we have a badminton club for staff. It has also included significant agency, with teachers supported to teach in the way that works best for them, flexible timetables to empower teachers' professional judgement, no formal monitoring and a culture of collaboration.

At a governance level, we have a Well Schools link governor and a link trustee for the trust. They have oversight of our work on health and provide support and challenge to keep this at the forefront of our strategy.

Challenges and successes

Children are demonstrably fitter and healthier than they were previously. In a recent survey, nearly 90 per cent of parents said that their child was active for 60+ minutes a day, compared to the national average of 47 per cent and the Newham average of 28 per cent.

Despite having a context where most families have close relatives living abroad, a very mobile population, which means significant mid-phase admissions (around 20 per cent in-year), and very real financial pressures for many, our attendance is above national averages.

It's hard to measure, but people never fail to comment on how happy the children are. In the same parent survey, 98 per cent said that their child was happy at school. The team has really bought into what we are trying to do; this is something in which everyone believes.

Physical space remains a challenge and one that we have little agency to change. We have just started work with OPAL (https://outdoorplayandlearning.org.uk) to maximise the use of outdoor space and ensure that children's play is the best that it can be.

Measuring a lot of this with numerical data is tough. We are working with the Youth Sport Trust and Well Schools on further research, but the reality is that there are many factors at play that impact learning, attendance and 'behaviour'. We take a long-term view , based on our collective professional wisdom, we have a high degree of confidence that this will positively impact our children, both now and in perhaps 20, 30 or even 50 years' time. Nonetheless, justifying our approach in a system that values SATs results, phonics outcomes, attendance figures and Ofsted judgements is an ongoing challenge.

Championing health and wellbeing

Sue Watmough, Headteacher, Manchester Communication Academy (MCA)

Understanding context

To effectively impact the health of our children, staff and community, it was essential to have a clear understanding of the context. Our starting point was data, including the Index of Multiple Deprivation, public health data and census data. Our next step was the voices of our parents and children, in order to understand the brilliance in the community and some of the challenges that they faced. The time taken to invest in those conversations cannot be underestimated; they were unbelievably important in gaining a rich understanding of the local community. Armed with this, we developed a strategic approach to improving the health and wellbeing of our children and families.

Deliberate leadership choices

The wishes of our learners were central. At MCA and across the Greater Manchester Academies Trust, the most important wish is for our learners to be safe, healthy, happy and loved. This is not to say that other matters are not important or to ignore our accountability measures but, ultimately, these are our wishes for our children. To bring these to life, we anchored our leadership decisions around health and happiness. We always consider the question 'Is this approach going to improve the health and happiness of our community?'. If it will, then we go for it. This comes from a shared understanding that in order for children to achieve academic success, they need healthy foundations upon which to build. For us, children being safe, happy, healthy and loved must come first.

Curriculum

We have a dedicated health and wellbeing faculty that teaches health explicitly. The faculty encompasses physical education, food and cookery, and our Aspire curriculum. The PE curriculum has five key influences:

1 what children know and what they can do as a result of their primary education

2 knowledge of what children need to know and be able to do at Level 2 qualifications
3 what the National Curriculum outlines
4 what our subject experts believe should be in that curriculum offer
5 the needs of the local area and how the curriculum can meet those needs.

All children at MCA understand how important movement, play, sport and physical activity are to their wellbeing. Food and cookery was deliberately placed within the health and wellbeing faculty as opposed to being part of the design technology curriculum, so that children fully understand the impact of a healthy diet on their wellbeing. All ingredients are purchased by the school from a local supermarket so that all children can access lessons and replicate dishes at home. Our Aspire curriculum is similar to a PSHE curriculum; however, this is driven by the needs of our learners and is responsive to any arising issues.

Wider strategies

Our mission is to mitigate the impact of social disadvantage, and one way in which we do this is through our Family Partnerships Team. They help to remove perceived or actual barriers that families may be facing that could prevent a child from attending, learning and thriving. This work includes supporting families that may be facing housing issues or who are at risk of becoming homeless. The team works with The Bread and Butter Thing (www.breadandbutterthing.org) to provide a low-cost food subscription service. The Family Partnerships Team also looks after our young carers and any children that may have a health condition, as well as running intergenerational activities through our Feel Good Friday offer.

MCA prioritises health and wellbeing as essential components of fostering an environment where children can achieve their full potential. By promoting physical and mental health through a variety of initiatives, including access to nutritious meals, regular exercise and emotional support, MCA ensures that children are equipped with the resilience and energy needed to succeed academically and socially. This focus on holistic development enhances children's overall quality of life and significantly improves their chances of success in the future, setting them on a path to reach their highest potential, both inside and outside the classroom.

Questions to consider

- Which curriculum focus is important for your children, your community and you? What is the right focus for your time, resource and energy?
- Do your children need improved physical fitness, confidence or teamwork?
- Is this just a tweak to your PE lessons or are you changing other aspects of your provision, such as uniform, breaktimes, competitions, extra-curricular activities, vision and ethos? Which aspects are going to create the greatest resistance? How much resource will each change take? Where are the low-hanging fruit?
- How do you make this change stick through building it into processes and systems?
- Where is this change aligned with your ethos and are there other systems that actively rub up against it – for example, negative views on running on the premises?

Further reading

Public Health England's report 'What works in schools and colleges to increase physical activity' (2020)

Ratey's book *Spark: The revolutionary new science of exercise and the brain* (2008)

Youth Sport Trust's report 'PE and school sport: The annual report 2025'

14 Lunchtimes: How lunchtimes can enable learning experiences for our young people
TIM STAYNER

In this chapter, I explain how lunchtimes and breaktimes can be learning experiences for children and a rich part of the school curriculum. I describe our family-style dining and focus on playful outdoor learning at breaktimes. I also talk about the challenges that we have faced in making lunchtimes a community dining experience and incorporating play into breaktimes.

> **The author**
>
> I am a learning coach at School 360, a state primary in Newham, London. I wanted to be part of a community with a passion for play-based learning and I am currently working towards becoming a teacher at the school.

The lunchtime 'problem'

At School 360, we felt that the traditional cafeteria-style lunches and playground breaktimes that most schools have were missed opportunities for learning. The staff team were keen to create an environment that was more than just an opportunity for learners to fill their stomachs and get some fresh air. Considering a Head, Heart and Hand balance, we wanted to explore opportunities to use this time to develop learners' character, strengthen relationships between peers and foster a school community by enabling our school values of joy, kindness, responsibility, courage and curiosity to extend beyond our classrooms.

We planned to focus not only on the learners' dining experience but also on their access to outdoor play and provision. We knew that this was important for our learners' development, as the majority of our learners do not have natural outside spaces: many live in flats and may only have a balcony as an outside space. Similarly, we felt that lunchtimes can sometimes be an unpleasant experience for both learners and adults, due to behaviour problems, arguments, first aid incidents and the dreaded wet play. This was something that we also wanted to tackle.

This goal was part of our wider desire to shift the balance of power between teachers and learners, stepping away from an 'us and them' culture as a school. We wanted to be approachable and be seen as mentors, people that learners could trust, so that they did not feel afraid of making mistakes – because, ultimately, schools are places for both personal and academic growth.

Transforming lunchtimes

Family-style dining mimics the types of meals that families may have at home. Rather than merely receiving a pre-portioned plate of food, learners are given opportunities to lay the table, pour water for one another and serve themselves from large bowls of food in the centre of the table, creating a relaxed and familiar environment. Having family-style dining also provides learners with the opportunity to develop their oracy skills by asking about each other's day or asking for food to be passed.

A family-style dining setting has a few key components:

- **Round tables:** Instead of long rows of tables, our learners sit at round tables. This seating encourages conversation and teamwork, fostering group interaction and community.
- **Shared platters:** A variety of food is placed in large serving dishes at the centre of the table. These may include salad, pasta dishes, rice and vegetables. Learners take turns serving themselves, passing food around and ensuring that everyone gets fed.
- **Learner roles:** In our setting, we have learners in mixed-year groups at our tables. Older learners help with pouring water and passing heavy food bowls, something that younger learners find difficult. Younger learners help with laying the table. This shared responsibility teaches learners that every member of our school can help others and that lunchtime isn't just about them – it's about the collective.

- **Adult supervision:** Every table has an adult who is eating with the learners; this is part of the school day and is not taken from staff's lunch breaks. This not only ensures that learners are encouraged to try new foods and eat a varied and balanced diet, but they are also there to facilitate conversation. This includes showing curiosity about where the food has come from – at times, many of the vegetables that our learners have grown in our roof garden are in their food, something that always gets the learners excited. These conversations allow them to deepen their relationships with their friends and broaden their oracy skills.

This journey begins in our Reception classes, where we have a snack area that replicates our dining hall, with a circular table and the same plates and utensils that they would have at lunchtimes. Here, they can explore and play at laying a table, chopping fruit for their friends, pouring water for each other and washing their own dishes.

But it doesn't end there. Once the learners get outside, there are plenty more learning experiences. We are a school with a motto of 'there's no such thing as bad weather, just bad clothing' so, in each year group, learners are provided with a rain-suit, and all that parents are asked to supply are the wellies. We do not have wet play in the traditional sense, where learners stay in a hall playing games or in a classroom watching something on a screen, while quietly colouring. Instead, our learners jump in puddles, play in the mud kitchen or build outdoor shelters using tarpaulins and rope in the den-building area. They experience playing in the rain not only together but also with the adults that are on duty that day. Adults on duty do not merely supervise the fun but are modelling by joining in the play in their own waterproofs.

We knew that playtimes could sometimes be boring for learners and that this boredom could cause arguments and behaviour problems. This was one of many reasons why we made the choice to encourage risky play at the school. As research has shown (Sandseter and Kennair, 2011), not allowing learners to take calculated risks and problem-solve on their own (especially when adults say 'don't do that' or 'that's not safe') can instil fear and potentially damage self-esteem and confidence.

Instead, we coach learners and ask questions: 'Do you feel safe?' or 'I wonder how you're going to get down from there?' This approach has not only helped them to overcome challenges outside but also has authentically come into the classroom, in that learners are not afraid to question and show courage by doing new things that they once dreaded.

At lunchtimes, we wanted a collection of loose parts; for example, in our provision, we have den-building materials, large and small LEGO®, old pushchairs, trikes, large wooden construction blocks, hula hoops, used tyres, bags and old suitcases, allowing learners to explore and enhance their imaginative play. For instance, the large LEGO® bricks have been not only building blocks but also ice skates, bowls, helmets, a tray for collecting bugs, a shovel, containers for collecting water in the rain and road layouts for the trikes. The possibilities are endless. We took inspiration from the Outdoor Play and Learning (OPAL) project (https://outdoorplayandlearning.org.uk). We saw how this approach helped other schools to get learners of all ages to play alongside each other and to enable joyful lunchtimes. Because of this, we have less conflict and a reduced number of first aid incidents; instead, learners are engaged in their play.

The challenges and successes

There have been challenges, and our approach only works because we feel passionate about this issue. There was a running joke between us all that we were on plan 108 of 'how to do lunchtimes'.

Some of the challenges were around managing allergies. These learners now sit on an allergens table wearing a red lanyard and they are served their food on their own plate, prepared by our kitchen team, rather than serving themselves. By keeping the learners with allergies on specific tables, we reduce the risk of cross-contamination and ultimately keep them safe, which will always be our main priority. This has not, however, diminished their experience of family-style dining, as they are still expected to help to lay the table and clear their plates when finished and, more importantly, join in conversations with each other and the adults on their table. We also have a vegan and vegetarian table to cater for these dietary requirements but, on this table, learners can still serve themselves like the rest of the learners.

Teachers work together to create a table plan for where to place learners. This helps to manage behaviour, and directing children where to sit has the positive impact of encouraging them to make relationships with other children to whom they may not have spoken before.

We also had to think about children bringing packed lunches. As a school, we try to get all parents on board with school lunches, and in the past we have invited them in for a parents' lunch with their children so that they can experience lunchtimes for themselves. This has resulted in us having very few learners who bring in packed lunches in comparison to other schools. As one parent commented, 'No wonder you're not hungry when you come home from school if this is what you have.'

Another challenge was food waste and our efforts to reduce this. We always model to the learners what a portion size looks like when they first join our school, and explain to them that they can have more if they still feel hungry after they have finished. In fact, waste is minimal because learners have plated it up themselves, meaning that they haven't put food on their plate that they don't want or like, which would have gone straight into the bin.

Being a new school in London means that we have very little green space, and the cost of digging up all the concrete to develop play spaces has been difficult within the constraints of increasingly tight school budgets. We have had to fundraise and source from our community. As examples, this has helped us to dig up a small amount of concrete to position a fallen tree and monkey bars for learners to climb on, and also to bring in additional play equipment.

One of the biggest successes of family-style dining is a different kind of learner-to-teacher relationship. At School 360, we already have a close relationship with our learners, whether from using first names, our more practical and casual dress code or the messaging that we are just adults, navigating the world just as much as children are. Lunchtimes feel different to other schools. As teachers, it's an opportunity to know the learners on a deeper level and outside a school context. We talk about weekend plans, things that we are excited about or different celebrations. Since we all work in different areas of the school, lunchtime is a chance to hear what learners are learning about in their class. Having family-style dining abolishes the 'us and them' culture and deepens learner and adult relationships through the simple act of sharing food and having conversations.

I should also mention the genuine care that our learners demonstrate for the year groups below them, whether through helping them to cut their food or cleaning up some spilt water. They go above and beyond for them and are always there to celebrate each other's successes, getting excited when someone tries a new food and likes it.

Playtimes have been more joyful, with fewer accidents and medical incidents because our approach to risky play allows learners to take calculated risks. We have noticed that behaviour incidents are less frequent because the learners are fully engaged in play with the loose parts and use different zones in the playground. We have also noticed that allowing our learners to play in all weathers means that they have opportunities to expel any excess energy, enabling them to be more focused and present in our classrooms. We still have further ideas for our outside playground, including greater development of the mud kitchen and an enclosed sandpit area for the learners to play in.

Our learners take genuine interest in and care for our outside spaces, looking at plants and admiring the changes in seasons. This supports the school's wider focus on caring for the natural environment. With the very little green space that we have, we had to think creatively about how we could best enhance these areas and , with the fruits of some fundraising, we have begun to plant trees in our orchard area and sow seeds in the raised beds for vegetables and flowers. Having learners actively involved in this naturally and authentically supports them to develop a propensity for nurturing and a natural desire to be inquisitive. We also see this caring nature with our resident chickens at the school, where learners are taught how to care for and properly look after them. I wasn't joking when I said that we've thought about every possible use for our limited outdoor green spaces – every inch is put to good use, and all this has been made possible because of the generosity and determination of our parents/carers and wider school community.

Having a very small outside space hasn't stopped us from making big changes. In fact, it has made us question how we can do things, and it seems that with every hurdle we face, we come together as our school community to overcome it.

Play as a playground priority

Kathryn Puch, Deputy Head, Surrey Square Primary School

Why we did it

In our playground, we noticed that children who liked sport (predominantly football and basketball) were engaged, as we employed sports coaches; however, there was very little for other children to do. Some children didn't want to be outside in the playground, which led us to question how we could develop playtimes and make them more inclusive, purposeful and fun. In addition, we had children who were bored, and incidents with negative behaviours were high.

What we did

We had heard about OPAL and went to see how it worked in a local primary school. We spent that lunchtime talking to the curricular lead and observed children stacking palettes, pulling around suitcases, playing in mud and dancing to music. All children were engaged and happy. We came back excited to bring OPAL into our school, and signed up to the programme (a relatively small cost for a two-year programme, including mentoring, professional development, access to documentation and support).

- **Developing the playground:** With an OPAL advisor, we audited our playground, looking at space and equipment, and an action plan was created. Zones and areas were developed over time, resources were sourced and we advertised for donations. In addition, we purchased lots of welly boots and waterproofs for the children to wear.
- **Risk assessments and documentation:** As the OPAL approach is based on dynamic risk assessment, these were carried out on all equipment and zones, ensuring that all staff were clear on how to support children in their risk-taking and problem-solving.
- **Play assemblies:** We implemented a weekly play assembly so that certificates could be awarded, new equipment could be introduced and children could help to identify ways in which the equipment could be used to maximise enjoyment and minimise risk.

The challenges

We needed a staff shift in mindset from 'No, don't do that' to 'How can you keep yourself and your friends safe?'. We had to prioritise regular professional development around dynamic risk assessment.

Parents and carers needed to be supported to understand the OPAL approach and to value children being able to play in all weathers and taking risks. We held workshops with parents and carers, and OPAL features regularly on our newsletter.

Staff needed to be comfortable being outside in all weathers. We purchased large waterproof jackets for staff to use and wear over their own coats.

The impact

All children are now engaged and can play in any area of the playground. As a result, there are far fewer behaviour incidents. The majority of children are able to discuss risk and problem-solve as to how they can play safely or in a safer way. There are fewer first aid incidents.

The children have developed skills outside of sport, e.g. children are now able to ride bikes, roller skate, create mud pie dinners, make castles in sandpits and role-play with small world equipment. Through surveys, we have seen that the level of enjoyment is far higher.

Questions to consider

- How can you encourage staff to eat their lunch with the learners?
- What needs to change in the kitchen and dining hall to enable a move to family-style dining?
- How can you introduce risky play to learners in ways that adults feel comfortable with and that manage the dangers effectively?
- Will parents see the value of learners playing in the rain and mud, and how can you get them on board?

Further reading

Brussoni et al.'s article 'risky play and children's safety: Balancing priorities for optimal child development' (2012)
Fraser's book *Authentic Childhood: Experiencing Reggio Emilia in the classroom* (2011)
Sills and Watkins' book *The Power of Risky Play in the Early Years* (2025)

PART 3

Pedagogy

15 Play-based learning: Why play matters and how playful pedagogies improve learning

SARAH SELEZNYOV

In this chapter, I explain why play is an important pedagogy for learning and how we can use a play-based approach and playful pedagogies to improve learning for children.

> **The author**
>
> I have been working in inner-city schools for over 30 years, as a teacher, headteacher, school improvement consultant, professional development lead and researcher. I currently work as Associate Headteacher at School 360, alongside completing my PhD and developing a range of interesting education projects across the UK.

The problem

In September 2021, when we first opened School 360, a new state primary in Newham, London, we were just emerging from the COVID-19 lockdown. One of the things that we had all learned from lockdown was how important play is for children's wellbeing and learning (Rogers, 2022). Parents had seen their children struggle to stay happy when they could no longer play with their friends.

In the Early Years, play is seen as crucial to learning. At university, playing with ideas, experimenting and following your own lines of enquiry are seen as crucial to learning. Why does play lose credibility as a learning experience between the ages of 4 and 18? Research from the Real Play Coalition (2019) shows that children and parents believe that play is important:

- Ninety-three per cent of children say that play makes them feel happier, and 83 per cent say that they learn better when it feels like play.
- Ninety-five per cent of parents believe that play has a positive impact on the development of prosocial skills such as empathy, and 82 per cent believe that children who play more will be more successful in education and life.

And yet in recent years in England, we have seen opportunities for play reduced. Parents are less likely to let their children play out unsupervised, and many children's lives are fully scheduled with activities. Space for play inside school has been under threat, with reduced breaktimes, extended school days and direct instruction for children as young as four years old. This is in contrast to what happens in many high-performing Scandinavian and Asian countries, who focus on play-based approaches for longer and later. Just over the border in Wales, play-based learning until the age of seven was introduced in 2011, and studies found that both attainment and wellbeing improved (Taylor et al., 2015).

For some, their concept of play is one that is entirely child-directed and which involves a hit-and-miss approach to learning (Smith, 2015). This is a misunderstanding, since 'Having autonomy in a situation is about feeling ownership and making choices, rather than being free from all constraints.' (Jensen et al., 2019, p. 20)

Guided play offers a teacher-led version of play that merges the best of 'telling' and 'discovery' approaches to learning: the child has some free choice within a playful activity to make their own discoveries, and the adult provides guidance based on individual children's interests, needs and understanding, supporting them towards a predetermined learning goal (Skene, 2022).

Championing play

To make play one of the underlying pedagogical and curriculum principles of the school, we first reconsidered the classroom environment. If children were going to make choices, then the standard classroom setup of 30 chairs and some tables would not suffice. We needed to set up areas that reflected the choices for children: a creative area in which to choose art and design materials and activities; a construction area with various construction kits; a science area for investigations; and a role-play area reflecting children's current interests, which could become a doctor's surgery, a fire station, a shop... This meant that there was not a chair for every child, nor a table.

Free access to the outdoors was also crucial. Since children were going to go outside in all weathers, we bought sets of waterproof clothing and parents brought in wellies. We needed more green spaces, so we dug up concrete and planted trees. To include opportunities for the risky outdoor play offered in a Scandinavian learning environment, we bought climbing frames, monkey bars, climbing walls and woodwork benches. We introduced loose parts play, participated in a den-building workshop and collected old tyres, pushchairs, tarpaulins, cable reels and suitcases for imaginative and construction play.

While there is some time for direct teaching at the beginning and end of the morning and afternoon sessions, the rest of the day is COOL (Choose Our Own Learning) time. A progression of resources, skills and knowledge was carefully mapped out to support teachers to plan high-quality provision. We were cautious not to overload teachers with too much guided group work, as we knew that this would leave them with limited time in which to interact with children in play (Seleznyov et al., 2020).

Challenge and progression were created by using 'must do' tasks in COOL time. Linked to the short twice-daily whole-class teaching sessions, these were tasks for children to complete independently at a time of their own choosing during the week or day. Each one was linked to a QR code that children could access via the class tablets, so that they could relisten to the teacher explaining the task. The teacher would track the completion of the tasks via the tablet and remind children of the deadlines for completion. As they got older, the number of tasks increased and the time-frame for completion shrank. But, crucially, learners chose where, when and with whom to do the work, meaning that they shaped their own learning trajectory.

The challenges and successes

We knew that in Wales, extensive staff professional development had been needed to ensure high-quality play, and to avoid a slip back into formal learning (Rhys et al., 2015). One study warned against assuming that a play-based curriculum would solve the issue of underachievement unless the quality of interactions with adults was high for all children (Power at al., 2019).

We included teachers and teaching assistants in our professional development sessions on the effective interaction of adults and children in playful learning. This involved learning about the role of adults, videoing ourselves interacting with children in play and reflecting on these videos collectively, offering constructive feedback and agreeing joint next steps. In this way, professional development offered teaching staff a chance to play around with their practice, take risks and explore possibilities.

The TRAIL (Teachers Reflecting on Agency in Learning) materials developed by the University of Cambridge provided brilliant support for us, and we used them to structure our reflection sessions. The five 'trails' (Figure 15.1) were broken down into individual strategies (Figure 15.2), with descriptions and brief vignettes. These were really easy for staff to use when planning playful activities and when analysing videos of their practice.

We had to consider how assessment would enable learning progress while maintaining children's independence. We taught children how to use tablets to take pictures, videos and audio clips to record learning independently. During whole-class sessions, teachers planned in time to look regularly at children's work and supported children to give each other feedback.

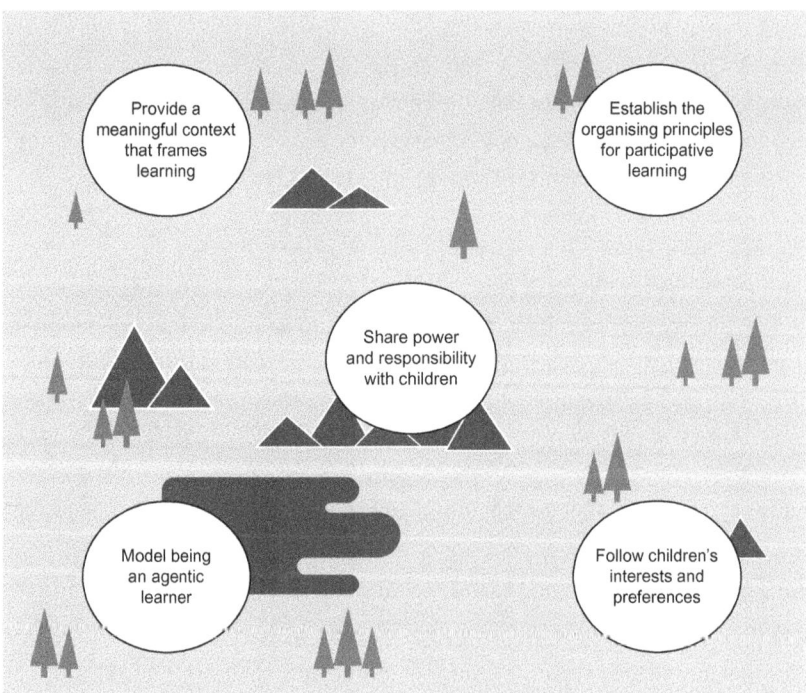

Figure 15.1: Five 'trails'

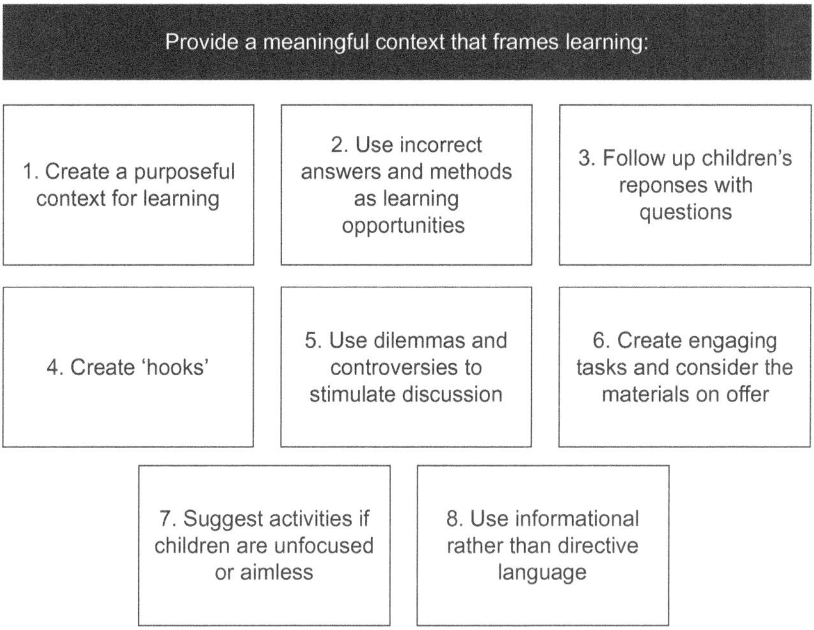

Provide a meaningful context that frames learning:

1. Create a purposeful context for learning

2. Use incorrect answers and methods as learning opportunities

3. Follow up children's reponses with questions

4. Create 'hooks'

5. Use dilemmas and controversies to stimulate discussion

6. Create engaging tasks and consider the materials on offer

7. Suggest activities if children are unfocused or aimless

8. Use informational rather than directive language

Figure 15.2: Strategies for trail one

We managed COOL time by having adults inside and outside. Staffing levels are therefore crucial, and recent budget cuts made this challenging. Staff have helped us to make it work by being flexible with their own timetables because they see the benefits for children.

This is still a work in progress and we do not yet have a perfect model of learning through play, but walk into our classrooms and you will see a general atmosphere of happy purposefulness. All children are engaged in playful learning tasks, adults are interacting with small groups and those not with an adult are engrossed in learning in the various areas of the classroom. We have some children with special needs and disabilities, but you would not immediately notice them. In fact, the time at which we notice them most is during the short whole-class carpet sessions, when they struggle to focus and sit still.

Our children are confident speakers and good listeners, able to collaborate and support each other and happy to have a go, even when learning is tricky. They are creative learners, producing the most wonderful art, woodwork, scientific investigations and design projects. They are learning to read, write and do mathematics as well as – if not better than – their peers in more formal learning environments.

Parents say that their children love coming to school, have happy, productive friendships and are making progress in their learning. Learning is open-access to all parents via the Seesaw app, and they can also use this to upload evidence of learning at home.

And what about staff? We do not want to give the impression that this has been an easy journey for us: teaching this way is more difficult. Staff have needed to work hard on their practice, ask for lots of help and give each other more feedback. But the wellbeing and learning of the children are visible, and that is what really motivates them to continue:

'I believe play is just as important for adults as it is for children… Play isn't a tick box: it is the core of everything we do and it's the heartbeat of our school.'
(Teaching assistant)

We are now beginning to think about what happens in Year 3 (seven to eight years old) and beyond. How will we develop play as the children mature and the learning becomes more challenging? The key pedagogical principles that will help us to embed play into the curriculum as we grow and expand are as follows:

- Any concept, skill or knowledge can be taught playfully.
- Giving children choices enables them to take charge of their own learning and become more engaged.
- Play spans free play through to more structured guided play: all are valid and important.
- Skilful adult interactions in play are crucial for high-quality learning.
- Playful learning requires staff to rethink the classroom environment, including spaces, furniture and equipment.

As long as we remain true to these principles and continue to value wellbeing and creativity as highly as literacy and mathematics, then we hope to offer children at School 360 an experience in which play is integral to learning at all ages, and where learning is hard but fun and something that you self-manage rather than something that is done to you.

Making school a happier place

Polly Shields, Headteacher, Hanover Primary School, London

Why we did it

When I joined Hanover as deputy head in 2016, I noticed that we had a significant group of learners for whom school learning felt irrelevant, and who struggled to socialise positively, particularly the younger ones, those with SEND and those from less-advantaged backgrounds. Teachers were exhausted and demoralised. Parents told us that their children, who had loved Reception, weren't keen on school any more.

What we did

- **Decluttering:** Fewer tables, chairs and cupboards meant space for classroom zones: creative 'making' areas, construction, small world play, maths and writing zones, role-play, water trays, inviting book areas, cooking areas, geography zones and resources to explore the natural world, including a growing area.
- **Developing the shared outside area:** We developed challenging climbing apparatus, a huge sandpit, growing zones, a mud kitchen, large-scale painting, a zone for ball games and bikes, water play, a woodwork area and musical instruments.
- **Reviewing the curriculum:** We separated out National Curriculum objectives that we felt could only be covered through direct teaching and those that could better be covered through direct experience. Direct teaching sessions for reading, phonics and maths were short, focused and timetabled at the beginning or end of the day. Learning is responsive to the interests of the learners, while ensuring that the curriculum is covered – but we often found that the children's interests led the class beyond the National Curriculum.

The challenges

The biggest challenge was proving that every child was covering the curriculum to the satisfaction of external advisers and, in particular,

Ofsted. We are currently investigating using technology (Seesaw or Tapestry, for example) to record learning in all its wonderful variety (although we will also keep some exercise books!).

Another difficulty was helping staff to understand what 'teaching and learning' means in a play-based context. Teachers learned that when given choices, children will often choose to learn something new. Staff had to accept that we would often never know exactly what a child had learned, but that the fact that they were absorbed in a self-chosen task for an extended period of time meant that deep-level learning was taking place. Staff needed to learn how to build in challenge through adult interactions and to choose when to intervene and when to step back, supporting thinking, exploration and learning.

A further tension is that a higher number of SEND learners with more complex needs means that the available adult attention sometimes has to ensure that they are safe, regulated and appropriately stimulated, which inevitably leaves less adult time to support the wider class. On the flip side, it means that these learners, as long as they have the right preparation, become increasingly self-managing and independent.

While many parents support and value our approach, particularly those brought up outside the UK, some were sceptical. It has been important to listen to their concerns and to explain the philosophy behind our approach. Having strong outcomes (an 85 per cent phonics screening pass rate in 2024 against a national average of 80 per cent) helps to reassure the sceptics!

The impact

Children's wellbeing has rocketed. They get on well and are competent problem-solvers and creative and enthusiastic learners. Levels of focus and engagement are higher and they can stay on a task for much longer. They are more active and seem physically fitter.

Assessments at age seven years show that learners achieve generally in line or slightly above the national average. Teachers enjoy their jobs: as one Year 1 teacher told us, having moved from a more traditional system, 'It just seems kinder.'

Questions to consider

- What does playful learning look like in your context and how might it benefit learners?
- What would be the barriers to implementing playful pedagogies in your context: accountability systems, buildings, resources, staff skills and attitudes, or parental views?
- From what kinds of play would learners in your setting gain the most learning?
- What might progression in play look like from age 4 through to 18?

Further reading

Durning et al.'s book *Empowering Play in Primary Education* (2024)
Seleznyov and Silvain's article 'School 360: Doing education differently' (2023)

16 Imagination matters: Shaping the conditions for creative learning experiences
TOM DOUST

In this chapter, I introduce the concept of imagination pedagogy and connect it to classroom education, focusing on creative learning through physical making as a way in which to engage children in deeper, more meaningful learning experiences.

> **The author**
>
> I am Associate Director at iOi, a charity that designs powerful learning experiences that empower children to believe that they can build a just, fair and sustainable world. A social innovator, I have spent over 20 years devising creative programmes with children, young people, families, schools and communities in the education and cultural sectors, and I am also a Design Council Expert, a LEGO® Education Academy Certified Trainer and a Fellow of the RSA.

Why imagination matters

'The world needs innovation and, more importantly, innovative people. Imagination and creativity are exactly what is needed to succeed in our future.'
(Learner aged ten, St Lukes Primary School, Newham)

Children today are growing up in a world that is becoming increasingly uncertain and liable to disruption, impacting the way in which they will live, learn and work. As Vincent-Lancrin and van der Vlies note, 'In the digital era, complex skills that are less easy to automate become increasingly important. Creativity and critical thinking are becoming increasingly important in the labour market, and contribute to a better personal and civic life.' (2020, p. 11)

What role does imagination have to play in this rapidly evolving world? Imagination is a unique human faculty, a fundamental aspect of human cognition that actively shapes our understanding of the world (Chambliss, 1991). It enables us to create the world that we inhabit, rather than merely existing within it (Robinson and Robinson, 2022). In short, imagination has the potential to support and aid younger generations as they navigate this evolving world, and this is why it matters to their education.

To stay physically healthy, we actively encourage children to eat a balanced diet and spend time being physically active. Do we do the same when it comes to nurturing children's imagination? Arguably not, particularly in heavily assessed education systems where the curriculum is narrow. And yet imagination can help children to problem-solve, innovate and build resilience to change. Imagination allows us to reimagine our society and circumstances.

In particular, imagination nurtures creativity, fuelling the construction of new ideas and differing perspectives. Creativity is essentially 'applied imagination' – it's putting your imagination to work. Creative thinking is more than coming up with unexpected ideas: it is a tangible competence grounded in both knowledge and practice. And this competence supports people to achieve better outcomes, especially in constrained or challenging environments. It is through creative learning experiences that we can hope to foster children's freedom to imagine new possibilities and ultimately help to build a more positive future.

Bringing creativity to life

At the heart of iOi's work lies creativity. This can be a divisive and emotive word, because some have the self-perceived idea that people are not very creative. However, we are all born with the capacity to be creative, with an incredible ability to dream up new ideas (it's what differentiates humans from most other species on the planet). While often associated with the arts, iOi believes that creativity can be applied across all subjects and disciplines. Albert Einstein was a brilliant physicist and mathematician, but it was his imaginative and creative flare that sparked his eureka moments.

iOi's learning experiences draw inspiration from a number of learning pedagogies, including constructionism (Papert and Harel, 1991). Constructionism takes the constructivist theory (Piaget, 1966) towards applying one's imagination through a creative action. Within this theory, cognitive learning happens inside the learner's head, but it also happens more reliably when the learner is engaged in a personally meaningful activity outside their head, which makes the learning real and shareable. This shareable construction may take the form of a robot, a musical composition, a papier mâché volcano, a poem, a conversation or a new hypothesis (Martinez and Stager, 2013).

We believe that it is vital to nurture creativity beyond just the early years of a child's life. We do this in two ways:

- by creating the conditions for creativity, designing highly immersive creative learning experiences using a constructionism approach that empowers children to tinker and make
- by empowering children to think creatively through the generation of new ideas, often framed through divergent thinking (the inception of many ideas or solutions to problems).

iOi offers this approach across the UK in three domains:

1. **in school (formal learning):** in partnership with children and teachers
2. **in the community (informal learning):** in partnership with children, caregivers and community leaders
3. **at live events (informal learning):** in partnership with civic spaces and venues for family events.

In primary schools, we provide support for teachers to develop new approaches to teaching practice by building confidence in tactile, hands-on, minds-on learning. A learning platform called ImagineEd (https://ioi.thinkific.com) houses a repository of STEAM-based (science, technology, engineering, arts and mathematics) learning activities. In the 'Imagine Me, Imagine You' theme, for example, you can learn and experiment with 'balancing me sculptures', an activity that considers children's similarities and differences through the making of a balancing sculpture that tells the story of what makes you who you are. iOi also supports children directly through in-person and live broadcast workshops. In 'Wild Eco Builders', for example, children can be inspired by animals' traits and characteristics to design new inventive buildings and spaces that might improve their local community (think octopus-inspired hospitals!).

Beyond the formal school environment, we work in partnership with a broad spectrum of organisations to nurture and reinforce the same principles. The Power of Play, for example, is a collective partnership programme that aims to improve access to quality 'learning through play' opportunities for children across the London Borough of Tower Hamlets. Supported by the LEGO Foundation and in partnership with the LEGO® Group, this multi-year project develops children's holistic skills through learning via play-based interventions and a well-established pedagogy (LEGO Foundation, 2017) that includes the development of children's holistic skills:

- **physical:** being active, practising sensory-motor skills, developing spatial understanding
- **social:** collaborating, communicating, understanding other people's perspectives
- **cognitive:** problem-solving and flexible thinking
- **emotional:** expressing and managing emotions, tackling challenges with confidence
- **creative:** coming up with new ideas and bringing these ideas to life.

Central to the success of The Power of Play is co-production with audiences and the collaboration between a range of organisations able to bring a systemic approach to change. The programme's unique partnership includes the involvement of a museum (Young V&A, with a focus on place-based activities), a social enterprise (EasyPeasy, with a focus on digital activities for caregivers) and charities (iOi, with a focus on schools and their immediate surroundings, and Save the Children UK, with a focus on supporting established local community groups).

We also believe that families can play a critical role in supporting and bolstering the notions of creativity and imagination. iOi therefore convenes family audiences around central themes of ideation, rapid prototyping, crafting and constructing. From local libraries to major institutions, these events invite audiences to curate and exhibit outputs. For example, inspired by Kara Walker's large *Fons Americanus* installation in the Turbine Hall, which inverted the usual function of a memorial and questioned narratives of power, iOi devised a weekend of making digital and physical mini-monuments at Tate Modern. Using a broad range of tools and materials, including augmented reality and 3D printing, children with their caregivers reimagined and constructed their own monument.

Challenges and successes

Under the coalition government (2010–15) and the Conservative government (2015–24), the emphasis on creativity in education has largely been removed. Curriculum and exam focus have prioritised numeracy and literacy and, as a result, this has made the case for creativity harder among teachers, caregivers and school trusts.

However, schools can – and should – feel confident to champion creativity and put time and resources into this work. In 2022, for example, the OECD (Organisation for Economic Co-operation and Development) recognised creativity's centrality by introducing creative thinking into its PISA assessment. PISA already assesses its 38 member countries' schools on numeracy, literacy and scientific thinking, but now regards creative thinking to be as important. Meanwhile, the World Economic Forum (WEF, 2025) has stated that analytical thinking, creative thinking, AI (artificial intelligence) and big data will be the top in-demand skills by 2027. In essence, the WEF considers characteristics like curiosity and competencies like problem-solving to be as important as knowledge.

Further, there is measurable evidence to show the impact that creativity programmes can have. In 2003, iOi partnered with Harvard University academics to trial a creative thinking tool. Called the 'Divergent Association Task', it was a short activity that assessed divergent thinking (the ability to generate diverse solutions to open-ended problems), in which participants were invited to think of ten words that were as different from each other as possible. In an adapted study with 17 primary school classes and 500 learners, iOi measured learners' divergent thinking skills before and after their intervention, and after the intervention there was an 80 per cent increase in creative thinking skills across the classes. Measuring creativity is challenging, but these results go some way towards understanding how we can capture children's imagination and creativity through divergent thinking.

Championing imagination

Katarzyna Wasielewska, Teacher, St Joseph's Primary School

It all starts with imagination. If you think about any subject that we teach at school, nothing would truly be possible without imagination. How long can a child sit and listen to a list of facts without imagining them and putting them into a broader perspective? At St Joseph's Primary School, imagination is at the heart of everything that we do, fostering a dynamic, engaging and enriching learning environment.

What has helped to bring children's imagination to life? Having that spark – that moment where we can bring their ideas to life through the curriculum. In science, children have used their creativity to repurpose junk, recreating natural structures like beehives, coral reefs and bird nests while learning about sustainability and the natural world. These tactile projects connect abstract concepts to tangible experiences, leaving a lasting impact.

Walking through our school, you'll see the power of imagination displayed on every wall. Our 3D displays, often created by our learners, bring current or past topics to life, transforming corridors into living galleries of their learning journeys. In our classrooms, learners don't just sit and listen; they actively participate, bringing lessons to life in ways that are as diverse as they are meaningful.

Take our religious education lessons, for example. When Year 5 (aged nine to ten) learned about the story of David and Goliath, we encouraged them to imagine themselves as part of the story. This immersion inspired them to create a digital movie that reimagined the biblical tale. But it didn't stop there – our music lessons added a new layer of creativity, as children composed an original soundtrack to complement their film. They explored the sounds of the battlefield, the tension of the crowd and the ultimate triumph, giving life to their imaginations through music.

Imagination extends to every corner of our curriculum. In computing, with coding and problem-solving at the heart of the lessons, we've discovered that creativity plays an equally vital role. At St Joseph's Primary School, coding isn't just about algorithms; it's about expressing ideas. Our robotics lessons are a prime example. Learners not only program robotic animals but also build their faces using LEGO® bricks or craft outfits for them through knitting and crocheting. One learner summed it up perfectly: 'You don't have to worry about what job you'll do in the future. As long as you have imagination, you can always come up with a solution!'

At St Joseph's Primary School, imagination doesn't just enhance learning – it drives it. It bridges subjects, connects learners and prepares them for a world where creativity and problem-solving are invaluable. It's not just a method; it's a mindset that empowers every child to think beyond today's boundaries and imagine tomorrow's possibilities.

Questions to consider

- What are the opportunities to talk to learners about imagination and ask them for their ideas? Imagination provides greater opportunities to amplify a learner's voice.
- Imagination can be seen as frivolous and intangible. How can you create the conditions for learners to express their ideas and creativity in order to provide innovative approaches to teaching and learning?
- How can you utilise and maximise the support from charities and not-for-profits in providing educational programmes, activities and resources?

Further reading

Aronica and Robinson's book *Creative Schools: The grassroots revolution that's transforming education* (2016)

Brown et al.'s book *Creativity in Education: International perspectives* (2024)

Martinez and Stager's book, *Invent To Learn: Making, tinkering, and engineering in the classroom* (2013)

OECD's publication 'Supporting students to think creatively: What education policy can do' (2022a)

Wilkinson and Petrich's book *The Art of Tinkering: Meet 150 makers working at the intersection of art, science & technology* (2014)

17 Outdoor learning: How outdoor learning can improve engagement and progression

GEMMA GOLDENBERG

In this chapter, I explain the research proving that time outdoors can boost children's attention and engagement, and reflect on why it's important to consider which learning environments are optimal for different children.

> **The author**
>
> I worked in state primary schools in London for 15 years before retraining as a psychologist and researcher, completing a PhD on the impact of indoor and outdoor learning environments on children's stress, attention and behaviour. I have since published two books and currently work at the Institute for the Science of Early Years and Youth (ISEY) at the University of East London.

The problem

Recent research shows that indoor classrooms are often noisy, crowded and overloaded with visual materials that children have to process. This makes them difficult places for children to focus, listen and self-regulate (Fisher et al., 2014; Shield and Dockrell, 2003; Visentin et al., 2023). Meanwhile, there's a growing body of evidence suggesting that time outdoors supports children's learning, behaviour and attention. Unfortunately, children increasingly spend most of their time indoors. In recent years, school playtimes and outdoor play outside school hours have both reduced (Baines and Blatchford, 2019; Natural England, 2009). The current generation of children are facing a disconnect with nature and limited opportunities to be outside in an environment that might support their development (Louv, 2008).

What we did

Curious about whether the impact of an outdoor learning environment could be scientifically proven, I left my job as an assistant headteacher to design my own PhD research project, comparing children's noise levels, stress, attention and behaviour across indoor and outdoor settings. In the first research of its kind, we fitted children with wearable equipment such as head-mounted cameras, microphones and heart rate monitors to gain new insights into their experiences of indoor and outdoor environments.

Children in the Reception classes of four state schools in Newham, East London took part in eight indoor sessions in their usual classroom and eight outdoor sessions in whatever outdoor space was available at their school. Activities, resources, pedagogy and staff were carefully matched across both settings to isolate the specific impact of the environment.

Effects of being outdoors

Noise and stress

Using a decibel meter, we found that outdoor sessions were significantly quieter than indoor ones, both when the children were seated listening to a story and when they were actively learning and playing. This was true across all the schools studied, even those in urban locations close to road traffic. This is likely to be because outdoors there are no classroom walls and ceilings for noise to reverberate off, so noise dissipates more quickly. Excess noise has been shown to have a negative effect on children's learning and can particularly affect reading, comprehension and communication (Shield and Dockrell, 2003; Visentin et al., 2023).

On average, children's resting heart rates were also lower outdoors, suggesting lower levels of stress (Goldenberg et al., 2024). Indoors, noise levels and heart rate were correlated: as noise levels increased, children's heart rates went up. But interestingly, this wasn't the case outdoors. Being outside appeared to buffer children from the stressful effects of noise.

Attention and engagement

The impact on children's attention and focus was mixed. Some children were more on-task and engaged in their indoor classroom, whereas others paid much better attention outdoors. Boys were over three times as likely as girls to be more on-task outside, whereas children with a general preference for being outside were almost seven times as likely to focus for longer outdoors.

Further analyses revealed that the children who struggled *most* with their attention indoors showed the greatest improvements outside. On average, across eight indoor sessions, these 'low baseline attention' children were on task for 53 per cent of the time, but when they were presented with the same activities *outside*, their on-task time increased to 74 per cent. Children who found it hard to sustain engagement with an activity indoors (maximum engagement periods of 1.5 to 12 minutes) showed marked improvements outside, sometimes reaching up to 20 minutes of engagement.

These results demonstrate the importance of knowing children's preferences and observing them in different environments to see where they shine. No single environment is optimal for all children, but by locating almost all learning indoors, we deny some children the opportunity to learn in the environment that suits them best.

Children's self-regulated behaviour

The same patterns were observed with behaviour. Children who struggled to behave prosocially indoors (e.g. to engage in actions like sharing or inviting a child to join in) were more prosocial when they were outside (by around 50 per cent on average). Children also spent significantly more time engaged in self-directed play and talk with their peers outdoors.

On average, children were involved in the same number of antisocial interactions both indoors and outdoors. However, when looking *specifically* at the children who were the *most antisocial* in their usual indoor classroom, their antisocial behaviour decreased significantly in the outdoor environment. On average, they were involved in half as many antisocial interactions outside.

Why does being outside have a positive effect?

There are various pathways through which being outdoors has a positive effect on our minds and bodies. Exposure to natural light affects every cell in our bodies, regulating sleep patterns and improving mood. The ability to move around more can also support focus and self-regulation. Outdoors there are lower levels of noise and less visual clutter, reducing distractions and cognitive load. The presence of natural features like trees and plants has also been shown to improve wellbeing and enhance learning and behaviour.

We do not yet know exactly why being outside benefits some children more than others, although some research suggests that being in nature has equigenic effects (i.e. it benefits economically disadvantaged people more, thus narrowing the disadvantage gap).

How we do it

To enable all children to experience the potential benefits of the outdoors, it's important to build more opportunities for outdoor time into the school day – but how can this be done practically?

The good news is that the research suggests that schools do not need to subscribe to a particular approach in order for outdoor learning to be beneficial. A systematic review found that almost all outdoor learning had a positive impact on defined outcomes, particularly when activities were longer-term and included good preparation and follow-up (Fiennes et al., 2015).

The following tips can help you to increase outdoor time with your learners:

- Use tarpaulins so that children can sit outside even when the ground is damp.
- Consider investing in covered areas so that children can be outside when it's raining.
- Think about everyday routine activities that could be moved outside: independent reading, story time, circle time, etc.
- Evaluate the number of outdoor breaks that children have – in Finland, children have a break outside every 45 minutes!
- Let go of the notion that 'real learning' has to happen inside a classroom. Anything can be done outside: phonics groups, assessments, maths lessons, etc. You might find that some children's results are much higher when they are outside (see evidence from Mancuso et al., 2006; Mason et al., 2022).
- If there are no tables and chairs outside, use clipboards for written work.
- When you cannot get children outdoors, consider bringing the outside in. Indoor plants (Han, 2009), images of nature (Beute and de Kort, 2014) and nature soundscapes (Shu and Ma, 2019) have all been shown to have a positive effect on learning and behaviour.

- Consider fundraising opportunities for improving outdoor learning spaces; there may be specific funds available or it might be a project in which your parent teacher association (PTA) would like to get involved.

Challenges and successes

There are some barriers to spending time outside: lack of weatherproof clothing for children and a lack of outdoor resources (tables, chairs and canopies) are commonly cited as issues. It can be difficult to find funding. However, given the research evidence, it is arguably cheaper to be proactive in providing supportive environments for children than to deal with potentially avoidable issues further down the line. Sharing the benefits of the outdoors with parents and governors can help to gain momentum.

The research project involved creating an outdoor classroom, using whatever the children usually had access to indoors. This meant carrying tables and chairs, resources and often rugs, cushions and role-play areas outside. It was surprisingly quick to do this and children were keen to help. Their responses when they were told that today was an 'outdoor day' were usually very positive! Seeing daily activities moved outdoors provided a model for staff and enabled them to see that it's achievable to relocate almost any activity outside. Many teachers were keen to continue with this after the research project had ended, commenting that they had seen children who were often challenging indoors being noticeably more regulated and focused outside.

There are still some cases where outdoor playtime is removed from children as a punishment for misbehaviour or for not completing learning. This is often counterproductive because outdoor time supports children's focus and self-regulation, so taking it away can make it harder for them to achieve expectations. Sharing the value of time outdoors and reframing it as a child's right rather than a privilege can help to build awareness of the implications of taking playtime away.

The findings from the project have raised awareness of the significance of the physical learning environment and how, sometimes, challenges with behaviour or attention are not only situated 'within the child' but are the result of a learning environment that doesn't always suit the child's needs.

Prioritising nature engagement

Claudia Bellwood, Teacher, School 360, Newham

Why we did it

We knew from research that getting children to feel nature-engaged improves wellbeing and encourages them to care about tackling the climate crisis. We also knew that children are generally more focused when learning activities take place outside. We therefore wanted to create classrooms and creative learning experiences that prioritised outdoor learning to enhance our curriculum.

What we do

Reception, Year 1 and Year 2 are able to choose the indoor or outdoor area from 9.30–11.00 am and 1.30–3.00 pm every day. We make sure that one adult goes outside straight after each teaching session. This responsibility rotates through all the adults in the classroom.

Teachers plan for a balance of learning experiences in both indoor and outdoor spaces, collaborating in professional development sessions to work through obstacles and share ideas.

We teach the children how to choose and put on suitable clothes for outdoor play. Our learners all have access to wellies, waterproofs and aprons for water play or outdoor art, and there are covered areas for when the weather is bad. The children are explicitly taught how to tidy and care for the outside environment, including maintaining the gardens and feeding the chickens.

The challenges

- **Weather:** There is no such thing as bad weather, just bad clothing! It was crucial that we provided the learners with everything that they needed to play safely and comfortably outside.
- **Resources:** It might not be possible to double up on resources for outdoor maths and literacy areas, but this is where the great outdoors comes to your rescue. Being creative with tools helps to add to the experience. Chalk is a great, environmentally friendly way in which to replace pens and paper. Sticks, conkers or rocks are excellent tools for early counting.

- **Motivation:** Time to plan outdoor experiences and set up meaningful provision is important. You cannot just add an outdoor space and hope that it will happen by itself. Explicit planning for the outdoors is vital, and sharing the research and evidence behind the approach is a great way in which to get buy-in from staff. When adults show excitement about what's outside, even the most reluctant of children will follow.

The impact

Outdoor learning supports all kinds of learners. Reluctant writers can be easily persuaded to practise letter formation when they can do it with a paintbrush and mud or using chalk on the tarmac. We have found that moving an activity that is usually inside to the outside attracts a whole different group of children. Outside learning also provides children with the opportunity to develop gross motor skills, something that can be overlooked in a traditional classroom.

We know that sensory breaks are important for many children, and the outdoors has enabled this. Children who are easily overstimulated use the outside to self-regulate or to access learning that felt unachievable indoors. Having access to both spaces also means that it's generally quieter, allowing for more manageable small-group work or interventions.

Questions to consider

- Why do we do this activity/lesson indoors? Is there any feasible way in which this can be done outside instead?
- Who is struggling and have we seen them in an outdoor environment? Was being in an outdoor environment supportive for them?
- Do we know and talk to children about their environmental preferences? Where and how do they like to learn best: indoors or outdoors, sitting still, lying down or moving around, in quiet places or in noisy ones?
- When should we use short periods of outdoor time as a detox from noise or over-stimulation for individuals, groups or whole classes?
- How can we share the importance of the outdoors with parents, staff and other stakeholders?

Further reading

Atkinson et al.'s article 'Differential Effects of an urban outdoor environment on 4–5 year old children's attention in school' (2025)

Goldenberg et al.'s article 'Outdoor learning in urban schools: Effects on 4–5 year old children's noise and physiological stress' (2024)

Louv's book *Last Child in the Woods: saving our children from nature-deficit disorder* (2008)

Wass and Goldenberg's book *Take Action on Distraction: The definitive guide to improving attention and focus in the Early Years and Key Stage One* (2025)

Williams' book *The Nature Fix: Why nature makes us happier, healthier, and more creative* (2017)

18 Oracy: Progressively developing learner talk to build confidence and raise attainment

DANIEL THOMAS AND EMILY THOMAS

In this chapter, we explain the importance of an oracy education and the powerful impact that this has had on our schools. The chapter includes case studies, practical examples and lesson ideas that can be implemented in both primary and secondary sectors.

The authors

Emily is the oracy and Key Stage 1 leader at Pinner Wood School, a three-form-entry primary school in Harrow in Greater London. In 2022, her research was highly commended in the Douglas Barnes Award, and in 2024 they were accredited as a Centre of Excellence for Oracy with Voice 21.

Daniel arrived at School 21, London in 2016, and soon after became the head of oracy 4–18 and subsequently assistant headteacher. He has always been passionate in driving forward the development of oracy practice within the school and has also worked extensively with schools nationally to develop and embed oracy.

What is oracy?

Oracy is the ability to articulate ideas, develop understanding and engage with others through talking and listening. It is learning to talk and learning through talk. It can elevate learning, deepen understanding, enable us to connect with others and help to form how we see ourselves and how we are seen by others.

Despite the phrase being coined in the 1960s, over the past decade oracy has seen a surge in popularity. Recent global events have increased public consciousness surrounding the importance of young people having a voice. Education increasingly recognises that fluent, articulate and authentic communication is vital to empower learners to thrive in a future dominated by technology.

We are two very different schools with very different journeys, but we both agree that embedding oracy at the heart of everything that we do will best serve our learners and our communities.

Placing oracy at the heart of the school

At Pinner Wood, our vision is for all our learners to be confident, articulate individuals who are equipped with the tools with which to express themselves and collaborate effectively with others. Oracy is at the centre of our school. It is the golden thread that runs through teaching and learning, the curriculum, our behaviour strategy, pastoral support and wider opportunities. We explicitly teach the learners that oracy is important so that they are able to speak up for their rights, protect democracy and express their thoughts, opinions and individuality. We want all the learners to find their voice and use it to be civic and community-minded. We use oracy teaching tools and scaffolds to actively engage learners in debate and discussion, providing them with opportunities inside and outside the classroom.

School 21 is a pioneering, state-funded, inclusive 4–18 school in Stratford, East London, which is part of the Big Education Trust. Opening in 2012 with a mission to empower young people to change the world, the school believes that communication – both as a set of skills and as a method of learning – is not valued sufficiently alongside literacy and numeracy. We want oracy to underpin all teaching and learning, as well as be at the heart of how a school community functions.

How we do it

The implementation of oracy can be organised into three strands: teaching and learning, curriculum and school culture.

1. Teaching and learning

Oracy is designed to be woven into the DNA of teaching and learning: learning to talk, learning through talk and learning about talk. Practical strategies, lesson plans and classroom routines are at the centre of a dialogic classroom. Dialogic teaching is where talk is used to 'engage their interest, stimulate thinking, advance understanding, expand ideas and build and evaluate arguments empowering them for lifelong learning and democratic engagement' (Alexander, 2020, p. 1). It is at its most impactful when talk has been thoughtfully planned into the lesson, where talking strategies have been carefully considered to elevate the learning and where there is collaborative talk between teacher and learners.

One of the largest pieces of research conducted by the University of Cambridge (2019) measuring the impact of oracy on academic outcomes highlights two key tenets of high-quality oracy practice. Firstly, the teacher and learners equally deploy talk through structured tasks (this is not simply the teacher at the front using questioning, however sophisticated it may be). Secondly, the talk most frequently associated with academic progress comprises invitational types of dialogue:

- **IRE (Initiate-Response-Evaluate):** inviting others to explain, justify and/or use possibility thinking relating to their own or another's ideas
- **IEL (Interactive-Exploratory-Listening):** inviting others to elaborate and build on ideas.

At Pinner Wood School, oracy is our pedagogical approach, meaning that lessons are taught in a dialogic way. Some lessons are solely talk-based and we use a range of strategies and lesson plans to do this, although not all lessons have an oracy outcome.

At School 21, we have developed the Oracy Triangle (Figure 18.1), using the analogy of a fire triangle. This provides a codified shared language requiring three elements necessary for good oracy to exist: expectations, intentionality and reflection.

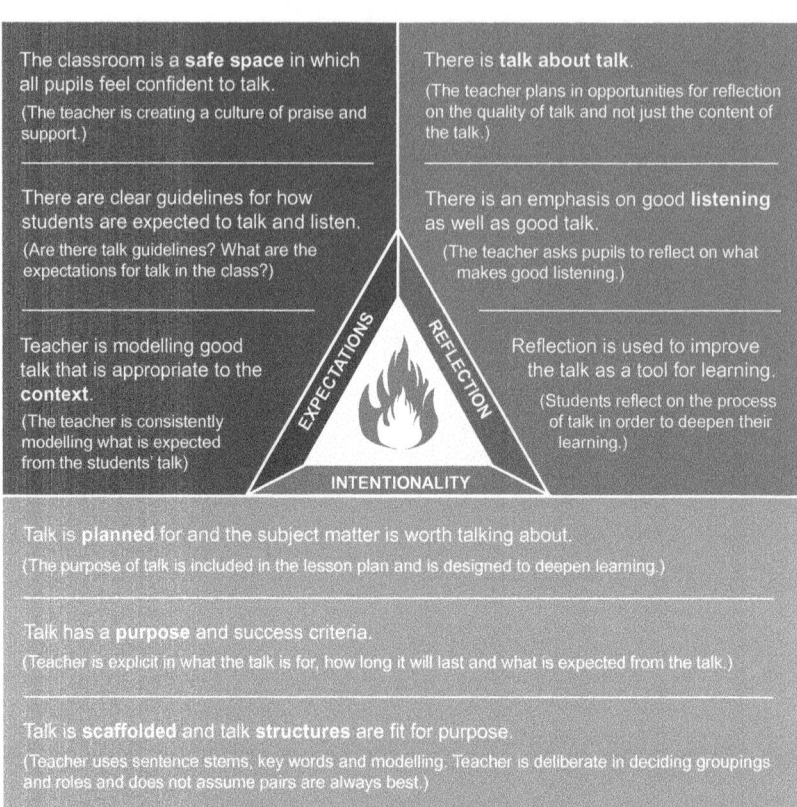

Figure 18.1: Oracy Triangle, developed by School 21

Setting high expectations for talk is at the centre of an oracy education. What are the expectations for talk in the classroom? How can we complain that learners cannot do something if we have not taught them to do it? How often do we spend time explicitly teaching protocols or specific roles? How much time do we spend reviewing the expectations? Rules, routines and expectations for talk must be created in collaboration with the learners and the teacher. To support this, some schools choose to have a set of school discussion guidelines for a cohesive approach (see Figures 18.2 and 18.3), which can be adapted for Early Years, primary and secondary schools.

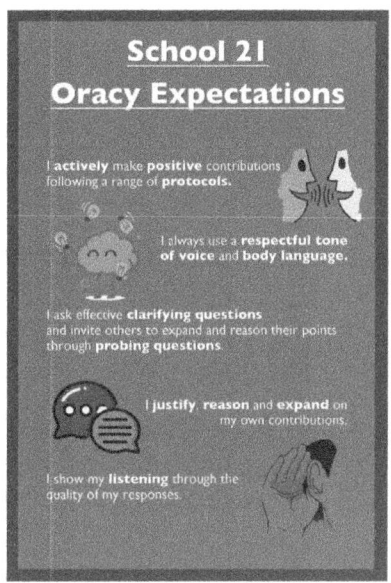

Figure 18.2: Talking Time poster, developed by Pinner Wood School

Figure 18.3: Oracy Expectations, developed by School 21

2. Curriculum

Oracy is unique in the sense that it is both content and pedagogy. When it comes to curriculum, it is important to define when you wish to teach oracy explicitly as knowledge and skills and when it should be embedded as a pedagogical practice in order to most effectively deliver the existing curriculum.

At Pinner Wood, our speech-making curriculum benchmarks learners' journey through the school. The progression grid in Table 18.1 maps this curriculum.

Throughout their time at Pinner Wood, learners will experience a progressive range of opportunities within the speech-making curriculum. These moments expand from Nursery to Year 6 (from age 3 to 11), with the learners delivering speeches to wider, larger audiences and having more freedom

Table 18.1: Oracy progression grid

Nursery	Reception	Year 1	Year 2	Year 3	Year 4	Year 5	Year 6
End-of-year report speech							
	'My interest' speeches		Debate speeches		SPARK speeches		Change speeches

Progression throughout their time at school
How do we build on skills and prepare the children for real-world situations?

Recorded and shared with families on an online platform	Performed to families on speech night	Performed to a larger audience of experts and the wider community	Secondary school transition
Families post comments	Audience asks prepared questions to which the children have answers	Audience asks unprepared questions and experts give feedback and insights into the topic	

Figure 18.4: Pinner Wood speech night progression

to speak on topics about which they are passionate. In Year 4, for example, the learners learn about the rainforest. At an evening event, learners deliver these speeches to their families and parents ask questions to which learners have pre-prepared answers. This then progresses into Year 6, where learners explore how they would like to change the world. Professionals, members of the community and their families are invited to attend the speech night and ask unprepared questions.

One of our first initiatives when embedding oracy was to change our end-of-year report comments to speech (see Figure 18.4). While previously the learners had written a reflection on their year, now they write a speech. This takes place during the whole-school Speech Week, where the learners learn about speeches, looking at and analysing what makes a good oration. They then move on to planning, writing and orally rehearsing, before recording their speech, which is then shared with their families. Every child in the school, from age three to 11, performs a speech, with adaptations being made where appropriate. These can include using speech and language therapy resources such as Alison Bryan's Colourful Semantics (2003) to support sentence construction. Some children may need to perform their speech in a quiet room with an adult rather than a larger audience. Others may benefit from recording each sentence of the speech in segments, which an adult can edit together before it is sent to families. For children who are selectively mute at school, a written copy of their speech can be sent home, allowing them to perform it in a more comfortable setting.

At School 21, every Key Stage 3 learner has an oracy lesson each week. In term 1, for example, learners may work on how to have an effective exploratory discussion, in term 2 on speech-making and in term 3 on how oracy can help them to become more employable. Drawing on a knowledge base of explicit tools that teachers have learned, we apply oracy into talk tasks and carefully designed assessments to measure the progress of all learners. Having collective success criteria for the different curriculum modules allows us to standardise the quality of talk so that all learners know what good talk sounds like. The benefit of having an explicit oracy curriculum that functions in the same way as other subject areas means that it raises its value for learners and parents.

3. School culture

School culture is the environment that we create through shared values, policies and practices. In order for oracy to truly be embedded, it must feature in all aspects of school life. For this to happen, oracy must be prioritised in school improvement plans and by senior leaders. The conversation is the culture.

Continuous professional development

Continuous professional development is delivered through an oracy approach. This is integral for the continuity of staff expertise, ensuring that oracy is not only embedded but also modelled and sustained in the culture of the school. Talking tasks are central to professional development, not only when developing oracy strategies but also for subject-specific training and wider teaching and learning development.

School council

Oracy is a fundamental part of democracy. At Pinner Wood, our school council meetings are designed with an oracy approach at the centre. Each year, two learners from each class are elected to represent their peers on the council, and those seeking election prepare speeches outlining their aims and ideas for the school. During the meetings, learners are divided into three discussion circles containing ten learners, and the circle discusses, provides feedback and debates ideas. Before each session, participants are reminded of the discussion roles and are provided with sentence starters to structure their ideas effectively. Two of the oldest learners act as chairs for each circle, facilitating participation and ensuring that everyone's voice is heard and valued. The chairs then feed back to the group and write up the meeting notes, which are shared with the wider school. Using oracy in the school council allows young people to advocate for themselves and others, as well as stand for change.

Being a member of the school council at School 21 means that you are an Oracy Ambassador, expected to be on hand to give tours, meet and greet visitors, participate in learner panels and act as hosts during any big events. Consultation is a big part of the school council's role, whether with the school chef on new menu ideas or on a working group creating a learner charter for discriminatory language. To bring rigour to the council and to develop oracy skills through the process, each meeting is seen as a developmental oracy moment, utilising key tools including effective chairing, summarising and challenging.

Restorative practice

At School 21, we employ a restorative approach to behaviour issues, which is underpinned by dialogue. When things go wrong, we place an emphasis on creating deliberate and structured reflective points for young people and teachers to discuss, as well as what steps can be taken to improve things. Rather than a detention, if a learner is removed from a lesson, they must meet with that teacher in a shared reflective space to 'restore'. We are an 'acknowledge first' school, meaning that any point of interaction between staff and learners should seek out positive intent, spotlighting and modelling what we want to see. This is in itself a deliberate skill that requires training and an awareness of body language, choice of words and tone of voice.

Challenges and successes

Currently, there is a lot of discussion around the potential problems when it comes to oracy – not what works but what doesn't work. Teachers say that they try to set up discussion and debate but the learners argue, behaviour becomes challenging, there is too much planning or it is somehow too risky. However, these outcomes depend on the teacher's understanding, ability to trial strategies and willingness to embrace a different way of doing things.

Some teachers misunderstand how oracy is embedded into the curriculum, believing that it can only be used during English lessons or that some subjects are better suited to using talk. However, the fact remains that, at its heart, oracy is a pedagogical tool, which is at its most powerful when embedded across the curriculum and into wider school life.

At primary level, common challenges that we face include speech and language development, participation and collaboration. From our observations, we have seen that many children who enter Reception may be used to one-on-one attention, where their questions are answered immediately and conversations revolve around their interests. As a result, this can mean that in the classroom, skills including listening, waiting and turn-taking are skills that need to be explicitly taught. Children benefit from structured opportunities to practise staying on topic, knowing when to speak and when to listen, and engaging others in conversation.

One of the unique challenges that we face at secondary level is the increasing volume of content to 'get through' as learners move towards their GCSE exams (taken at age 16). Time to plan and implement oracy strategies is often cited as a key barrier for teachers. We work extensively with middle leaders to ensure that oracy is embedded at the point of curriculum design for the team. This takes the workload away from individual teachers planning it into each of their lessons. Secondly, the sheer fluidity and frequency of different teachers in different rooms means that having any collective, quality-assured criteria for high-quality oracy is difficult. Having shared language, such as our School 21 Oracy Expectations and centrally designed template slides as an online resource, supports all learners to be exposed to a consistent diet of oracy, whatever the classroom and whoever the teacher. Finally, the social dynamics of a secondary school, together with adolescent self-consciousness, can have a significant impact on learners' motivation to use their voice in public. One strategy that we use to combat this is to 'scaffold confidence'; we deliberately build in low-stakes talk in smaller groups as stepping stones into more expansive, wider group talk or public sharing.

However, any gains far outweigh these challenges. When you realise how failing to develop oracy skills impacts the young people in front of you, it becomes a challenging but necessary pursuit.

The impact of oracy has been transformational in rethinking teaching and learning and learners' confidence and collaborative and communication skills. Our learners are confident, articulate speakers who want to share their ideas with the world. They are developing into compassionate, collaborative citizens who are able to participate in any discussion. They are able to look objectively at talk and discuss challenging topics beyond their years. Oracy is a tool for challenging global issues, fostering the need to listen as well as to talk.

Parents say that oracy has been helpful in enabling their children to better communicate their ideas, become more articulate and put arguments together. They think that oracy builds their confidence and, most importantly, nurtures their development as human beings.

Placing oracy at the heart of our school

Nicky Pear, Deputy Headteacher, Cubitt Town Primary School, Tower Hamlets, London

Why we did it

We began our oracy journey a number of years ago, as we realised that our learners, while well-behaved and attentive, were also very passive. Our curriculum was helping to develop great readers, writers, mathematicians and thinkers, but not equipping learners to successfully and confidently communicate. We saw this as a crucial missing link, and it became our intention to change the culture of our school and ensure that learners' days were talk-rich from the moment at which they arrived at the gate in the morning to when their parents collected them at the end of the day. As part of this transformation, we looked closely at our structure for assemblies and decided that the way in which we were delivering them was not fit for purpose, with learners sitting largely in silence, listening to a lecture from the front. We decided to radically change the way in which we assembled, developing a dialogic approach in which adults facilitate but learners do the talking.

What we did

We devised a structure of assemblies in which learners from two different classes sit in one large circle and are then grouped into trios. We pair year groups up together so that learners can have discussions with and get to know other learners from older and younger years. Each assembly is 30 to 45 minutes long and is based around an engaging stimulus: this could be a short film, a poem, a piece of music or a philosophical idea. The adults in the room act as facilitators, setting up a sequence of open-ended discussion points relating to the stimulus, which the learners discuss firstly in their trios and subsequently as a whole group. This enables them to develop both their conversational and presentational oracy skills. Ongoing feedback is provided by adults and peers, based on a set of commonly agreed discussion guidelines, and sentence stems are provided as a scaffold. While meticulously planned, there is an organic element to the assembly structure, in that conversations lead in original and interesting directions. Throughout the year, different subject leaders take responsibility for planning oracy assemblies and they have now become a truly cross-curricular experience.

The challenges

An initial challenge was one of changing mindsets: rows of children was what people expected in assemblies. However, once staff became used to the structure, the old way of doing things soon became a thing of the past and oracy assemblies became universally popular with both learners and staff.

Timetabling oracy assemblies is also a challenge in a three-form-entry school, and we have had to dedicate a lot of time in the hall each week. By reducing the number of traditional whole-school assemblies, we have managed to make this work.

The impact

Six years later and we still run almost all our assemblies in circles. It has become the norm. The communication skills that learners develop in oracy assemblies are then developed in classrooms, with teachers providing opportunities to talk in every lesson of the day.

An unintended consequence has been that assemblies have become a form of professional development for staff. Particularly for those new to teaching and the school, observing colleagues running oracy assemblies and utilising a range of tools and resources has helped them to develop skills to use more broadly in their classroom practice. The same applies for support staff, who are an integral part of assemblies.

Oracy is now the golden thread in teaching and learning at Cubitt Town, weaving through every aspect of learners' school experience. Assemblies are a crucial part of this – a visible expression of our talk-rich learning culture, in which learners are supported to find their voice and given the confidence to use it.

Questions to consider

- What oracy work is already planned into your curriculum?
- What expectations are there for talk in and outside the classroom?
- Do teachers in your school value oracy as highly as literacy and numeracy?
- What professional development might teachers need if they are to both teach learners *to* talk and teach *through* talk?
- How can leaders build oracy into the wider fabric of the school to show that they value it highly, e.g. relationships management, democratic structures like school council or professional development systems?

Further reading

Alexander's book *Towards Dialogic Teaching* (2008)
Gaunt and Stott's book *Transform Teaching and Learning Through Talk: The oracy imperative* (2019)
Knight and Poultney's book *Classroom Talk: Evidence-based teaching for enquiring teachers* (2020)
Mercer's book *Oracy: The transformative power of finding your voice* (2025)

19 Mantle of the Expert: Using drama and role-play to bring learning to life
TIM TAYLOR

In this chapter, I explain the teaching and learning approach called Mantle of the Expert (MoE) and how it can be used to transform learning in the primary classroom. We discuss the challenges associated with implementation and consolidation and recommend solutions to address these challenges.

> **The author**
> I started teaching in 1990 and discovered MoE through Luke Abbott. Inspired, I implemented it in my classroom, leading to successful external recognition and a government-funded research project. This propelled me into full-time training, publishing *A Beginner's Guide to Mantle of the Expert* in 2016 and supporting schools globally.

What is the Mantle of the Expert?

Developed by Dorothy Heathcote in the mid-1980s, MoE is about creating stories as contexts for exploring and developing curriculum learning. In the story, the learners take on the role of a team of experts with responsibility to fulfil a commission – a project or assignment – for a client. It is from the responsibilities of the expert team that the name 'Mantle of the Expert' comes.

Here's an example. Imagine a class of seven-year-olds entering a story as a castle restoration team commissioned by National Heritage to restore a ruined castle. Their first task is to visit the ruin, discuss the commission with a representative from National Heritage, and then map the castle and make a list of jobs that need doing immediately. In the classroom, the learners are introduced to the story using a narrative opening:

There is, on the top of a wind-blasted hill, an ancient and long-empty stone building. Its towers are crumbling, its once-solid walls broken and decayed, and its great wooden doors hang ajar, rotting on rusted hinges. Vines and moss cling stubbornly to the ruins, weaving through cracks where mortar once held strong. Whispers of the past seem to echo through the broken archways, carried by the howling wind. Once a proud fortress, it now stands as a forgotten relic, a monument to time's relentless passing. Shadows darken within its hollow shell as the sun sinks low, casting long, jagged silhouettes across the ground. Something about the place feels heavy, almost alive, as if it remembers the stories of those who once dwelled there – their triumphs, their fears and their secrets now lost to history. Standing outside the building is a woman in a long raincoat, her hood pulled up against the wind. The woman works for National Heritage, and in her hand she carries a brown leather briefcase. She is waiting for a team of experts in castle restoration, commissioned by National Heritage to repair the castle and open it to visitors. Suddenly, she hears the sound of an engine and sees a large green van making its way up the winding country road to the castle. Written on the side of the van are the words 'Castle Restoration Team'.

The teacher pauses and asks the listening learners, 'If you were this team, what kind of equipment do you think you might carry in your van?'

Working in small groups, the learners discuss the question and create a list, combining drawings and writing with the teacher's guidance and support. To expand the learners' knowledge, the teacher displays a prepared list on the whiteboard using a slide.

Stepping now into the fiction, the teacher takes on the role of the woman in the story: 'Ah, it's good to see you. Sorry about the weather – it's often like this, I'm afraid. I expect you'd like to get started and see what you're up against! Shall we go inside the walls? Watch out for fallen masonry – it's a bit slippery, I'm afraid.'

Returning to the narrator voice, the teacher reads, 'Carefully, the team makes their way through the crumbling gateway and inside the broken walls of the castle. There they find a courtyard filled with fallen masonry and twisted weeds. Here and there, they catch sight of rusted machinery and other artefacts that hint at the castle's long history.'

The teacher stops and asks the learners to imagine what they see. Showing them pictures on the whiteboard and giving them a list of castle vocabulary, she asks the learners to draw what they find in the ruin and to make a note of anything dangerous that needs urgent attention. Once again, the learners get to work in groups, with the teacher's continued support.

Once the task is complete, the team discusses the order in which to carry out the repairs. Stepping into the fiction, the learners enact the team at work, using their equipment and taking care to avoid accidents. The teacher uses a drama convention to hold the moment, saying to the learners, 'I'm just going to take some photographs of the team at work for our website. I'll count down: three, two, one. When I reach one, I'm going to ask you to hold the moment, as if you are in a photograph. See whether you can get the faces of the team while they are at work, the effort they are putting in, the care that they are taking. Ready? Three, two, one…'

Returning to their desks, the teacher says, 'Let's take a look now at the letter that the team received from National Heritage. This will give us an idea of what's ahead.' She then displays the letter on the whiteboard:

Dear Castle Restoration Team,

We are thrilled to confirm your role in restoring Stormwatch Castle, a vital project to preserve its history and ensure its safety for future generations. Below are the key tasks requiring your expertise:

1. **Site assessment**
   Conduct a thorough evaluation of the castle's condition, including structural stability, areas of damage and overall documentation.
2. **Work evaluation**
   Develop a detailed plan for necessary repairs and restorations, addressing immediate safety concerns, preservation strategies and required resources.
3. **Castle restoration**
   Restore the castle to structural soundness while preserving its historical significance, using authentic materials and modern techniques for safety.
4. **Visitor safety**
   Ensure visitor safety by addressing hazards like unstable masonry and slippery surfaces, implementing signage, pathways and barriers.
5. **Historical research**
   Investigate the castle's history to uncover its stories, architectural evolution and cultural importance.
6. **Visitor experience recommendations**
   Offer ideas to share the castle's history through displays, tours, interactive media and educational programmes.

Your contributions will shape Stormwatch Castle into a site that honours its heritage while securing its future.

Yours sincerely,

Dr Eleanor Hughes
Project Manager

The teacher asks the learners whether they have any questions. To answer the questions, she will step into the role of Dr Hughes.

'Let's imagine that we've set up a meeting with Dr Hughes at our offices. I expect that we have a meeting room for such purposes. How would you like the meeting room to look? What kinds of things are on the walls? How should the seats be arranged?'

Before she starts, the teacher encourages the learners to take notes, explaining that there will likely be a lot of important information to remember.

The learners ask questions and write down notes. The teacher answers the questions in role as Dr Hughes and comes out of role to give the learners support and time to write. At the end of the meeting, Dr Hughes asks the team to write her a short report on their first visit to the ruins, including a list of the repairs completed so far. Stepping out of the fiction, the teacher guides the learners in writing these reports. Each learner writes their own.

In this way, the teacher creates a fiction, casts the learners as an expert team, commissions them to work on a project and assigns various tasks to fulfil the work. The context of the castle and the restoration team's responsibilities requires the learners to learn about castles and their history, while developing curriculum skills – such as research, note-taking, report writing and drawing – in meaningful and purposeful ways that integrate subjects across the curriculum.

In Mantle of the Expert, the learners' tasks have immediate meaning and purpose within the fiction. There is a sense of urgency and importance to what they are doing because of their relationship with the client.

That is not to say that we should attempt to teach everything using MoE. Some subjects or specific areas of study are best taught discretely. However, once a carefully planned context is up and running, it can offer all kinds of opportunities.

- exploring the castle's structure to check whether the walls and towers are safe
- writing reports to explain what needs fixing and how the work is progressing
- drawing maps of the castle
- spotting dangerous areas, like loose stones or slippery paths, and planning how to fix them

- finding out about the materials used to build the castle and thinking about what to use for repairs
- digging into the past by examining old objects and working out what they were for
- measuring and calculating how much wood, stone or other materials are needed for repairs
- presenting their discoveries clearly as if speaking to visitors
- creating signs and posters to help visitors to understand the history of the castle
- exploring how plants and weather have damaged the castle and thinking about how to protect it
- developing stories about the people who once lived in the castle and writing them down.

Challenges and successes

Despite its benefits, implementing MoE can present challenges. One is time: integrating a fictional context into a packed curriculum is daunting, especially for beginners. One solution is to view subjects as interconnected. For instance, writing stories about castle inhabitants engages learners in both English and history, providing content, purpose and audience.

Learning MoE requires time and effort, involving study, practice and reflection. I suggest that you start small with online resources like *A Beginner's Guide to Mantle of the Expert*. Progress to professional trainers offering workshops, support and demonstration lessons to embed the approach effectively.

Curriculum demands can also discourage schools from exploring new methods. However, Mantle of the Expert makes learning meaningful by connecting it to learners' interests, fostering creativity and problem-solving while achieving excellent results.

The MoE approach transforms classrooms into engaging communities, ensuring that learning is both purposeful and enjoyable.

Mantle of the Expert at Woodrow First School, Redditch

Richard Kieran, Headteacher

Why we did it

Implementing MoE at Woodrow came from a whole-staff desire to create authentic contexts in which the learners could engage with the curriculum. We wanted learners to have a point of view, ask more questions and make links within their learning – bringing about a voice in their school life.

What we did

We had a go at using plans from the MoE website (www.mantleoftheexpert.com) and decided which areas of the curriculum might best lend themselves to using imaginative contexts. We watched each other in class, we planned together and mistakes were seen as learning points and developmental. Learners were talking more about their work and could be heard in classrooms – building islands, investigating sinkholes and stopping rail disasters.

We spent time finding out about the work of Dorothy Heathcote, deciding how it could best work for our learners and the school community. The school opened its doors to share opportunities that the work brought with its community. Governors would come in and meet with children and staff, and parents had opportunities to see their children engaging with the work and each other.

Developing the practice

We read more about the approach and considered how we could use drama to reflect and develop. Learners might be in a coal mine as a team investigating child labour for Queen Victoria, taking a trip to Canada as a team of rewilders to track wolves, or repatriating a leather slipper to Egypt, discovered when they were wall-watching in Northumberland. We worked with key individuals who knew the approach and got to know the school.

We held study days where staff, learners and visitors could work together in class and in workshops. This built a growing network of schools and organisations with whom we could work.

Reviewing

We review constantly. Scenarios are never repeated, and this ensures that they are always constructed with – rather than taught to – learners. As we have developed a stronger understanding of how the system works for learners and staff, we continue to develop how narrative with drama can be even better implemented using MoE. We also spend time returning to the 'why' – why MoE is at the heart of our curriculum.

The challenges

As the prescriptivist demands of education policy have increased, staff have had to be more creative in when and how we can teach using MoE, making more links across the curriculum, while never shoehorning or contriving content. It is vital to adapt and be open to its evolution.

A weather eye is always kept on how external bodies, such as Ofsted, will regard our work – Mantle of the Expert can be considered a niche approach and is by no means an 'off the shelf approved' published scheme.

Impact

Wandering around the school, you will see and hear classes of children suspending their disbelief. The community is fully on board with the approach and value the way in which the learners love to learn new things.

They know that these contexts are not real but are more than happy to imagine that they are. There are newly refreshed maps, notes and pictures on the walls, floors and ceilings. Displays are not just wallpaper – they tell the story. Learners' talk is purposeful and they know that their tasks in MoE are important and often urgent. They value what they do and they value the fact that they have influence and agency.

Teachers want to teach at Woodrow because they can work with Mantle of the Expert – consequently, we only lose teaching staff when they retire.

Questions to consider

- How could Mantle of the Expert approaches help to create activities for curriculum learning in your setting?
- How much confidence and knowledge do teachers in your setting have about the use of drama as a pedagogical tool?
- To what extent do learners experience learning in your school as purposeful and authentic? Could an approach like Mantle of the Expert help to enhance this?
- How much of the learning in your school is currently taught as cross-curricular? Could a rigorous approach to cross-curricular learning like Mantle of the Expert help your teachers to develop more opportunities for cross-curricular learning?

Further reading

Aitken's book *Real in All the Ways That Matter: Weaving learning across the curriculum with Mantle of the Expert* (2013a)
Aitken's chapter 'Dorothy Heathcote's Mantle of the Expert approach to teaching and learning: A brief introduction' (2013b)
Aitken and Taylor's book *Try This: Unlocking learning with imagination* (2022)
Heathcote and Bolton's book *Drama for Learning: Dorothy Heathcote's Mantle of the Expert approach to education* (1995)
Taylor's book *A Beginner's Guide to Mantle of the Expert* (2016)
Taylor's article 'Introducing Mantle of the Expert' (2018)
Mantle of the Expert: www.mantleoftheexpert.com
Mantle of the Expert Network: www.mantlenetwork.com
Woodrow First School and Nursery: www.woodrowfirstschool.co.uk

20 Design thinking as pedagogy: The importance of the Maker{Cycle} in practical subjects

ALISON BUXTON

In this chapter, I explain a pedagogical tool – our Maker{Cycle} – for supporting making in the classroom, and share the many ways in which this tool underpins our work, supports children's learning and transforms educators' practices.

> **The author**
>
> I am the director of Maker{Futures} at the School of Education at the University of Sheffield, UK. This ambitious programme is leading an innovative change in schools, libraries and museums by supporting educators to develop their maker education provision and practice. As well as having over 20 years of experience in STEAM and maker education, I have authored several practical maker books and sit on international advisory boards for LEGO® Education and the FIRST® LEGO® League global robotics programme.

Fostering creativity

My background is in construction and design and I began to notice a phenomenon when supporting schools with STEAM-based provision in around 2014. Whereas younger children (three to six) demonstrated generally high levels of confidence in their own creative ideas and responses, proudly showing off their drawings and models, I noticed that the children became less creatively confident the older they became. By ten years old, children were asking, 'Miss, is this the right answer?', expecting me to assess their creative ideas. They increasingly lost the idea that they could bring their own creativity to how they responded to a design brief, and instead were drawn to following someone else's instructions to build someone else's product. When children came up against a problem, they seemed to have no idea how to solve it independently. The queue for the teacher's help grew longer, and the children became less resilient. When things did not go right, the children were often left feeling frustrated and lost confidence in their design and making abilities.

This left me wondering what happens when the problem changes. Perhaps it is time to start thinking about *how* we creatively solve problems rather than *what* the correct answer is. When teaching practical subjects, many schools use a linear design process: research, design, make, evaluate. With this model, children are being asked to design a product of which they have no prior experience or expertise, make it by following their own instructions or design annotations, and then evaluate it to say whether it met the brief and what improvements they would make. Can you imagine asking a chef to design a new menu without trying out ideas along the way? Or asking an engineer to oversee the construction of a new bridge without a range of physical and digital models for testing a range of approaches? It is just not how things work in the real world. Every design-based sector has its own version of a cyclical approach to the design process.

The Maker{Cycle}

One of the tools that underpins all our work at Maker{Futures} is the Maker{Cycle} (Figure 20.1). In order to help children to respond to real-world challenges, we needed to look at how innovators in different areas of society and in different communities effectively solve problems. The Maker{Cycle} draws on a range of existing design cycle models used in the real world and has been adapted to work in early Years and primary education. In fact, it is so effective as a method of improvement and innovation that we use it at every level of our work. The Maker{Cycle} is integral to the entire Maker{Futures} programme. We live and breathe it at all levels. Whether research, development or working closely with educators, we approach every aspect of our work as makers. This cyclical, iterative process means that we are always evaluating and looking for ways in which to improve what we do.

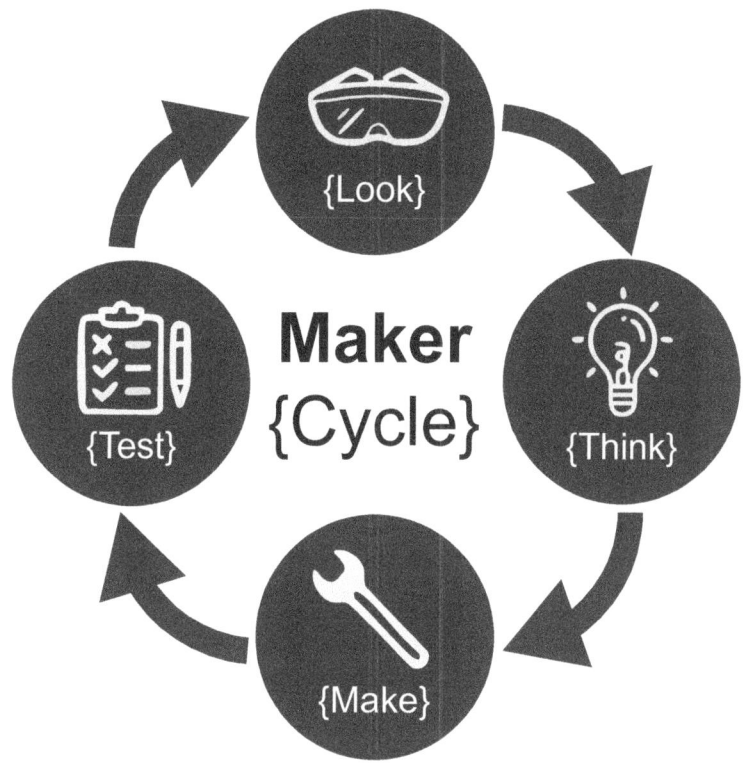

Figure 20.1: The Maker{Cycle}

Using the Maker{Cycle} in school

The Maker{Cycle} guides us through four stages: LOOK, THINK, MAKE and TEST. It is designed to be used multiple times – if we only work through the four stages once, then we have essentially gone back to a linear process.

To illustrate, I will describe one lesson that I developed with a class of nine- and ten-year-olds, which drew together a number of themes and subjects: sustainability and design technology. The children were tasked with the challenge of designing and creating a gift that money could not buy. In this lesson, we included opportunities to work through the Maker{Cycle} many times.

Maker{Cycle} 1: Gathering ideas

Sometimes, the Maker{Cycle} can be carefully structured and is facilitated by the teacher to support learning. For example, in this lesson, I used the structure of the Maker{Cycle} to support children in gathering and generating ideas:

- **LOOK:** Children were shown a photograph of a child at Christmas time sitting inside a cardboard box, with an untouched pile of new toys lying to one side. Children looked at the image closely.
- **THINK:** As a class, they thought about what they were seeing and I asked some open-ended questions: What is significant about the picture? Why is the box of value to the child? Are more expensive gifts more valuable? What kind of gift might you give that money cannot buy?
- **MAKE:** Children were encouraged to make suggestions in response to these questions, drawing on their lived experiences and cultural contexts. For example, the child was enjoying the box because it was playful and open-ended.
- **TEST:** The children were supported through careful questioning to reflect on their responses and test out their ideas through discussion with others. Some responses were met with positivity, providing affirmation that encouraged others to make suggestions. Other responses were not heading in the right direction so were redirected through gentle rewording of the question. For example, in response to the question 'What kind of gift might you give that money cannot buy?', one child suggested a limited edition pair of very expensive trainers. I asked them whether anyone might be able to give this as a gift and another child suggested that someone famous could. I then responded by asking them to think of things that could not be bought by anyone, even if they were very rich. Another learner suggested that doing something fun with our families was a gift that money can't buy. I said that this was a great suggestion, and very quickly, hands shot up with other similar suggestions.

Maker{Cycle} 2, 3, 4 and beyond… Exploring and combining materials

At other times in the lesson, the Maker{Cycle} was iterative and driven by children's curiosity and interests, rather than being explicitly guided by the teacher. This occurred in rapid succession, and could be observed as the children began to explore and combine materials. In their groups, children were given 'a gift that money did not buy'. This was a box filled with an assortment of unused items, including fabric scraps, discarded plastic, old containers and widgets. Children began to LOOK closely at what they had in their box and at the project brief. They began to THINK about the possibilities and discuss ideas together as they explored the materials. They began to MAKE connections (physically and metaphorically) between the characteristics of the materials and their lived experiences. For example, one child picked up some blue fabric and said that it reminded them of the ocean, and another child picked up an orange bottle lid, thought about it and made the suggestion, 'This could be the sun.' They also began to TEST ways of combining the materials together, seeing what worked and what didn't.

At this point of the process, it is hard to keep track of the number of times that children naturally iterate their ideas as they start to physically make their model. If they come across a problem, the Maker{Cycle} encourages them to LOOK closely and THINK about what is happening and why. Do they need to MAKE an adjustment or try something different? They MAKE changes and TEST things out as they go.

By responding to the brief or challenge in this cyclical way, children formulate their own ideas. For some children, the physical representation of their ideas centred on a trip to the beach with , where they could spend quality time together. Others in the class responded differently, with examples including creating a board game to play together, with a similar focus on quality time with family. Other children also reflected on the theme of sustainability and wanted to help people to make good decisions that would help the environment, creating a model home representing a safe place in which to live.

The challenges and successes

While we see children adapt naturally to this learning approach, it is teachers who ensure that it happens. By considering how children might work through the Maker{Cycle} at every stage of their project, it is teachers who facilitate the learning opportunities.

However, some educators fear a loss of control. How can they plan if they don't know what children will make and how? The reality is that planning is relatively easy once you let go of the reins. A skilled teacher can pose thoughtful questions that support children to find their own particular outcome. They can provide a range of materials and tools that children can utilise. Children learn to adapt their ideas to cater for the constraints of the resources and their own limitations in terms of skills and understanding of the materials and tools available to them.

For larger projects, time can be a limiting factor. Very few schools have any spare time in their curricula to introduce a new subject or project. Our most successful Maker{School}s integrate the Maker{Cycle} and physical making across the curriculum by adapting how they teach rather than what they teach. They provide opportunities for children to make early in the term, which in turn provides time for deeper engagement across a subject. Making supports their understanding of a subject, and this then manifests in other areas of their work, such as writing.

If physical making goes beyond a single lesson, there is an issue of where to put half-finished projects. Schools have responded to this need by freeing up shelves, window sills and the tops of bookshelves for 'projects in progress' displays.

The teachers in our Maker{School} programme also use the Maker{Cycle} to introduce 'makerspaces' and maker pedagogies into their practice and curriculum. We do not ask or expect teachers to implement whole-school changes in one go – they start small, with a simple project or maker-based play. They LOOK closely to notice how children are learning and THINK about the way in which children are engaging. What is it about the making process that affects these changes? What changes would they like to make next? This organic and reflective approach to change helps teachers to make positive changes and keep things manageable.

The Maker{Cycle} is very much aligned with how children naturally learn and explore the world around them: by doing (Dewey, 1933) and through play (Vygotsky, 1967). Through this iterative approach, children develop curiosity, creativity and innovative ideas. They become comfortable with uncertainty and build resilience as they think and make their way through problems that they encounter. They collaborate with each other as they seek each other's expertise. They have the creative freedom to experiment, trust their instincts and bring their ideas to life. Children self-differentiate when using the Maker{Cycle}, meaning that it is an inclusive teaching method. We have also found that by handing elements of control and agency over to the children, they respond positively, leading to greater participation, motivation and improved behaviour. It is worth noting that the Maker{Cycle} does not only need to be utilised in practical subjects like DT; increasingly, we are seeing teachers utilise this methodology across the curriculum and as a whole-school approach.

Introducing the Maker{Cycle}

Debra McFarlane, Headteacher, St Joseph's Academy, UK

Why we did it

We were having a particularly challenging time with engagement and behaviour, and some of our children were at serious risk of exclusion. We were looking for solutions to tackle this and were recommended Maker{School} by our school improvement officer. At the start of the new school year, we had a full day of professional development led by Alison and the Maker{Futures} team, where they introduced how children learn through making.

What we did

Our Year 4 teacher tried a simple maker project with her class: stop-motion animation to create short stories. Children began making almost immediately and the children were hooked! There was full engagement and lots of learning as they figured out what worked and how to create a simple animation. While all learners got a lot out of it, the children who really shone were the group of children who usually struggled to focus and behave. This was our first experimentation in using the Maker{Cycle} to change our approach. As we began to notice the effects of this change, we reflected on what it was about this teaching that had led to such positive engagement. We then redesigned our curriculum to embed a range of physical and digital making elements linked to our current topics.

We also introduced child-led making into other areas. For example, we created more making opportunities in our Forest School provision, as well as opportunities to make in our alternative provision area for those children who struggle to be in the classroom for sustained periods.

The impact

We are in our second year as a Maker{School}. The whole school is making! Other teachers across the school have adopted the approach, and making is now actively used as a learning methodology across the school and across the curriculum. Children are more actively engaged in learning and we no longer have a need for children to access alternative provision off site. No children are at serious risk of exclusion. We are noticing our children becoming more resilient, creative and thriving, solving problems through their making.

Questions to consider

- How do you currently approach practical projects in the classroom: a linear or cyclical approach?
- How could you use the Maker{Cycle} to introduce a new approach to physical or digital making?
- What small changes could you make in your classroom to introduce the Maker{Cycle}?
- How might you use the Maker{Cycle} to shape your planning of lessons?
- How might you measure or assess the learning, skills and attributes shown during the making process?

Further reading

Provenzano's book *The Nerdy Teacher Presents: Your starter guide to makerspaces* (2016)
Resnick's book *Lifelong Kindergarten: Cultivating creativity through projects, passion, peers, and play* (2017)
Maker{Futures}: makerfutures.org

PART 4

Assessment

21 Competency progression: How can we teach and assess transferable competencies?

ROBERT LOBATTO

In this chapter, I explain why developing transferable competencies is a neglected yet critical dimension of education in today's world, and how this can be successfully implemented in schools.

> **The author**
>
> I am a longstanding headteacher. For the last decade, I have been head of King Alfred School, London – an all-through independent school and pioneer within the progressive education movement. Prior to that, I was the headteacher of a large inner-city London comprehensive school, which won awards for achievement and innovation.

The importance of skills

To thrive beyond school, young people need well-developed transferable skills – what we might call the Hand aspect of education. Read any report from an employer's organisation (DfE, 2022) or any paper from national or global bodies on how education needs to evolve (e.g. Deloitte, 2018) and the need for competencies such as communication, creativity and metacognition is writ large.

In English schools, however, these Hand competencies have become marginalised. Over the last 15 years, the primacy of a knowledge-rich curriculum assessed through academic exams has become dominant, and focusing on skills has been seen at best as irrelevant, and at worst as harmful (Bennett, 2014; Christodoulou, 2011; Young, 2014). This has been reinforced by our high-stakes accountability system, which places almost all emphasis on exam-based assessment of academic knowledge alone.

As a result, growing numbers of young people feel inadequately equipped for life beyond school. Many learners who are academically unsuccessful leave school with neither a set of meaningful qualifications nor well-developed transferable competencies that would open up other post-school pathways (ASCL, 2019). Conversely, while academically successful learners have become very effective at passing exams, they may find themselves lacking critical skills required for the workplace, such as teamwork and creative thinking.

The system's challenge, therefore, is to recognise the necessity and importance of traditional academic learning but also the importance of other kinds of more expansive learning – to find a new synthesis between subject knowledge and transferable skills, teacher direction and learner agency, 'traditionalist' and 'progressive' approaches.

This is more complex than choosing one approach or the other. Walk into any school, however, and you will see the best teachers seamlessly transition from directing learning to facilitating self-directed learning and back again. How, then, to build this balance into sustainable school structures and cultures?

Integrating skills into the curriculum

After studying practices across the world, we first identified the skills and personal qualities that we sought to develop in our Deeper Learning Wheel (see Figure 21.1). Working through this identification phase was important, both for the outcome achieved and for the deeper understanding gained by the process. Although tempted by off-the-shelf models, such as Skills Builder (www.skillsbuilder.org), we required an approach that fitted our own context: one that entwined the transferable competencies with knowledge, was applicable across the 4-to-18 age range and connected to the ideas of 'thriving', which had been an area of development for some years. It was important that the underpinning architecture did not become too unwieldy. There were trade-offs to make here, but experience of various iterations taught us that, ultimately, 'less is more'.

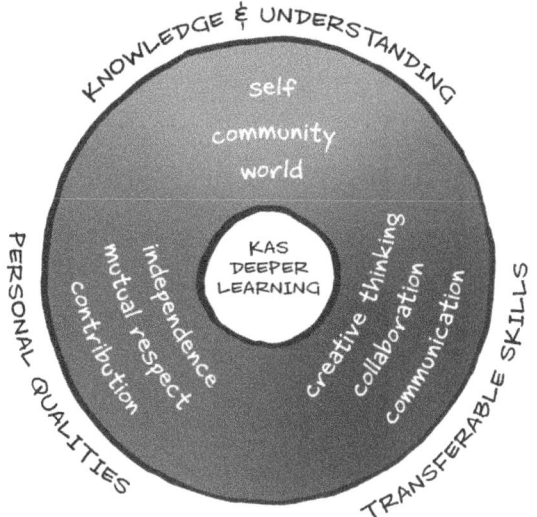

Figure 21.1: The King Alfred School Deeper Learning Wheel

Second, we needed to develop our *curriculum* so that it created time for competency development. This led to our Explorations Programme in Years 6, 7 and 8 – a set of structured, interdisciplinary inquiry projects, each lasting a term and inspired by Ron Berger's work (https://eleducation.org/who-we-are/people/ron-berger), XP School's Expeditions and the IB MYP (www.ibo.org/programmes/middle-years-programme/curriculum/interdisciplinary). Each Exploration leads to an outcome on a 'Big Question' shown in a public exhibition, such as 'Should we embrace or fear AI?', or a real-world practical project, such as 'How should we design and build a wellbeing garden for a local community centre?'.

For each Exploration, learners build subject knowledge, learn discipline-specific skills and focus on identified transferable competencies of the wheel. Running the complete programme over three years means that the moments of focus for each competency can be carefully planned over time. Each Exploration is allocated a significant slot within the timetable (five hours or a day per week). For the rest of the week, which is the significant majority, learners follow a conventional curriculum, which acts to support rather than drive these competencies.

Third, we needed to support staff to develop their *pedagogy*. One of the benefits of being an all-through school is the capacity to bring primary and secondary specialists together, enabling a blend of inquiry-led approaches with subject specialisms. Secondary colleagues have had to pivot towards a more inquiry-led pedagogy, involving a greater degree of open-ended questions, learner choice and learner-directed research and development time. Notably, this has supported their teaching and learning approaches in lessons outside of the programme.

Fourth, we needed to create our *assessment* system:

- Should we picture competency development as 'progression ladders'?
- Should assessment be a purely formative tool or should it include a summative element?
- How should we balance teacher, peer and self-assessment?

Our experience of trialling various rubrics led us towards reflection rather than assessment, and away from using ladders. We found that the development of skills was not necessarily a linear process, and ladders gave a false expectation that it should be. For many competencies, we also found that growth came from carrying out the competency with greater skill, confidence and depth, rather than by adding something new. We also found that some rubrics quickly tended to include too many value-laden adjectives and adverbs that were difficult for both learners and staff to interpret consistently. Therefore, instead of rubrics:

- The relevant competencies, carefully broken down, are identified to learners at the start of the Exploration and returned to at regular intervals.
- Learners journal each week to record and reflect on their development, as well as making ongoing observations on their collaboration and creative thinking.
- At the end of the unit, learners self-assess on a four-colour mastery scale, based on how successfully, confidently and independently they have been able to apply the identified competency.
- The teacher both comments on their progress and gives feedback on their self-assessment.

Fifth, we needed to consider *reporting*. Over the last few years, our school-wide reporting system has been developed to reflect the Deeper Learning Wheel. In the primary years, reports to parents include progress on the competencies, and the children conduct learner-led conferences with parents and teachers in which they share and reflect on their progress.

This approach comes into the secondary school via digital portfolios. Using Google Sites, learners collect evidence of their practice in each skill area, from Explorations, subject lessons and other school experiences. This evidence includes videos, images, sound and written work, and is accompanied by self-reflection and teacher comment. As the portfolios are organised by competency, learners are able to see how their skills have developed over time and can understand the similarities and differences in the way in which they are applied in different contexts. These portfolios become the centrepiece of learner-led conferences with parents and teachers, where, as in the primary years, learners share and reflect on their progress using their Google Site as evidence.

Challenges and successes

The first challenge was to decide on our aims. We knew that developing transferable competencies was important, but it was not until we developed our Deeper Learning Wheel that we were able to define exactly what we wanted to do and why.

The second challenge was to work through how we would develop competencies in parallel with strong subject knowledge. This required careful interweaving of the two within the Explorations and an intentional approach in other curriculum areas. While the Explorations drove the development of the competencies, more conventional teaching played the support role.

The third challenge was designing the Explorations themselves. This work was outside the direct experience of many of our staff, and required significant professional input, including visits to other schools, support from experts and collaborative planning time.

The fourth challenge was pedagogy. Many staff were well trained in teacher-directed learning but less familiar with high-quality enquiry-based practice. Learning from different phases was important here, alongside CPD and professional collaboration.

The fifth challenge was assessment. In many ways, this was the hardest nut to crack. On the one hand, there are fundamental questions about the value and authenticity of ascribing 'levels' to this kind of learning. On the other hand, learners and parents find themselves in a system where unless something is measured, it can feel as though it lacks value. In addition, without levelling, how do we measure progress and impact?

This links to the sixth challenge: reporting. To be seen to have value, reporting is necessary, and we had to think hard about how to integrate this into our existing systems.

The seventh and final challenge was commitment. Like the development of the competencies themselves, progress is not linear – there will be moments of joy and success and moments of disappointment and frustration. When learning is freer, the range of possible outcomes is greater. Growing competencies requires commitment over a sustained period of time, and courage and determination with learners, parents and staff are needed in order to navigate the challenging moments.

Despite the challenges, this work is unquestionably worth it. Imagine a scene: you walk into a hall alongside parents, staff and learners of many ages. In front of you, there are rows of exhibition desks, each dedicated to the impact of AI over the next 20 years. On one stand, you are taught about how healthcare will be transformed and how you will be looked after in the year 2050 by a robot, who will gently stroke your forearm. On another, you see the role that AI will play in settlement on Mars. In another, you see a piece of AI-infused art on the human brain that would not look out of place in a professional gallery. It is at this point that you check yourself and realise that every stall is staffed by an 11- or 12-year-old.

Imagine another scene: the final of a competition for the statue on the fourth plinth in Trafalgar Square. You chair the judging panel for six proposals for a memorial to the slave trade. Grounded in a detailed grasp of the history, and drawing on sophisticated concepts about power and equality explored through literature, each presentation fluently articulates their vision of remembrance and the physical embodiment of what it will look like. Again, you check yourself and remember that everyone talking is a 12- or 13-year-old.

And imagine a final scene: you see a group of 12- and 13-year-olds in a French lesson. The task is to write a script to show a French visitor around the school. The teacher explains the vocabulary and the learners ask whether they can work in groups, arguing that it will improve the quality of their work and be more fun. The teacher gives a shrug and, in a flash, the learners are collaborating constructively, thinking creatively about what to say and how to say it, and communicating with confidence and self-awareness. Before your eyes, you see that these competencies, when done right, can be truly transferable.

Our work in this area is too recent to establish its impact on exam results and academic progress measures. However, we have conducted regular external and internal evaluation of the Explorations, and learners report high levels of satisfaction with their progress, engagement and enjoyment. They have also given honest feedback and, in true enquiry fashion, have appreciated working collaboratively with teachers to develop the Explorations for the learners who follow.

Developing confident, curious and compassionate learners

Jeremy Hannay, Headteacher, Three Bridges Primary

Who we are

At the heart of our vision is a belief in education as a transformative experience – one that nurtures curiosity, character and connection. We believe that we need to go further than knowledge, developing confident, curious and compassionate individuals who are equipped to navigate an ever-changing world. Therefore, at the core of our approach, we foster a culture of enquiry, creativity and shared discovery.

What we do

Teachers at Three Bridges are seen as facilitators and co-learners, guiding children through research projects, structured discussions and philosophical enquiry. They seek to encourage learner-led learning, where children take ownership of their education, ask meaningful questions and seek out their own answers.

As part of this, innovative qualitative tools play an important role in understanding and assessing learner growth – especially in terms of attitudes toward learning. Learner journalling in mathematics has become a central part of our assessment approach, enabling children to reflect regularly on their experiences, emotions and questions. These written reflections help both learners and teachers to identify moments of insight, perseverance or challenge, allowing for responsive and personalised support.

Alongside journalling, we have also used video to capture authentic learning moments. By filming collaborative activities, discussions and problem-solving sessions, we gain insight into interpersonal dynamics, confidence levels and learner engagement that might otherwise go unnoticed. These recordings form a valuable resource for both staff development and learner self-awareness, as learners are often invited to reflect on their own participation.

Additionally, we have also conducted interviews with learners across different stages of their learning journey. These conversations are structured to draw out stories of growth, curiosity and resilience, revealing the internal dispositions that shape their approach to learning. Insights from these interviews are shared among staff and used to inform our teaching practices and pastoral care.

The challenges

Balancing deep, meaningful learning with external expectations is an ongoing challenge. The pressures of standardisation and accountability can sometimes limit the time and space needed for rich enquiry and reflection. Another challenge is ensuring that all learners – regardless of background – feel empowered to succeed and have equitable access to the opportunities that will help them to flourish.

Reflections

We understand that true learning cannot always be quantified. While we monitor academic progress, we also value the more intangible indicators of success: the confidence with which learners express their ideas, their ability to challenge perspectives and their commitment to making a positive difference. Our use of learner journalling, video ethnography and narrative interviews has significantly enhanced our ability to observe and assess these critical skills in a meaningful way.

These approaches are deeply embedded into our close-to-practice research and everyday routines. The insights that we gather inform not only individual support plans but also the ongoing evolution of our teaching practices. In this way, we strive to foster a learning environment where every child feels seen, heard and empowered to make a difference.

Questions to consider

- What transferable competencies do you want to develop and why?
- What types of learning experiences are required for learners' development and how will you build the space in your curriculum for these across different age groups?
- How will you upskill staff to enable them to give learners the levels of independence and agency required for meaningful competency development?
- How will you assess the development of the competencies? In particular, what assessment framework or rubrics will you employ, and will you use these to assign stages of development or primarily use them to enable reflection?
- How will you record the development of the competencies and then report these to learners and parents? What implications does this have for your existing reporting arrangements?
- How determined are you to navigate the tricky moments in order to fulfil your vision of what learners need to thrive in the world beyond school?

Further reading

DeLorenzo and Mourant's book *Competency-Based Education Ignited: A transformational systemwide approach for leaders* (2024)
Hess et al.'s book *Deeper Competency-Based Learning: Making equitable, student-centered, sustainable shifts* (2020)
OECD's publication 'Thinking outside the box: The PISA 2022 creative thinking assessment' (2022)
Skills Builder Partnership's 'Skills Builder Expanded Universal Framework' (2024)
Sturgis and Casey's book *Quality Principles for Competency-Based Education* (2018)
Victorian Curriculum and Assessment Authority's 'The Victorian Curriculum F-10: Version 2.0' (2024)

22 Learner profiles: Assessment that evidences the full breadth of learning
ROSIE CLAYTON AND FRAN WILBY

In this chapter, we explain how digital learner profiles provide the opportunity to capture the full breadth of learners' strengths: Head (academic learning), Heart (wellbeing and relationships) and Hand (creativity and problem-solving). Through a variety of assessment methods, they give children and young people the opportunity to evidence and articulate their development as reflective, creative and collaborative individuals. This chapter shares a small slice of the pilot work being done by schools and colleges across the country.

The authors

Dr Fran Wilby leads on the development of nationwide school-designed learner profile pilots for Rethinking Assessment. She was previously head of international implementation for Lumiar Education, a global innovative educational organisation based in Brazil. Previously, she taught across education and the Early Years, and taught culture and media courses in further and higher education. Rosie Clayton is head of Rethinking Assessment. She was part of the founding team setting up Studio Schools in England and was an associate director at the Royal Society of Arts, setting up the Cities of Learning programme. She is a research fellow with the World Innovation Summit for Education, working on learning ecosystems in the Middle East and Global South.

New assessment models for a new reality

The global discussion about assessment is changing. People around the world are recognising that our assessment systems and the way in which we measure and recognise learner achievement need to change (Lucas, 2021; UNESCO, 2021; UNESCO-IBE, 2023; OECD, 2024). Digital learner profiles are one method of evidencing and capturing, and can provide a holistic Head, Heart and Hand assessment of development. This broader and richer approach, which is valued by teachers and learners, is shared with parents and, later on, with higher education admissions bodies and employers.

In Australia, a focus on reforming assessment to better prepare upper secondary school learners for learning, work and life has led to learner profiles being state-level policy in some states (Lucas, 2023). Learner profiles are also being trialled in Wales and Scotland (Scottish Government, 2023). Elsewhere, the US-based Mastery Transcript Consortium (n.d.) is 'empowering students to showcase competencies and share evidence of their learning', with nearly 600 colleges accepting the Mastery Transcript, a replacement for the traditional US high school record and providing credentialling for competency-based learning.

In this chapter, we focus on the English education system and argue that capturing learner development via a learner profile can provide a more equitable and inclusive tool with which to empower children and young people as they learn about their own potential as creative and collaborative individuals. We will show how learner profiles can unlock wider assessment and pedagogical practices at school and system level by valuing and capturing wider skills and dispositions, such as creativity, critical thinking and collaboration, alongside curriculum subjects and other areas of learning outside the classroom.

Rethinking assessment

Since its launch in 2020, Rethinking Assessment has gathered a broad coalition of teachers, school leaders, education professionals, academics and policymakers, all committed to building a system that reflects the strengths of every young person. We undertake advocacy to support high-quality, evidenced-based debate and discussion to assist policy development, by submitting evidence to government reviews, committees and inquiries (e.g. House of Lords, 2023, p. 61). Alongside this, we work with teachers and school leaders across our Practice Networks to test out new assessment ideas and develop free resources, materials and toolkits for schools and colleges, to support innovation and collaboration. Our aspiration is for every young person to be supported to create a learner profile while in compulsory education, as recommended by the Times Education Commission (2022).

Our work builds on a groundswell of growing practice. Schools and employers in the UK and internationally are currently creating and using digital profiles and eportfolios as rich sources of information. Drawing on international research and evidence, Rethinking Assessment developed a framework of components in 2022 (Figure 22.1) in order to support the development of high-quality approaches to learner profiling. In this framework, a digital learner profile contains a record of academic achievement (grades or progress in a subject area), alongside evidence of wider intellectual enrichment (additional courses, specialised modules or project based qualifications). This is accompanied by links to portfolios of work and evidence of community/sports/music or wider enrichment experiences – from local interest clubs, teams, arts and cultural experiences through to organised experiences such as the Duke of Edinburgh Award. The learner profile also contains evidence of a learner's reflection on their development, strengths and areas for development. This can be supported by testimonials from others, including employers or trusted adults from community or enrichment activities.

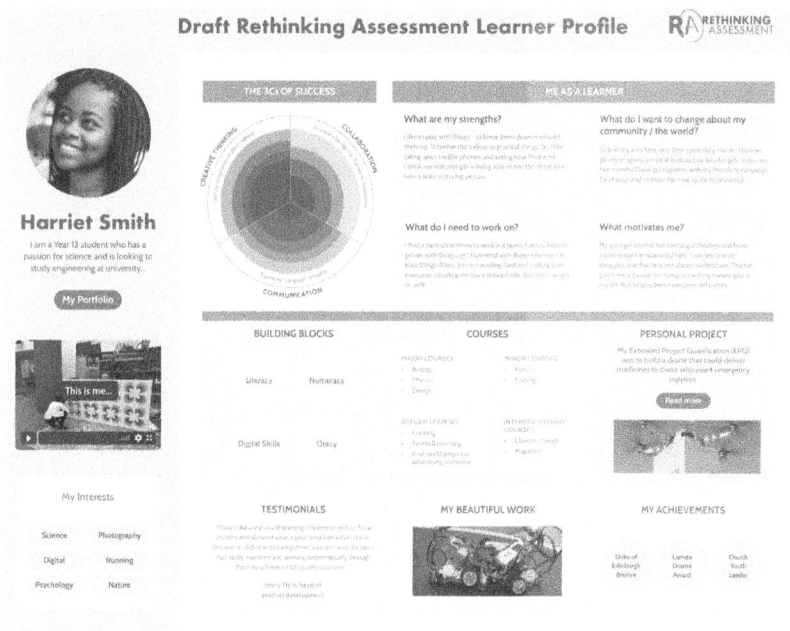

Figure 22.1: Draft learner profile

Since then, we have piloted and tested the concept across four programmes in England. Work is being carried out by schools and colleges across the country, with hotspots emerging in Greater London and Greater Manchester, alongside regional projects in Hertfordshire and Doncaster.

Our approach to learner profiling does not specify a certain digital product or tool that schools or colleges must use. Instead, we support schools to utilise existing tools, such as Google Sites or Slides or Microsoft SharePoint, Sway or PowerPoint, adapting the framework elements to their context and learners. Using a range of familiar and free (with schools' existing licences) tools, the emphasis is less on the mode of technology and instead on addressing the problem of a narrow assessment system that does not adequately evidence and showcase young people's strengths and development.

In a 2023 paper, Barthakur et al. investigate how learner profiles can be integrated to make personalised learning scalable and actionable. Barthakur et al., all affiliated with the University of South Australia, are experts in learning analytics and educational data science. They describe how 'the scaled adoption of Learner Profiles requires the capacity to work in the day-to-day messiness of teaching and learning' (2023, p. 8). Our pilot work has encouraged discussion around this 'messiness' and has attempted to identify the conditions for success needed for effective school-level implementation. Crucially, settings have different levels of readiness, depending on existing culture and practices, technological equipment, digital literacy and curriculum approaches, but some trends have begun to emerge:

- In primary schools, learner profiles are being used for holistic assessment approaches to capture development, extra-curricular learning, interests and achievement, and to enhance parent and carer reporting and communication.
- In secondary schools, they are being used as part of learner conferencing and formal presentations of learning; as part of formative assessment, where learners present and share their progress; for CIAG (careers information advice and guidance) planning and documentation, reflection and meta-learning; and for supporting transition to further study or employment, including university applications.
- In alternative provision (AP) settings, practices around learner profiling are often well developed. For example, Big Picture Doncaster uses learner profiles to assess the impact of each learner's 12-week period and serves

as a tool with which to empower learners to articulate their attributes, skills and knowledge (using their ASK framework).
- In region-wide approaches, there has been excitement and consensus from both educators and employers on the value and potential of learner profiles. In our projects with HLF Education in Hertfordshire (HFL Education, 2024) and with the City of Doncaster Council (Rethinking Assessment, 2025), there was evidence of the impact of groups of schools and colleges developing a shared language, practice and approach to developing profiles together, which can support learners across multiple ages and stages.

Challenges and successes

While we are still at the very beginning in supporting schools and colleges in England to test out the learner profile concept, we have gathered valuable learning and insight so far.

Digital device access and IT connectivity can be a challenge. The pilots uncovered technical considerations, including equity of access to technology, devices and broadband connectivity. At a school level, digital device and broadband access is a necessary precondition and, as is the case across the UK, learners will not necessarily have routine access to digital devices.

The development of learners' digital literacy and confidence is important. Gradual familiarity with the tool (e.g. Google Sites or Slides) is essential; however, once this knowledge is in place, learners can work independently on their profiles, with teachers checking content once or twice per half-term and always before any presentations to parents and carers.

Teacher confidence in the school's choice of technology needs careful consideration and support, with structured implementation. There should be a focus on staff capacity and expertise, with an emphasis on professional development. Careful groundwork is needed to share the rationale and benefits with staff before changes are made to everyday classroom practices.

Learner profiling needs a whole-school approach to curriculum and assessment, rather than a focus on implementing a 'tech tool'. Developing learner profiles needs to become a core part of teaching and learning, requiring substantial practice change over the longer term.

In England, the school system is currently highly fragmented, and wider system readiness is also a critical consideration. The transition of information across parts of the system – between different institutions, with different types of profile and management information systems – is an implementation challenge. Looking ahead, developments such as the piloting of a Department for Education Record for post-16 transitions, which contains limited data at the moment but is akin to the National Health Record, suggest that broader national systems may in the future provide the technical infrastructure needed. It is anticipated that the Royal Society of Arts Digital Badging Commission will make recommendations for a national digital skills wallet.

Teachers who have been involved with piloting a learner profile in their school have shared their experiences with us:

'We chose [to do] a learner profile as it gives children more autonomy over their learning. Pupils can take control over target setting, recognising their strengths and realising what they need to work on. These are the skills that will help them in later life, in careers where they will need to set goals on a regular basis.' (Michael McMorrin, Pinner Wood Primary)

Employers like the NHS have also shared their perspective:

'I am delighted to support the introduction of the new skills profile, developed in Doncaster... I anticipate that it will not only support the application process for new roles but will also be the foundations for onward personal development and learning. The Skills Profile celebrates the range of skills an individual brings to the world of work.' (Professor Sam Debbage, Director of Education and Research, Doncaster and Bassetlaw Teaching Hospitals NHS, Foundation Trust)

To find out more about the impact of our pilots for learners themselves, a survey was conducted with a sample of learners from three of the schools involved in one of the pilot programmes. From 119 learner responses, on a one-to-four scale, with one being 'strongly agree', 80 per cent said that they strongly agreed (39.5 per cent) or agreed (39.5 per cent) that a learner profile is a good way in which to show what they know and can do. Seventy-four per cent agreed or strongly agreed that the learner profile is better than a test at showing what they are good at, and 63 per cent agreed or strongly agreed that they enjoy working on their learner profile.

Our first set of pilots has also enabled the development of an online Learner Profile Starter Kit, which has already had over 9,500 visitors to the landing page since September 2023. Sign-ups for the Starter Kit span the UK and also internationally, including from countries across Europe, Australia, New Zealand, USA, Canada, India, Singapore, Qatar, South Africa and Vietnam.

Although it is likely to be a three- to five-year journey of change to embed learner profiles effectively within a school, it is worth it. They support – and perhaps require – a change in mindset, which enables children and young people's achievement to be presented in a comprehensive strength-based way, committing to the idea that learners are more than just their grades.

No tests, no matter

Matt Morden, Headteacher, Surrey Square Primary School (SSQ)

The school took the opportunity given by the cancellation of statutory tests for 11-year-olds during the COVID-19 pandemic to rethink what the end-of-primary assessment could look like. Following a year of research and consultation with stakeholders, including staff, parents and learners, they created a digital portfolio template as a way for each young person to capture their learning beyond SATs. It contains a homepage and six additional pages: writing, reading, maths, oracy, teamwork and passions (see Figure 22.2). Learners curate the portfolios in Google Sites and independently collect evidence throughout the year, giving them autonomy to choose the evidence that they wish to include. Teachers block out time in the curriculum for learners to work on the portfolios, meeting with them one to one to help to unpick their strengths and development areas.

At the end of their school journey, learners present their portfolios in groups of four, and parents are invited to make up a small audience along with the staff team. Each learner presents their home page and one other page of their choice. The audience asks questions and gives feedback. Since launching this practice in 2022, parents have been hugely positive about the presentations, with parents often overwhelmed by what their children are sharing. For learners, the process of creating and presenting the profile enables them to confidently articulate their learning, and they leave the school feeling positive about themselves, recognising and valuing their achievements.

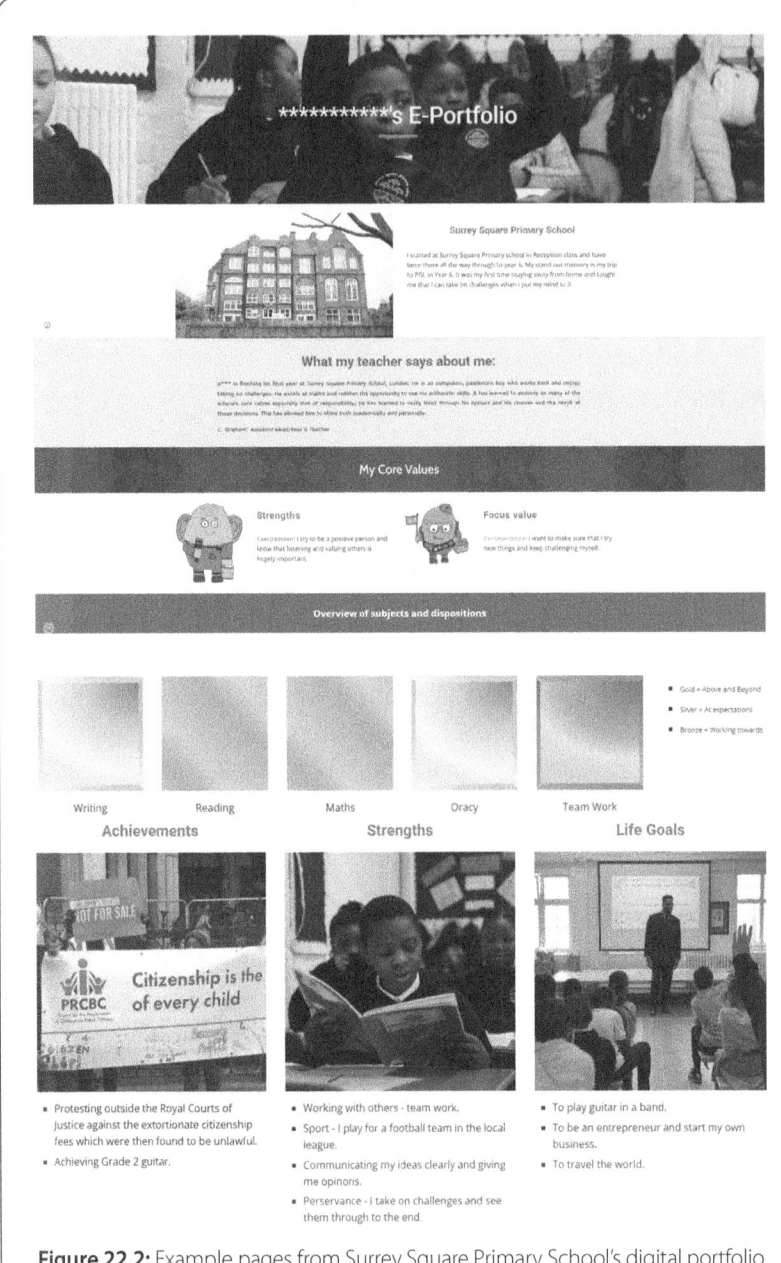

Figure 22.2: Example pages from Surrey Square Primary School's digital portfolio

A richer picture of learning and development

Serra Sanders, Assistant Head, Wapping High School

School leaders were firstly keen for their learner profile to revamp outdated reporting systems and to shift the focus of parent events from teacher-centred meetings towards learner-led interactions between the school and parents and carers.

Wapping High secondly had a focus on careers and PSHE provision, and wanted to develop one of the Rethinking Assessment Google Site templates in order to empower learners to showcase the work of which they were most proud, using a combination of text, image, video and sound. Their aim was to assist learners in charting career pathways and making informed choices beyond Key Stage 4, providing a centralised

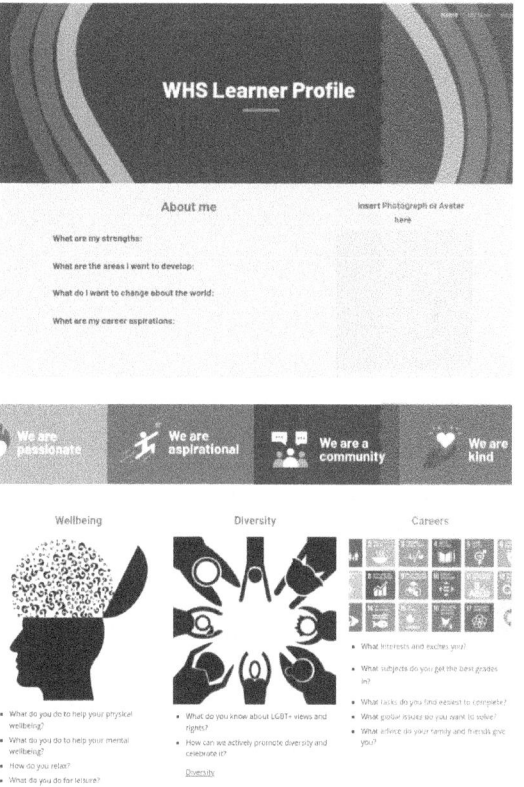

Figure 22.3: Example learner profile at Wapping High School

record of their journey. This was aligned with the Gatsby Benchmarks (2025) and supported GCSE selections and post-16 transitions.

As seen in Figure 22.3, the profile was also used to capture the development of essential skills that are often overlooked by the traditional curriculum but are intrinsic to the development of the whole child. As the school uses the nationally recognised Skills Builder programme, learners are able to develop their knowledge and understanding of skills through workshop lessons. One of the final aims was for learners to journal their 'personal growth' and have a space in which to reflect on the PSHE curriculum and record their thoughts and reflections on the promotion of British Values, which is carefully delivered to all learners through a blend of expert-led seminars and peer coaching opportunities.

Questions to consider

- *Why* are you doing it? Ensure that you have a clear intent and purpose for your learner profile, one that complements and supports your wider school vision, strategy and goals.
- *How* will you embed it within your school? Consider the access points for implementation. Where in the curriculum and timetable might you choose to first introduce lessons to develop and build a profile? Which curriculum areas might then benefit the most from a profile to capture learning and development?
- *How* will you involve key staff and stakeholders in the testing and development of a profile? Which staff might be your advocates and curious innovators?

Further reading

Darling-Hammond's report 'Developing and measuring higher order skills: Models for state performance assessment systems' (2017)

Lucas's publication 'Rethinking assessment in education: The case for change' (2021)

OECD's publication 'What students learn matters: Towards a 21st century curriculum' (2020)

Shepard's article 'The role of assessment in a learning culture' (2000)

23 Interdisciplinary qualifications: New qualifications for future-facing schools
BERTIE CAIRNS

In this chapter, I explain the creation of new interdisciplinary assessments that are directed by schools and which seek to step away from the national structures of examinations. They are practical and experiential in their approach.

> ### The author
> Bedales is an independent school located in the Hampshire village of Steep, England. It has 800 learners aged between four and 18, and a rich history of innovation. Established by John Badley in 1893, it aimed to provide a humane alternative to the authoritarian regimes prevalent in late-Victorian British public schools. Notably, Bedales was among the first boarding schools to become co-educational. The school has had a student council in place since 1913, making it probably the oldest in the world. I am deputy head (academic) at Bedales and have taught across the state and private sectors in England.

Addressing the narrow nature of GCSEs

In the early 2000s, we felt that GCSEs (exams for 16-year-olds) were not aligned with the ethos of the school. We found them to be too restrictive and narrow in both content and assessment. They limited our learners' educational experience – especially because the school's underlying belief was that we need to educate learners through a balanced focus on the Head (academic learning), the Heart (relationships and wellbeing) and the Hand (creativity and skills building).

The school decided to create its own assessments for Key Stage 4. The first Bedales Assessed Course (BAC) was launched in 2005, and currently, our learners take a limited set of GCSEs (English language, maths, science – double or triple – and a foreign language) and can select up to 5 from the 14 BACs.

BACs are graded like GCSEs from 9 (high) to 1 (low). They are externally moderated by GCSE examiners and are recognised by universities and employers. We have created BACs in the following subjects:

- ancient civilisations
- art
- dance
- design: product and fashion
- digital game design
- English literature
- geography
- global perspectives
- history
- music
- outdoor work
- philosophy, religion and ethics
- sports science
- theatre.

We are currently designing BACs in science and MFL (modern foreign languages).

How we do it

This section looks at two interdisciplinary BACs: outdoor work and humanities.

Outdoor work

Outdoor work covers the learning that might be required to run a smallholding, with a focus on traditional skills: blacksmithing using a traditional and induction forge, timber-framed building, creating wooden shingles for roofs, concrete laying, fence mending, livestock husbandry, willow and wool work, welding, renovating and repurposing farm machinery, stained glass and baking (there is a pizza oven and bakehouse). The qualification touches on what we might traditionally call food tech, design technology and agriculture studies, but with a real-world approach and outcomes. Apples from the school orchard and honey are harvested and used in the bakehouse to make consumables that are sold in the farm shop. Sows' piglets are reared and made into sausages. Buildings are improved on the school site: an ornate handrail outside a building needs designing, creating in the forge, welding together and placing in situ. Learners also think about sustainability in outdoor work. A recent project recycled corrugated iron from an old roof into a shutter for the pizza shack; trees like willow and hazel are coppiced and used to make borders or hanging baskets; and learners make charcoal and use it in art. Each project is learner-led. Learners are assessed on their knowledge, applied skills and achievement, as well as their participation, engagement, initiative and independence. We have used Instagram to help learners to capture their progress through a project journal, and now use Microsoft's OneNote. An external assessor speaks to each learner about their work as part of the standardisation and moderation process.

Humanities

Global perspectives comes closest to being a fully interdisciplinary course, blending geography, politics, economics, law and history. It focuses on teaching research, critical thinking and cross-cultural communication. Learners explore human rights, the global arms trade, genocide, social entrepreneurship and the global economy. It is assessed in various ways but most notably in a real-world project, where small groups of learners develop a campaign or solution addressing a global issue, applying the design thinking model. This includes community action, a 5,000-word portfolio and a final viva, where learners defend their work. Some learners have raised money for a local refugee charity through an art sale, while others have addressed school issues around recycling and others have drawn the school community's attention to global issues.

Challenges and successes

Creating new courses takes time. Teachers had the expertise, but needed time and space in which to apply it. Departments have opted to move to BACs over the past 20 years. This decision not to mandate a change is important because it allowed colleagues to be drawn to the project and meant that they were happier to take on the extra responsibility that comes with being an exam board. Making your own qualifications relies heavily on staff expertise, especially from middle leaders – with freedom comes huge responsibility. Mandating science and MFL in the last few years to create BACs meant that the process needed to be managed differently.

Maintaining standards can be challenging because the courses rely on the skills, drive and knowledge of middle managers. The external levers for maintaining standards, like benchmarking against other schools, is not possible. We use external moderators with Key Stage 4 examining experience to help to keep external rigour.

Becoming a de facto exam board is also a challenge. Decisions about scheduling, for example, are the school's remit and not that of some distant exam board. Stakeholder trust in the qualification must be earned and sustained in a way that is not necessary with national qualifications. It can also be expensive, limiting and time-consuming if you want to accredit the courses nationally (something that we have avoided).

We evaluated the impact of the BACs a few years after their launch. We conducted various statistical analyses, comparing the A level results of departments with BACs to those without. We observed clear improvements in outcomes and university offers for subjects with BACs. Universities and employers recognise and respect BACs.

Additionally, we collaborated with researchers from Harvard's Research Schools International (2024) on a project focused on motivation. They stated that:

'The vast majority of students at Bedales report being "a good amount" or "very" motivated in academic courses. In addition, students at Bedales describe how the school culture supports them to be independent learners. Further, Bedales students tend to report having a genuine love of learning and describe a school culture that inspires curiosity.'

BACs offer us the opportunity to offer a broader range of subjects than GCSE, allowing us complete freedom in what we choose to teach and learn. Featuring continuous assessment and a final exam, they emphasise collaboration, research, creative thinking and problem-solving. Teachers can tailor the syllabus to current events, their expertise, the local environment or learner interests, extending far beyond the GCSE curriculum.

Reimagining assessment to prepare for next steps in education

Tony Emmerson, Senior Deputy Head, English College in Prague, Czech Republic

Why we did it

I joined the English College in 2007 and GCSE was simply what we did. Nobody ever claimed that it was a good course; it just was, and everyone – parents, learners and teachers alike – accepted it. However, changes in the Czech national curriculum made it increasingly difficult to align this UK-centric qualification with a locally influenced curriculum, prompting us to ask why. Why devote so much time and effort to a specification that did not truly prepare learners for the International Baccalaureate (IB), which disadvantaged them as second-language learners and which no teacher particularly enjoyed? Where our learners needed aspiration, the GCSE route imposed limits; where they deserved stimulation, it was too often bland; and where they needed to develop skills and a broad understanding, it focused on recall and knowledge silos. In our context, the GCSE was simply not fit for purpose. It had to go.

What we did

We decided to retain GCSE English and mathematics, as well as a qualification in modern foreign languages. All other syllabi would be replaced by our own pre-IB (International Baccalaureate) course.

1 **Clear vision:** I asked subject leaders to imagine the ideal IB learner on the first day of the diploma programme. What did they know? What skills did they have? What was their attitude to learning? What assessments had they practised? With those questions in mind, I instructed them to design a Key Stage 4 course that would develop that ideal learner – and to keep improving it until it did!
2 **Mapping:** We plotted our new Key Stage 4 curriculum subject by subject. Cross-curricular links jumped out immediately. Assessment

was mapped over two years, with end-of-year exams accompanied by tasks mirroring coursework and the extended essay. At the same time, we introduced a pre-IB version of CAS (creativity, activity, service).

3 **Communication:** Although the shift from GCSE to our own Key Stage 4 programme may look obvious in retrospect, it felt risky at the time, making clear communication with families, learners, colleagues and governors vital.

Successes and challenges

Setting up the courses is a real challenge. Time, time, time! Asking colleagues to create new courses and become de facto exam boards requires a huge time commitment but also an emotional one. It is daunting. However, the payback is huge: teachers are using their expertise and are able to run with their passions. It has helped us to recruit and retain excellent colleagues.

Learners are happier and more independent. They feel listened to and valued because teachers can respond to their needs. They enter the IB diploma better prepared, with stronger knowledge, skills and familiarity with IB-style assessments.

Keeping consistency within departments is difficult. School life and learner life are full of exceptional events, and making sure that learners are treated fairly when deadlines for coursework are changed can be difficult. We have to carefully schedule assessments throughout the year to avoid bottlenecks, both with assessments and also with other extra-curricular events like trips, plays and concerts. The central success has been that the school has continued to offer these innovative courses, which attract teachers from across the world to see what we do.

Kierkegaard's aphorism that 'Life can only be understood backwards, but it must be lived forwards' (1967–1978, p. 14) comes with the reminder that we are all, in a sense, making things up as we go. In hindsight, the impact of our decision has been overwhelmingly positive: teachers feel liberated by writing their own courses, striving to make them the best that they can be. Our blended Humanities course is undoubtedly the jewel in our crown, allowing learners to see the world through multiple perspectives at the same time, and not through individual lenses.

This was one of the best decisions that we have made as a school. When idealism and aspiration guide your moral compass, it is hard to go wrong.

Questions to consider

This section is broken into four sections: setting the foundations, building the assessment map, building the subject content map, and starting and running.

Setting the foundations

- Why do you want to do this? How does it fit into your setting's ethos?
- What do your stakeholders expect or want? Are there conflicting priorities or expectations that need to be resolved or negotiated?
- Is this for some of the learners or all the learners?
- Has anyone done anything similar? Would being part of a consortium of schools, such as the SDCC (Schools Directed Course Consortium), support the work and its credibility with stakeholders? Do you want to accredit the courses that you create?
- What expertise do you have in your setting and who is supportive of the project? Listen to resistance: it is feedback.

Building the assessment map

- What are the different ways in which to assess? How do other countries assess? Do you have modules? Are they always terminal exams?
- Do you need to have written assessments? How do you assess other responses: performance, artefacts, speaking, listening? In what ways can you record progress/attainment? Could you use methods already out there, e.g. the Extended Project Qualification (EPQ)?
- What prior knowledge of alternative systems does your setting hold? For example, languages have listening units that are pre-recorded because a national assessment requires standardisation across a huge number of settings. It is easy to assume that you therefore need a recording for your languages assessment. However, English GCSE listening was assessed by teachers observing conversations and how learners responded to each other. How do you find and share this sort of organisational knowledge?
- How long will your course be? Six terms? Two terms? What are the pros and cons of short courses?
- How do you grade? Do you keep 9–1 or A–U, or do you have pass or fail? What about distinction, merit, pass or fail? First, second or third?
- How do you measure attainment in group projects? Do vivas help? Are you clear about the difference between project-based learning and learning that has a project in it?

- How do you protect against the use AI if you are not using terminal examinations?

Building the subject content map

- What assumptions do you make about subject areas? Are the current siloed subjects fit for purpose? Could you have completely new ones? Could you assess across subjects where learners combine knowledge? How much real-world learning should there be?
- How do you decide what to include and what to exclude from the curriculum? Does this decision need to include learner voice? Should it include parent voice? To what extent do your proposed choices reflect unconscious class or racial bias?
- What do other countries do?
- What organisations are there to help to develop your courses? Are there teacher-based communities like the National Association for the Teaching of English (NATE)? Are there national subject bodies like the Royal Society of Chemists? Or more general bodies like the Royal Society, the UK's national academy of sciences?
- Are there specific needs in your local area – maybe there is ship building as a key industry locally? Could that industry feed into your curriculum planning?

Starting and running

- How long will it take to create a course? How many teacher hours will it take? What resources do you need?
- Do you mandate or ask for volunteers?
- How do you make sure that the courses are of a high quality and consistent in the setting?
- You are now the exam board. How do you deal with re-marks, extensions, sickness, late starters, plagiarism and all the other vagaries of assessment?
- How do you sustain the courses (especially if you have a high turnover of staff)?

Further reading

DeLuca's article 'Assessment in education: Looking back, looking forward' (2025)
Girgla et al.'s report 'Developing a teachers' assessment literacy and design competence Framework' (2021)

24 Beyond the curriculum: Qualifications that enable learners to explore their own lines of enquiry

JOHN TAYLOR

In this chapter, I explain how projects can be incorporated into the curriculum in a manner that gives children the freedom and structure to learn more deeply about questions and challenges that are personally engaging and stimulating.

> **The author**
>
> I am director of learning, teaching and innovation at Cranleigh. I work closely with staff in Cranleigh's family of schools worldwide to promote deeper learning through project work. I have worked on the creation of the EPQ and other project-based qualifications in the UK.

The unintended consequences of testing

I came into secondary school teaching from a background in higher education, and one of the first things that struck me was the extent to which learners expected to be spoon-fed. For quite understandable reasons, their focus was on achieving the grades that they 'needed' in order to advance to the next stage of education. This is the effect of assessment and accountability pressures, exerted with increasing intensity at all points of the learning journey and from younger and younger ages. In itself, this might seem unproblematic, but the problem arises as learners progress through education, and the need for critical thinking, independent inquiry and creative development of personal perspectives grows.

This was nicely described in a report published in 2012 by IPSOS Mori on behalf of Ofqual, in which academics and admissions officers lamented the fact that in higher education, learners' thinking about learning had come to be dominated by what they termed a 'right answer' model: learning simply means knowing the right answer. The report traces out the implications of the right answer model: as learners progress along the education pathway, their sense of curiosity is dulled, their love of learning and their formation of a confident sense of one's own capacities for self-directed inquiry or creative problem-solving evaporate, and we are left with a residue of acquired factual knowledge in a fragmentary mode. In a colourful phrase, one interviewee likened exam-dominated education to a 'joyless little bean counter' process (Higton et al., 2012, p. 79).

Exploring alternatives

At Cranleigh School, we have been using the EPQ to address the challenge of equipping our learners with skills that will prepare them well for future work and study. We offer the EPQ to sixth form learners aged 16 to 18. We also now offer the GCSE-level Higher Project Qualification (HPQ) to our 14- and 15-year-olds, while - to 12-year-old learners are offered the iPQ, an age-appropriate project qualification that embodies a similar model of learning. In this way, we aim to provide learners with the opportunity to develop their skills as independent learners over time, and thus to learn to 'think beyond the test'.

So, for example, a learner with an interest in sport could devise a programme to assist their netball team in their training, with video evidence of exercises and analysis of their impact on performance. If a learner wants to deepen their knowledge of psychology, they could explore different theories of the impact of social media on teenage psychology, including in their research interviews with their peers and with trained counsellors. Alternatively, the stimulus might come from a local charity, which commissions a learner to produce multi-media resources to support a forthcoming event.

These project qualifications are supported by teachers from across a wide range of subject areas, and project qualification work happens during timetabled lessons. With the EPQ, we support a wide range of different types of projects, ranging from the standard dissertation through to creative projects such as film-making, podcasting, dressmaking, 3D design or cake creation (Cranleigh School, 2019).

How we do it

Our EPQ, HPQ and iPQ programmes are underpinned by a specific approach to project-based learning.

1. We encourage learners to follow their heart

Perhaps because it is so unusual, learners can take some persuading that they really can choose to pursue their passion through their project. They sometimes feel lost when invited to say what they would like to focus on. We ask them to consider their plans for the future. What could they do to develop skills or deepen their knowledge of a field that relates to their aspirations for future work or study?

Encouraging learners to follow their heart also includes choosing the mode of expression for their ideas. Some learners love essay-writing; for others, their natural mode of expression might be artwork, drama, dance or film-making. There is no intrinsic reason why projects should culminate in a written report. Allowing learners to follow their heart means embracing the exciting but challenging idea of multi-modal assessment.

2. Using open questions leads to deeper learning

The choice of question is of fundamental importance to the success of a project. The question need not be academic and may be better expressed in the form of a creative challenge: can I make a film to promote awareness of the challenge of teenage mental health? It matters that the learner chooses a question rather than simply exploring a broad topic area. A project on the Vikings or the Egyptians could be enhanced, for example, by sharpening up the initial focus: what does Egyptian art reveal to us about their beliefs?

With a question, a line of inquiry comes into view. But inquiry alone may simply lead to a project in which information is collated or compiled. Deeper learning stems from asking a question that is open, in the sense that there is no obvious, easily searchable, right answer.

3. A project is a process

If learners are to engage with challenging, complex, open-ended questions, as well as having a heartfelt interest, then they need time: to explore in depth, to acquire new knowledge and skills, to frame their own ideas and to revise them in the light of critical evaluation of alternative points of view. In short, carrying out a project is not simply a task; it is a process, a journey that you undertake. We need to give learners freedom to follow their heart, and we need to give them time to find their own path. Therefore, we timetable project work and we set deadlines to mark the main stages of the project process.

4. Mentors maintain momentum

Implicit in the fact that rich, interesting, open-ended, deeper learning projects unfold over an extended timescale is the risk of losing momentum and motivation. The initial surge of enthusiasm that comes with being able to choose a question that is personally engaging and stimulating often does not last, and the learner finds themselves coming to a halt, far from either shore.

It is here that mentoring is of vital importance in helping the learner to maintain their momentum. This can happen in various ways, but at the heart of mentoring is the skill of asking well-judged questions. The right question can help the learner to see the path more clearly, and once the path is clear, it becomes possible to resume the journey.

5. A clear project model supports both learning and assessment

While we wish to give learners the freedom to find their own pathways, there are some elements that are best provided by the mentor or project course leader. One of these is a helpful structure that can be used to organise both the learning process and the formatting of the final project prior to assessment. Each project qualification has incorporated some variant of the following basic project model:

- plan
- research
- create
- review.

Breaking a project down in this way makes it possible to assist learners along the way: teaching research skills, for example, when they are about to be needed, or setting up a process for review at the end of the course, perhaps through learner presentations. In terms of assessment, having a structure enables the writing of clear assessment criteria that relate to the core activities of planning, researching, creating and reviewing, and also helps the learner to make decisions about how to format their work at the point of assessment. A written project may contain planning documents followed by a literature review and a discussion section, where the learner creates their own arguments in response to their chosen question. A film-making project could begin with mind-maps and story-boards for planning purposes, and then include practical research addressing the process of film-making, followed by documentation of the filming process and a final presentation of the work accompanied by a reflective review.

Similarly, assessment should embrace both the product and the process. We want to be able to discern the development of qualities such as the capacity for self-directed research, critical evaluation of sources and creative revision of early drafts. It is therefore necessary to put in place a framework for learners that facilitates the collection of evidence of their developing skills.

The challenges and successes

Staffing a sizeable project programme year by year is an ongoing challenge, as is ensuring that staff are equipped with appropriate professional development and guidance. Staff need to be confident in taking on a new role as a mentor, supporting learners who may very well be working outside their own area of subject specialism.

We potentially ask any teacher in the secondary school to take on a period (or sometimes a small number of periods) of project supervision. This means that staff with gaps in their timetable become the pool from which EPQ mentors are drawn, and thus the EPQ mentor team varies from year to year, an arrangement that has the advantage that, over time, a large cross-section of staff gains some experience of project mentoring. The challenge, of course, is in the provision of professional development. While some of this happens through dedicated EPQ mentor training sessions, much guidance is provided in the form of 'just-in-time' email updates with key messages for the coming week. Both mentors and learners are also supported by a bank of short guidance videos, exemplar projects and project resources.

A significant proportion of our learners who take the EPQ receive lower-tariff offers from higher education institutions, who have recognised the value of the qualification as a preparation for independent study.

But it is not simply about outcomes. There is also value in the learning progress. We see children genuinely developing as independent learners, discovering that learning can be so much more than just a matter of getting ready to jump through the next assessment hoop.

The highlight of many of the extended projects is the final presentation, as this is the moment at which the learner demonstrates that they have become if not an expert then at the very least a well-informed source, someone with the knowledge and confidence to answer questions and, in one sense, surpass their mentor. But even where the outcomes are less dazzling, something significant can be achieved. Learners realise that they can learn for themselves, and this is a remarkably empowering discovery – hence, perhaps, why outcomes from qualifications such as the EPQ tend to be associated with higher levels of performance in subsequent academic challenges (Gill, 2024).

So how about primary schools?

Joe Hallgarten, Education Consultant

To our secondary colleagues, primary schools may feel like enlightened beacons of care, creativity and fun. To most primary practitioners, it doesn't feel this way. The excessive emphasis on summative assessment linked to school performance measures and the strong focus on literacy and numeracy can severely constrain opportunities for learners to deepen and broaden their learning, and connect that learning to the world outside the classroom. Primary learners need and deserve time to deepen their learning, develop their own interest and talents, and foster a broader range of dispositions that extend beyond what the primary National Curriculum and assessments currently value, but which are recognised by teachers, parents, employers and wider society as vital to a thriving childhood and adulthood. This is not just about becoming 'secondary-ready' but about celebrating the intrinsic value of the primary experience – the incredible potential of our primary learners as creative changemakers.

In 2022, The Centre for Education And Youth, in partnership with Big Education and six schools across England and Wales, designed a new Primary Extended Project Award (PEPA). We aimed to create a rigorous, flexible and scalable assessment instrument, guided by the following design principles:

- **complementary:** not an alternative to SATs
- **embedded:** not (just) for post-SATs time
- **inclusive:** not only for the academically able
- **additional:** not achieved (only) through standard subject-based lessons
- **connected:** not taught or assessed by teachers alone.

Similar to EPQs, the PEPA aims to give Year 5 and 6 learners a structured opportunity to explore a self-selected topic. With guidance, they set themselves their own inquiry question. Areas of interest could range from interrogating a political issue to exploring and fixing electrical equipment. They would receive meaningful, formative feedback from peers, teachers and one external mentor with expertise relevant to their inquiry. They would document and reflect on their own learning through a digital record and present the project using a range of media. Five dispositions would be assessed: research skills, presentation skills and the creative thinking dispositions of imagination, inquisitiveness and persistence. Informed by self- and peer assessment, learners would receive a bronze, silver or gold award. At the culmination of the project, learners would present their work to the local community through a range of media, receiving further feedback. Throughout the project, teachers and mentors would participate in professional development and form a powerful community of practice.

In discussion with teachers, we agreed on a small number of flexible pedagogical starting points for the PEPA:

1. prioritising *oracy and dialogue*
2. making deliberate space for *metacognition and self-regulation*
3. creating opportunities for *playful inquiry* that stretch and challenge the way in which children approach tasks and develop new ideas
4. valuing the role of *direct instruction* – for instance in (but not limited to) the teaching of research and presentation skills
5. ensuring a focus on *responsive teaching*, using relevant assessment for learning approaches
6. building genuine time and space for ongoing *self- and peer assessment*.

Our next piece of work is to prototype, pilot, evaluate and scale the PEPA (Robertson et al., 2023), with many schools interested in participating.

Questions to consider

- To what extent does your curriculum prepare learners for the skills that they will need in their next phase of learning?
- What opportunities do learners have to follow their own interests and passions in your curriculum?
- Is it possible for your school to create space within the timetable for project-based learning in order to develop associated independent study skills?
- To what extent does your school make use of assessments – other than tests – that value process as much as the 'right answer'?
- What professional development might staff need in order to support learners' independent learning?

Further reading

Kohn's book *The Schools our Children Deserve: Moving beyond traditional classrooms and 'tougher standards'* (1999)
Taylor's book *Think Again: A philosophical approach to teaching* (2012)
Taylor's book *Bloomsbury CPD Library: Independent learning* (2018)

Conclusion

Working on this book has been inspirational. It has shown that there are many people within our education system who recognise the need for a Big Education – one that values equally the Head, the Hand and the Heart. They see that a narrower approach does not work for many of their learners and neither does it prepare them well for the world as it is developing.

They are also showing that it is possible to do something about it, even within the constraints of the state school system and accountability to parents and statutory bodies like Ofsted. In leadership and curriculum, in pedagogy and assessment, in primary and secondary, we see example after example of what is possible. Some are fully developed, some are still developing but all are determined to bring the vision to life.

Three themes emerge that cross over the different parts of the book:

1. An approach based on the Head, the Heart and the Hand creates an inclusive, high-achieving, human and sustainable **school culture**.
2. Initiatives that **start with the Heart** support rigorous learning. The two are not in competition.
3. If we want our children and young people to be **prepared for the future**, then we have no choice but to embrace all three elements of the Head, Hand and Heart in our education system.

School culture

The chapters within the first part on leadership have a clear common thread. Each lays out different tools that enable long-term sustainable development of the school culture. The Big 8 tools equip the leaders of the future, design thinking provides a specific practical methodology for engaging stakeholders, and embedding evidence-based practices in an institution creates ongoing curiosity and progress. Approaches to professional development and peer review where staff 'do' rather than are 'done to' create empowered colleagues who shoulder their own responsibility for improvement. A whole-school strategy on DEIB, meanwhile, profoundly impacts not just the learners and the parents but staff too. We see the threads of these approaches in many other chapters, and one headline is writ large: if you want a personally and professionally thriving staff who stay in your institution and stay motivated, then attend to the Head, the Heart and the Hand.

Start with the Heart

It has long been established that learners – and indeed adults – learn more effectively when they feel safe, secure and supported. Paying attention to the whole of a person – or, in contemporary speak, *seeing them* – is an end in itself. Magically, it is also a means to another end: strong progress and achievement, including test scores.

Life at school has many parts, and the chapters on lunchtimes, health and outdoor spaces show how relatively small changes can make a big difference. As seen in the chapters on non-punitive management of behaviour and collaborative pastoral teams, support that fully understands the individual is a crucial ingredient for success. And surely now is the moment for us to reclaim the pivotal role of play in personal development and learning.

We live in a world where, unfortunately, some will instantly label these approaches as 'soft', 'too liberal' or 'embodying low expectations'. On the contrary – we have seen in these chapters that they are creative and practical strategies that are deeply serious and effective in enabling the best learning and achievement for every child.

Preparation for the future

It is perhaps no coincidence that the largest number of chapters cover this area. Maybe, just maybe, it is because it is so evident that the current system is failing to do this. What we also see in these chapters is teachers and leaders having the courage and determination to be true to their vision, which often entails working beyond the mainstream norms.

We see how this preparation for life can be nurtured by building on existing structures, such as in the chapters on oracy, Mantle of the Expert, the role of the imagination and design thinking. We also see how it can be provided through standalone initiatives that sit alongside the current provision, such as project-based learning and the promotion of passion projects. And we see more extensive transformation, such as in the chapters on real-world learning, the creation of new qualifications and the institutional adoption of an entrepreneurial mindset. The chapters on the development of transferable skills and learning portfolios demonstrate how we can give internal value and external validation to the work – these play a critical role in supporting academic and personal progress, and also recognise that attending to formal assessment and qualifications is a pragmatic reality of the world in which we live.

Underpinning all these chapters on preparation for the future is the recognition that we live in a changing world, and we are doing a disservice to our learners if we do not do our best to equip them for it.

We also see that connecting these three themes are two fundamental beliefs. First, education is fundamentally about people. It is not about data points on the spreadsheet. Second, every chapter champions agency. Agency for learners, agency for staff, agency for leaders. But this is not unrestricted agency without limits; it is agency with significant scaffolding and accountability. This requires effort and commitment to build and to sustain and, when in place, can unlock the creativity and motivation of all.

So, what should you do as a result of reading this book? You are probably already doing great things in your work, and the suggestion is to try something new. This could be something small, such as buying a set of outdoor clothing for the Reception class. It could be massive, such as reorienting the whole mindset of your institution. Or it could be anything in between. The late Tim Brighouse famously spoke of 'the gaps in the hedges' – the spaces to innovate even in a system that does not encourage it. So our invitation is to find your hedge, find the gaps and step through. In this way, we hope that you will embrace the holistic vision of the Head, the Heart and the Hand, and connect to the powerful motivations that drew you to be an educator in the first place.

RL and SS, April 2025

Networks supporting schools to develop a Head, Heart and Hand approach

Big Education runs the Rethinking School project (https://bigeducation.org/rethinking-school). This project invites ten schools to join each year. A Change Team from each participating school is nominated. Participants visit each other to share good practice, learn about implementation science (making change stick) and hear from a range of inspirational speakers. They also use design thinking to collaboratively work on shared problems of practice and to produce useful resources to share with other schools.

Edge Foundation (www.edge.co.uk) works to inspire the education system to give all young people across the UK the knowledge, skills and behaviours that they need to flourish in their future life and work. Edge believes in a broad and balanced curriculum, interactive and engaging real-world learning, high-quality technical and professional training and rich relationships between education and employers. They provide lots of online resources to support best practice development, lobby for policy change and conduct and publish research into innovation in the education system.

Rethinking Assessment (https://rethinkingassessment.com) is also part of Big Education and works with schools to design assessment systems that help every young person to thrive. They are the pioneers of learner profiles in the UK, offering a toolkit for schools wishing to implement these. They also campaign for change and run projects, conferences and events.

Schools of Tomorrow (https://schoolsoftomorrow.org) is a school membership organisation that works to achieve better outcomes by engaging with the communities in which schools work. Member schools commit to this vision: that the most effective schools are those that combine academic attainment with involvement at the heart of their communities and a broader vision of quality and purpose. They offer high-class professional development and practical peer support.

Well Schools (www.youthsporttrust.org/school-support/well-schools) is a movement of schools and trusts taking positive action to improve education outcomes by supporting the health and happiness of their staff and learners. Schools taking part can access self-review tools and dedicated support, connect with other Well Schools and Trusts across the UK, and keep up to date with the latest stories, events, podcasts and reports on how to create the healthiest, happiest schools.

Whole Education (https://wholeeducation.org) supports a network of confident and capable leaders who build schools that provide a rigorous whole education so that everyone thrives in a transforming world. Network membership provides structure, support and inspiration, with opportunities throughout the year to connect and collaborate with other schools across the country and beyond.

Bibliography

Aitken, V. (2013a), *Real in All the Ways That Matter: Weaving learning across the curriculum with Mantle of the Expert*. New Zealand: NZCER Press.

Aitken, V. (2013b), 'Dorothy Heathcote's Mantle of the Expert approach to teaching and learning: A brief introduction'. In: Fraser, D., Aitken, V. and Whyte, B. (eds), *Connecting Curriculum, Linking Learning*. New Zealand: NZCER Press, pp. 34–56.

Aitken, V. and Taylor, T. (2022), *Try This: Unlocking learning with imagination*. Norwich: Singular Publishing.

Alesandrini, K. and Larson, L. (2002), 'Teachers bridge to constructivism', *The Clearing House*, 75, (3), 119–121.

Alexander, R. (2008), *Towards Dialogic Teaching*. York: Dialogos.

Alexander, R. J. (2020), *A Dialogic Teaching Companion*. London: Routledge.

Aronica, L. and Robinson, K. (2016), *Creative Schools: The grassroots revolution that's transforming education*. London: Viking.

Association of School and College Leaders (ASCL) (2019), *The Forgotten Third*. Oxford: Oxford University Press.

Atkinson, M., Goldenberg, G., Dubiel, J. and Wass, S. (2025), 'Differential effects of an urban outdoor environment on 4–5 year old children's attention in school'. *Journal of Environmental Psychology*, 104, (12), 102589.

Axford, N., Berry, V., Lloyd, J., Moore, D., Rogers, M., Hurst, A., Blockley, K., Durkin, H. and Minton, J. (2019), 'How can schools support parents' engagement in their children's learning? Evidence from research and practice', Education Endowment Foundation, https://educationendowmentfoundation.org.uk/evidence-summaries/evidence-reviews/parental-engagement

Baines, E. and Blatchford, P. (2019), 'School break and lunch times and young people's social lives: A follow-up national study', UCL Institute of Education, www.nuffieldfoundation.org/wp-content/uploads/2019/05/Final-report-School-break-and-lunch-times-and-young-peoples-lives-A-follow-up-national-study.pdf

Barthakur, A., Dawson, S. and Kovanovic, V. (2023), 'Advancing learner profiles with learning analytics: A scoping review of current trends and challenges', *LAK2023: 13th International Learning Analytics and Knowledge Conference*, https://dl.acm.org/doi/10.1145/3576050.3576083

Bennett, T. (2014), 'I know therefore I can', *TES Magazine*, www.tes.com/magazine/archive/i-know-therefore-i-can-0

Berger, J. (2002), 'Exploring the connection between teacher education practice and adult development theory'. Doctoral dissertation, Harvard University Graduate School of Education, USA.

Berger, R. (2003), *An Ethic of Excellence: Building a culture of craftsmanship with students*. London: Heinemann.

Beute, F. and De Kort, Y. A. W. (2014), 'Natural resistance: Exposure to nature and self-regulation, mood, and physiology after ego-depletion'. *Journal of Environmental Psychology*, 40, 167–178.

Biesta, G. J. J. (2007), 'Why "what works" won't work: Evidence-based practice and the democratic deficit in educational research'. *Educational Theory*, 57, (1), 1–22.

Boaler, J., Wiliam, D. and Brown, M. (2000) 'Students' experiences of ability grouping – disaffection, polarisation and the construction of failure'. *British Educational Research Journal*, 26, (5), 631–648.

Brighouse, T. (2015), 'Seizing the agenda: Finding the gaps in the hedge', *Whole Education 6th Annual Conference*, YouTube, www.youtube.com/watch?v=IGUV5-NG8V8

Brown, N., Ince, A. and Ramlackhan, K. (eds) (2024) *Creativity in Education: International perspectives*. London: UCL Press.

Brown, T. and Katz, B. (2019), *Change by Design: How design thinking transforms organizations and inspires innovation*. New York: Harper Business.

Brussoni, M., Olsen, L., Pike, I. and Sleet, D. A. (2012), 'Risky play and children's safety: Balancing priorities for optimal child development'. *International Journal of Environmental Research and Public Health*, 9, (9), 3134–3149.

Bryan, A. (2003), 'Colourful semantics: Thematic role therapy'. In: Chiat, S., Law, J. and Marshall, J. (eds), *Language Disorders in Children And Adults: Psycholinguistic approaches to therapy*. Hoboken, NJ: John Wiley & Sons, pp. 143–161.

Cagliari, P. (2016), *Loris Malaguzzi and the Schools of Reggio Emilia: A selection of his writings and speeches, 1945–1993*. Abingdon: Routledge.

Cakir, M. (2008), 'Constructivist approaches to learning in science and their implications for science pedagogy: A literature review'. *International Journal of Environmental & Science Education*, 3, (4), 193–206.

Carothers, T. and O'Donohue, A. (2019), 'How to understand the global spread of political polarization', Carnegie Endowment for International Peace, https://carnegieendowment.org/posts/2019/10/how-to-understand-the-global-spread-of-political-polarization?lang=en

Center on the Developing Child (2025), 'Lifelong health and wellbeing', Harvard University, https://developingchild.harvard.edu/key-concept/lifelong-health

Centre for Social Justice (2025), 'School absence tracker (autumn term 2024 analysis', www.centreforsocialjustice.org.uk/wp-content/uploads/2025/08/CSJ-Absence_Tracker.pdf

Chambliss, J. J. (1991), 'John Dewey's idea of imagination in philosophy and education'. *Educational Theory*, 25, (4), 43–49.

Chapleau, S. (ed.) (2020), *Schools in their Communities: Taking action and developing civic life*. Citizen School and Big Education, https://citizenschool.org.uk/wp-content/uploads/2020/06/schools-in-their-communities-taking-action-and-developing-civic-life-final.pdf

Chapleau, S. (ed.) (2022), *Education – Power – Change*. Citizens UK, https://citizensuk.contentfiles.net/media/documents/EDUCATION_-_POWER_-_CHANGE.pdf

Chapleau, S. (ed.) (2023), *Hungry for Change*. Citizens UK, www.citizensuk.org/about-us/news/download-your-free-copy-of-hungry-for-change-and-other-publications

Chapleau, S. (2024), 'Schools as anchor institutions – a community organiser's perspective'. In: *Education – Power – Change*. Citizens UK, www.education-power-change.com/schools-as-anchor-institutions

Christodoulou, D. (2011), 'Skills and knowledge', *Daisy Christodoulou*, https://daisychristodoulou.com/2011/12/skills-and-knowledge

Claxton, G. (2008), *What's the Point of School? Rediscovering the heart of education*. Oxford: Oneworld Publications.

Coe, R., Rauch, C. J., Kime, S. and Singleton, D. (2020), 'Great Teaching Toolkit: Evidence review', Evidence Based Education, www.cambridgeinternational.org/Images/584543-great-teaching-toolkit-evidence-review.pdf

Copeland, M. (2014), 'The emerging significance of values based leadership: A literature review'. *International Journal of Leadership Studies*, 8, (2), 105–135.

Cortés, E. (2010), *Rebuilding Our Institutions*. Chicago: Acta Publications.

Covey, S. R. (2020), *The 7 Habits Of Highly Effective People: Revised and updated: 30th anniversary edition*. New York: Simon & Schuster.

Cranleigh School (2019), 'Academics: EPQ', www.cranleigh.org/school-life/academics/epq

Crick, B. and Advisory Group on Citizenship (1998), 'Education for citizenship and the teaching of democracy in schools: Final report', Qualifications and Curriculum Authority, https://dera.ioe.ac.uk/id/eprint/4385/1/crickreport1998.pdf

Cruddas, L. (2024), 'The schools accountability and regulatory system in England: Building an intelligent and compassionate system of accountability', Confederation of School Trusts, https://cstuk.org.uk/system/files/paragraphs/cw_file/2025-04/Schools_accountability_and_regulatory_system_-_2024-02-26.pdf

Cullen, M. A., Lindsay, G., Hastings, R., Denne, L. and Stanford, C. (2020), 'Special educational needs in mainstream schools: Evidence review', Education Endowment Foundation, https://educationendowmentfoundation.org.uk/education-evidence/guidance-reports/send

Darder, A. (2018), *The Student Guide to Freire's Pedagogy of the Oppressed*. New York: Bloomsbury.

Darling-Hammond, L. (2017), 'Developing and measuring higher order skills: Models for state performance assessment systems', Learning Policy Institute, https://learningpolicyinstitute.org/media/92/download?inline&file=Models_State_Performance_Assessment_Systems_REPORT.pdf

Davies, A. (2009), *The Gangs of Manchester: The story of the Scuttlers, Britain's first youth cult*. Preston: Milo Books.

Deloitte (2018), 'Power up: UK skills', www.ncub.co.uk/insight/power-up-uk-skills

DeLorenzo, R. A. and Mourant, R. L. (2024), *Competency-Based Education Ignited: A transformational systemwide approach for leaders*. Bloomington, IN: Solution Tree Press.

DeLuca, C. (2025), 'Assessment in education: Looking back, looking forward'. *Assessment in Education: Principles, Policy & Practice*, 32, (1), 1–4.

Department for Education (DfE) (n.d.), 'About us', www.gov.uk/government/organisations/department-for-education/about

Department for Education (DfE) (2020), 'School workforce in England: November 2019', www.gov.uk/government/statistics/school-workforce-in-england-november-2019

Department for Education (DfE) (2022), 'Employer skills survey: Calendar year 2022', https://explore-education-statistics.service.gov.uk/find-statistics/employer-skills-survey/2022

Department for Education (DfE) (2023a), 'Independent review of teachers' professional development in schools: Phase 1 findings', www.gov.uk/government/publications/teachers-professional-development-in-schools-phase-1-findings/independent-review-of-teachers-professional-development-in-schools-phase-1-findings

Department for Education (DfE) (2023b), 'School workforce in England: Reporting year 2022', https://explore-education-statistics.service.gov.uk/find-statistics/school-workforce-in-england/2022

Department for Education (DfE) (2024), 'Elective home education: Autumn term 2024/25', https://explore-education-statistics.service.gov.uk/find-statistics/elective-home-education/2024-25-autumn-term

Department for Education (DfE) (2025), 'Suspensions and permanent exclusions in England: Academic year 2023/24', https://explore-education-statistics.service.gov.uk/find-statistics/suspensions-and-permanent-exclusions-in-england/2023-24

Design Council (2019) 'The Double Diamond', www.designcouncil.org.uk/our-resources/the-double-diamond

Dewey, J. (1933 [2008]), 'How we think'. In: Boydston, J. A. (ed.), *The Collected Works of John Dewey* (Volume LW 8). Carbondale: Southern Illinois University Press, pp. 105–352.

Drago-Severson, E. and Blum-DeStefano, J. (2018), 'Building a developmental culture of feedback'. *Journal of Professional Capital and Community*, 3, (4), 62–78.

Durning, A., Baker S. and Ramchandani, P. (eds) (2024), *Empowering Play in Primary Education*. Abingdon: Routledge.

Edmondson, A. (2019), 'The role of psychological safety'. *Leader to Leader*, 92, 13–19.

Education Endowment Foundation (EEF) (2016), 'Do EEF trials meet the new "gold standard"?', *EEF Blog*, https://educationendowmentfoundation.org.uk/news/do-eef-trials-meet-the-new-gold-standard

Education Policy Institute (EPI) (2023), 'Annual report 2023: Disadvantage', https://epi.org.uk/%20annual-report-2023-disadvantage

Equality Act 2010, c. 15, www.legislation.gov.uk/ukpga/2010/15/contents

Fiennes, C., Dickson, K., de Escobar, D. A., Romans, A. and Oliveri, S. (2015), 'The existing evidence-base about the effectiveness of outdoor learning: Final report', The Blagrave Trust, www.blagravetrust.org/wp-content/uploads/2015/11/The-Existing-Evidence-base-about-the-Effectiveness-of-Outdoor-Learning-Executive-Summary-Nov-2015.pdf

Fisher, A. V., Godwin, K. E. and Seltman, H. (2014), 'Visual environment, attention allocation, and learning in young children: When too much of a good thing may be bad'. *Psychological Science*, 25, (7), 1362–1370.

Flavell, J. H. (1999), 'Cognitive development: Children's knowledge about the mind'. *Annual Review of Psychology*, 50, 21–45.

Foa, R. S., Klassen, A., Slade, M., Rand, A. and Collins, R. (2020), 'Report: Global satisfaction with democracy 2020', Centre for the Future of Democracy, www.cam.ac.uk/system/files/report2020_003.pdf

Fraser, S. (2011), *Authentic Childhood: Experiencing Reggio Emilia in the classroom* (3rd edn.). Toronto: Nelson Education.

Freire, P. (2018), *Pedagogy of the Oppressed: 50th anniversary edition*. New York: Bloomsbury.

Ganz, M. (2024), *People, Power, Change*. New York: Oxford University Press.

Gatsby (2025), 'Good career guidance: The next 10 years', https://cdn.gatsbybenchmarks.org.uk/app/uploads/2024/11/good-career-guidance-the-next-10-years-report.pdf

Gaunt, A. and Stott, A. (2019), *Transform Teaching and Learning Through Talk: The oracy imperative*. London: Rowman & Littlefield.

Gecan, M. (2018), *People's Institutions in Decline*. Chicago: Acta Publications.

Gess, A.H. (2017), 'STEAM education: Separating fact from fiction'. *Technology and Engineering Teacher*, 77, (3), 39–41.

Gill, K., Brown, S., O'Brien, C., Graham, J. and Poku-Amanfo, E. (2024), 'Who is losing learning? The case for reducing exclusions across mainstream schools', The Difference, https://static1.squarespace.com/static/5a6b53d0f43b55b9c64d99c8/t/66e1cc1f6d643f1fe141025e/1726073889332/Who_is_losing_learning_Sept24_2024-09-06-103617_euht.pdf

Gill, K., Quilter-Pinner, H. and Swift, D. (2017), 'Making the difference: Breaking the link between school exclusion and social exclusion', IPPR, www.ippr.org/articles/making-the-difference

Gill, T. (2024), 'The extended project qualification in England: Does it provide good preparation for higher education?'. *Oxford Review of Education*, 51, (4), 486–506.

Girgla, A., Good, L., Krstic, S., McGinley, B., Richardson, S., Sneidze-Gregory, S. and Star, J. (2021), 'Developing a teachers' assessment literacy and design competence

Framework', Australian Council for Educational Research, https://ibo.org/globalassets/new-structure/research/pdfs/assessment-literacy-final-report-en.pdf

Godfrey, D. (2017), 'What is the proposed role of research evidence in England's "self-improving" school system?'. *Oxford Review of Education*, 43, (4), 433–446.

Godfrey, D. (2020), *School Peer Review for Educational Improvement and Accountability: Theory, practice and policy implications*. Cham: Springer.

Goldenberg, G., Atkinson, M., Dubiel, J. and Wass, S. (2024), 'Outdoor learning in urban schools: Effects on 4–5-year-old children's noise and physiological stress'. *Journal of Environmental Psychology*, 97, 102362.

Golder, G., Briggs, D. and Child, F. (2019), 'The Plymouth oracy project: Its impact on non-academic measures of pupil success'. *Impact: Journal of the Chartered College of Teaching*, 7, https://my.chartered.college/impact_article/the-plymouth-oracy-project-its-impact-on-non-academic-measures-of-pupil-success

Gov.uk (2025), 'School teacher workforce'. *Ethnicity facts and figures*. https://www.ethnicity-facts-figures.service.gov.uk/workforce-and-business/workforce-diversity/school-teacher-workforce/latest/.

Guskey, T. R. (2002), 'Does it make a difference? Evaluating professional development'. *Educational Leadership*, 59, (6), 45–51.

Hall, G. E. (2013), 'Evaluating change processes: Assessing extent of implementation (constructs, methods and implications)'. *Journal of Educational Administration*, 51, (3), 264–289.

Hallgarten, J., Bamfield, L. and McCarthy, K. (eds) (2014), *Licensed to Create: Ten essays on improving teacher quality*. London: RSA Action and Research Centre.

Han, K. T. (2009), 'Influence of limitedly visible leafy indoor plants on the psychology, behavior, and health of students at a junior high school in Taiwan'. *Environment and Behavior*, 41, (5), 658–692.

Hargreaves, A. and Fullan, M. (2015), *Professional Capital: Transforming teaching in every school*. New York: Teachers College Press.

Hargreaves, D. (1999), 'The knowledge-creating school'. *British Journal of Educational Studies*, 47, (2), 122–144.

Hawkes, N. (2005), 'Does teaching values improve the quality of education in primary schools?'. Doctoral thesis, University of Oxford, UK.

Hawkes, N. (2010), 'Values education and the national curriculum in England'. In: Lovat, T., Toomey, R. and Neville, C. (eds), *International Research Handbook on Values Education and Student Wellbeing*. Dordrecht: Springer, pp. 225–238.

Heathcote, D. and Bolton, G. (1995), *Drama for Learning: Dorothy Heathcote's Mantle of the Expert approach to education*. Portsmouth, NH: Heinemann.

Hess, K., Colby, R. and Joseph, D. (2020), *Deeper Competency-Based Learning: Making equitable, student-centered, sustainable shifts*. Thousand Oaks, CA: Corwin.

HFL Education (2024), 'Rethinking Assessment: Collaboration for equity and inclusive learning for all: Assessment and curriculum approaches to support collaborative learning in the classroom', www.hfleducation.org/school-improvement/primary/assessment/rethinking-assessment?preview_key=0Q7xhpcue4Vxt6GiPmyVw_0iP3_PefjA-yOuur_3rxs

Hibbin, R. (2023), 'Relational responsibility, social discipline and behaviour in school: Re-orienting discipline and authority through a distributed network of relational accountability'. *Pastoral Care in Education*, 42, (4), 492–512.

Higton, J., Noble, J., Pope, S., Boal, N., Ginnis, S., Donaldson, R. and Greevy, H. (2012), 'Fit for purpose? The view of the higher education sector, teachers and employers on the suitability of A levels', Ipsos MORI Social Research Institute, Ofqual, https://assets.publishing.service.gov.uk/media/5a7dc46ce5274a5eaea66363/2012-04-03-fit-for-purpose-a-levels.pdf

Hill, D. (2012), *Dark Matter and Trojan Horses: A strategic design vocabulary*. London: Strelka Press.

hooks, b. (1994), *Teaching to Transgress: Education as the practice of freedom*. New York: Routledge.

House of Lords (2023), 'Requires improvement: Urgent change for 11–16 education', Education for 11–16 Year Olds Committee, https://publications.parliament.uk/pa/ld5804/ldselect/ldedu1116/17/17.pdf

IDEO (2015), 'The field guide to human-centred design', www.designkit.org/resources/1.html

Jameson, N. and Chapleau, S. (2011), 'Engaging citizens to ensure our democracy: The role and potential of educational institutions', Citizens UK, https://education-power-change.com/wp-content/uploads/2017/02/engaging-citizens-to-secure-our-democracy.pdf

Jensen, H., Pyle, A., Zosh, J. M., Ebrahim, H. B., Zaragoza Scherman, A., Reunamo, J. and Hamre, B. K. (2019), 'Play facilitation: The science behind the art of engaging young children', The LEGO Foundation, https://cms.learningthroughplay.com/media/ok2hjrbh/play-facilitation_the-science-behind-the-art-of-engaging-young-children.pdf

Kashefpakdel, E. T., Newton, O., Clark, J., Rehill, J., Emms, K. and Laczik, A. (2018), 'Joint dialogue: How are schools developing real employability skills?', Edge Foundation, www.edge.co.uk/documents/93/joint_dialogue_-_final_report_update-2_De4kkxs.pdf

Kawa, N. C., Arceño, M. A., Goeckner, R., Hunter, C. E., Rhue, S. J., Scaggs, S. A. and Moritz, M. (2021), 'Training wicked scientists for a world of wicked problems'. *Humanities and Social Sciences Communications*, 8, (1), 189.

Kierkegaard, S. (1967–1978), *Søren Kierkegaard's Journals and Papers* (ed. And trans. H. V. Hong and E. H. Hong). Bloomington, IN: Indiana University Press.

Kierkegaard, S. (1992), *Either/Or: A fragment of life*. London: Penguin.

Kiyosaki, R. T. (2017), *Rich Dad Poor Dad: What the rich teach their kids about money that the poor and middle class do not!* (2nd edn.). Scottsdale, AZ: Plata Publishing.

Knight, J. T. (2007), *Instructional Coaching: A partnership approach to improving*. Thousand Oaks, CA: Corwin Press.

Knight, R. and Poultney, V. (2020), *Classroom Talk: Evidence-based teaching for enquiring teachers*. Abingdon: Routledge.

Kohn, A. (1999), *The Schools our Children Deserve: Moving beyond traditional classrooms and 'tougher standards'*. New York: Houghton Mifflin Harcourt.

Kohn, A. (2006), *Beyond Discipline: From compliance to community*. Alexandria, VA: ASCD.

Laevers, F. (1999), 'The project Experiential Education. Well-being and involvement make the difference'. *Early Education*, 27, Discussion paper.

Lave, J. and Wenger, E. (1991), *Situated Learning: Legitimate peripheral participation*. Cambridge: Cambridge University Press.

LEGO Foundation (2017), 'What we mean by learning through play', version 1.2, https://cms.learningthroughplay.com/media/vd5fiurk/what-we-mean-by-learning-through-play.pdf

Liao, C. (2016), 'From interdisciplinary to transdisciplinary: An arts-integrated approach to STEAM education'. *Art Education*, 69, (6), 44–49.

Louv, R. (2008), *Last Child in the Woods: Saving our children from nature-deficit disorder*. Chapel Hill, NC: Algonquin Books.

Lucas, B. (2021), 'Rethinking assessment in education: The case for change', Rethinking Assessment, https://all-learning.org.au/app/uploads/2022/02/CSE-Leading-Education-Series2-04-2021b.pdf

Lucas, B. (2023), 'Beyond the baccalaureate: Learning from across the world', Edge Foundation, www.edge.co.uk/documents/432/Edge_RA_Principles_for_a_Baccalaureate_PROOF4.pdf

Lucas, B. and Spencer, E. (2020), *Zest for Learning: Developing curious learners who relish real-world challenges*. New York: Crown House Publishing.

Lucey, C., Lister, E., Robinson, L. and Parry, L. (2015), *Big 8 Leadership Foundation: The Research*. bit.ly/b8_rl25

Malaguzzi, L. (1998), 'History, ideas and philosophy'. In: Edwards, C., Gandini, L. and Forman, G. (eds), *The Hundred Languages of Children: The Reggio Emilia approach*. Greenwich: Ablex Publishing, pp. 49–98.

Mancuso, S., Rizzitelli, S. and Azzarello, E. (2006), 'Influence of green vegetation on children's capacity of attention: A case study in Florence, Italy'. *Advances in Horticultural Science*, 20, (3), 220–223.

Mardell, B., Wilson, D., Ryan, J., Ertel, K., Krechevsky, M. and Baker, M. (2016), 'Towards a pedagogy of play', Harvard Graduate School of Education, https://pz.harvard.edu/sites/default/files/Towards%20a%20Pedagogy%20of%20Play.pdf

Marks, R. (2016), *Ability-Grouping in Primary Schools: Case studies and critical debates*. St Albans: Critical Publishing.

Marr, B. (2024), 'How to embrace the Enterprise AI Era', *Forbes*, www.forbes.com/sites/bernardmarr/2024/09/27/how-to-embrace-the-enterprise-ai-era

Martinez, S. L. and Stager, G. S. (2013), *Invent to learn: Making, tinkering, and engineering in the classroom*. Torrance, CA: Constructing Modern Knowledge Press.

Mason, L., Manzione, L., Ronconi, A. and Pazzaglia, F. (2022), 'Lessons in a green school environment and in the classroom: Effects on students' cognitive functioning and affect'. *International Journal of Environmental Research and Public Health*, 19, (24), 16823.

Mastery Transcript Consortium (n.d.) Home page, https://mastery.org

Mccrea, P. (2018) 'Expert teaching: What is it, and how might we develop it?', Institute for Teaching, https://s3.eu-west-2.amazonaws.com/ambition-institute/documents/What_is_Expert_Teaching_-_Peps_Mccrea_1.pdf

Mercer, N. (2025), *Oracy: The transformative power of finding your voice*. London: The Bodley Head.

More, T. [1516] (2020), *Utopia* (Penguin Pocket Hardbacks). London: Penguin.

Most Likely to Succeed (2015), directed by Gregg Whitely. USA: One Potato Productions.

NAHT (2019), 'The principles of effective school-to-school peer review', www.naht.org.uk/Portals/0/PDF's/NAHT%20Peer%20Review%20Report%20(new).pdf?ver=2021-05-23-113106-710

NAHT Accountability Commission (2018), 'Improving school accountability', www.naht.org.uk/Portals/0/PDF%27s/Improving%20school%20accountability.pdf?ver=2021-04-27-121950-093

Natural England (2009), 'Report to Natural England on childhood and nature: A survey on the changing relationships with nature across generations', https://publications.naturalengland.org.uk/publication/5853658314964992

NFER (2023), 'New study suggests teacher autonomy over their professional development is strongly linked with job satisfaction and retention', www.nfer.ac.uk/press-releases/new-study-suggests-teacher-autonomy-over-their-professional-development-is-strongly-linked-with-job-satisfaction-and-retention

Niemiec, C. P. and Ryan, R. M. (2009), 'Autonomy, competence, and relatedness in the classroom: Applying self-determination theory to educational practice'. *Theory and Research in Education*, 7, (2), 133–144.

OECD (2020), 'What students learn matters: Towards a 21st century curriculum', www.oecd.org/content/dam/oecd/en/publications/reports/2020/11/what-students-learn-matters_555a22ec/d86d4d9a-en.pdf

OECD (2022a), 'Supporting students to think creatively: what education policy can do', https://issuu.com/oecd.publishing/docs/supporting_students_to_think_creatively_web_1_

OECD (2022b), 'Thinking outside the box: The PISA 2022 creative thinking assessment', www.oecd.org/en/topics/sub-issues/creative-thinking/pisa-2022-creative-thinking.html

OECD (2024), 'Curriculum frameworks and visualisations beyond national frameworks: Alignment with the OECD Learning Compass 2030', Working Papers no. 314, www.oecd.org/content/dam/oecd/en/publications/reports/2024/04/curriculum-frameworks-and-visualisations-beyond-national-frameworks_02ed384b/2a4bdce6-en.pdf

Ofsted, the Care Quality Commission, Her Majesty's Inspectorate of Constabulary and Fire & Rescue Services (HMICFRS) and Her Majesty's Inspectorate of Probation (2018), 'Protecting children from criminal exploitation, human trafficking and modern slavery: An addendum', https://assets.publishing.service.gov.uk/government/uploads/system/uploads/attachment_data/file/756031/Protecting_children_from_criminal_exploitation_human_trafficking_modern_slavery_addendum_141118.pdf

O'Leary, M. (2012), 'Exploring the role of lesson observation in the English education system: A review of methods, models and meanings'. *Professional Development in Education*, 38, (5), 791–810.

O'Leary, M. (2020), *Classroom Observation: A guide to the effective observation of teaching and learning*. London: Routledge.

Papert, S. and Harel, I. (1991), 'Situating constructionism'. *Constructionism*, 36, (2), 1–11.

Pedder, D., Storey, A., Opfer D. and Wolfenden, F. (2008), 'Schools and continuing professional development (CPD) in England – State of the Nation research project', synthesis report, Training and Development Agency for Schools, www.researchgate.net/publication/242118392_Schools_and_continuing_professional_development_CPD_in_England_-_State_of_the_Nation_research_project#fullTextFileContent

Piaget, J. (1966 [1980]), *The Psychology of the Child* (trans H. Weaver). New York: Basic Books.

Power, S., Rhys, M., Taylor, C. and Waldron, S. (2019), 'How child-centred education favours some learners more than others'. *Review of Education*, 7, (3), 570–592.

Price, M. (ed.) (2017), *Education Forward: Moving schools into the future*. Horley: Crux Publishing.

Provenzano, N. (2016), *The Nerdy Teacher Presents: Your starter guide to makerspaces*. Salem, OR: Blend Education.

Public Health England (2020), 'What works in schools and colleges to increase physical activity', www.gov.uk/government/publications/what-works-in-schools-to-increase-physical-activity-briefing

Public Health England (2024), 'The link between pupil health and wellbeing and attainment: A briefing for head teachers, governors and staff in education settings', National Association of Headteachers, https://assets.publishing.service.gov.uk/media/5a7ede2ded915d74e33f2eba/HT_briefing_layoutvFINALvii.pdf

Putnam, R. (2000), *Bowling Alone: The collapse and revival of American community*. New York: Simon & Schuster.

Ratey, J. (2008), *Spark: The revolutionary new science of exercise and the brain*. London: Quercus.

Real Play Coalition (2019), 'Value of play report', National Geographic, LEGO, UNILEVER and IKEA, www.ikea.com/ca/en/files/pdf/bb/2f/bb2f0627/the-real-play-coalition_value-of-play-report_a.pdf

Research Schools International (2024), 'Motivation', www.researchschoolsinternational.org/motivation

Resnick, M. (2017), *Lifelong Kindergarten: Cultivating creativity through projects, passion, peers, and play*. Cambridge, MA: MIT Press.

Rethinking Assessment (2023), 'Rethinking Assessment digital learner profile pilots: Learnings so far', *Rethinking Assessment Blog*, https://rethinkingassessment.com/rethinking-blogs/rethinking-assessment-digital-learner-profile-pilots-learnings-so-far

Rethinking Assessment (2025), 'Developing a digital skills profile for Doncaster', https://rethinkingassessment.com/rethinking-blogs/developing-a-digital-skills-profile-for-doncaster

Rhys, M., Waldron, S. and Taylor, C. (2015), 'Evaluating the foundation phase: Key findings on literacy and numeracy', Welsh Government, https://dera.ioe.ac.uk/id/eprint/20535/1/140506-evaluating-foundation-phase-reported-impacts-en.pdf

Rittel, H. and Webber, M. (1973), 'Dilemmas in a general theory of planning'. *Policy Sciences*, 4, (2), 155–169.

Roberts, R. (2024), 'Decline and fall? Students' perspectives on A-level English at 16', *BERA Blog*, www.bera.ac.uk/blog/decline-and-fall-students-perspectives-on-a-level-english-at-16

Robertson, A., Hallgarten, J. and Hasse (2023), 'The Primary Extended Project Award (PEPA)', https://cfey.org/reports/2023/05/the-primary-extended-project-award-pepa

Robinson, K. and Robinson, K. (2022), *Imagine if: Creating a future for us all*. London: Penguin Books.

Rogers, B. (2015), *Classroom Behaviour: A Practical guide to effective teaching, behaviour management and colleague support*. Thousand Oaks, CA: Sage.

Rogers, C. R. (1967), *On Becoming a Person: A therapist's view of psychotherapy*. London: Constable.

Rogers, S. (2022), 'Play in the time of pandemic: Children's agency and lost learning'. *Education 3–13*, 50, (7), 494–505.

Rohrbasser, A., Wong, G., Mickan, S. and Harris, J. (2022), 'Understanding how and why quality circles improve standards of practice, enhance professional development and increase psychological well-being of general practitioners: A realist synthesis'. *BMJ Open*, 12, (5), e058453.

Ryan, M., Ricardo, L. I., Nathan, N., Hofmann, R. and van Sluijs, E. (2024), 'Are school uniforms associated with gender inequalities in physical activity? A pooled analysis of population-level data from 135 countries/regions'. *Journal of Sport and Health Science*, 13, (4), 590–598.

Sandseter, E. B. H. and Kennair, L. E. O. (2011), 'Children's risky play from an evolutionary perspective: The anti-phobic effects of thrilling experiences'. *Evolutionary Psychology*, 9, (2), 257–284.

Sartain, L., Stoelinga, S. R. and Brown, E. R. (2011), 'Rethinking teacher evaluation in Chicago: Lessons learned from classroom observations, principal-teacher conferences, and district implementation', research report, Consortium on Chicago School Research, https://danielsongroup.org/wp-content/uploads/2022/02/Rethinking_Teacher_Evaluation_Chicago.pdf

Schein, E. H. (1999), *Process Consultation Revisited: Building the helping relationship*. Reading, MA: Addison-Wesley.

Scottish Government (2023), 'It's our future – independent review of qualifications and assessment: Report', Cabinet Secretary for Education and Skills, www.gov.scot/publications/future-report-independent-review-qualifications-assessment/pages/2

Sebba, J., Tregenza, J. and Kent, P. (2012), 'Powerful professional learning: A school leader's guide to joint practice development', National College for School Leadership, https://assets.publishing.service.gov.uk/government/uploads/system/uploads/attachment_data/file/329717/powerful-professional-learning-a-school-leaders-guide-to-joint-practice-development.pdf

Seleznyov, S. (2018), 'Lesson study: An exploration of its translation beyond Japan'. *International Journal for Lesson and Learning Studies*, 7, (3), 217–229.

Seleznyov, S. (2020a), 'Helping teachers to embed learning from research'. In: Brown, C. and Flood, J. (eds), *The Research-Informed Teaching Revolution: A handbook for the 21st century teacher*. London: John Catt.

Seleznyov, S. (2020b), 'Lesson study: Exploring implementation challenges in England'. *International Journal for Lesson and Learning Studies*, 9, (2), 179–192.

Seleznyov, S. and Silvain, A. (2023), 'School 360: Doing education differently'. *The Buckingham Journal of Education*, 4, (1), 55–63.

Seleznyov, S., Sprakes, A., Shields, P., Nakkas, N., Crank, A. and Finbow, K. (2020), 'Play based learning in Year 1: A practical guide for schools', London South Teaching Schools Alliance, https://drive.google.com/file/d/1Xdc2qDgKFAnnxRgsMiUL72FJgWTDbg_b/view

Shepard, L. A. (2000), 'The role of assessment in a learning culture'. *Educational Researcher*, 29, (7), 4–14.

Shield, B. M. and Dockrell, J. E. (2003), 'The effects of noise on children at school: A review.' *Building Acoustics*, 10, (2), 97–116.

Shu, S. and Ma, H. (2019), 'Restorative effects of classroom soundscapes on children's cognitive performance'. *International Journal of Environmental Research and Public Health*, 16, (2), 293.

Sills, Z. and Watkins, S. (2025), *The Power of Risky Play in the Early Years*. London: SAGE Publications Ltd.

Sinek, S. (2011), *Start With Why: How great leaders inspire everyone to take action*. London: Penguin.

Sismondo, S. (2017), Post-truth? *Social Studies of Science*, 47, (1), 3–6.

Skene, K. (2022), 'J: Juggling play and learning: The role of guided play', PEDAL, www.pedalhub.net/resource-library/resource/item/j-juggling-play-and-learning-the-role-of-guided-play

Skills Builder Partnership (2024), 'Skills Builder Expanded Universal Framework', https://hub.skillsbuilder.org/media/modules/2144/2144/Helpful-resource-3_Skills_Builder_Inclusion_Toolkit.pdf

Smith, S. (2012), *Sex and Sensibility: The Allure of Art Nouveau, Vienna*. [TV programme] BBC. Available at: https://www.bbc.co.uk/programmes/b01fd4z2 (Accessed 26 April 2025).

Smith, S. (2015), 'Playing to engage: Fostering engagement for children and teachers in low socioeconomic regions through science and mathematics play-based learning'. Doctoral dissertation, University of Notre Dame Australia.

Sprakes, A. and ap Hari, G. (2019), *How We XP*. Doncaster: XP School.

Stigler, J. and Hiebert, J. (2009), *The Teaching Gap: Best ideas from the world's teachers for improving education in the classroom*. New York: Free Press.

Stoll, L. and Brown, C. (2015), 'Middle leaders as catalysts for evidence-informed change'. In: Brown, C. (ed.) *Leading the Use of Research and Evidence in Schools*. London: Institute of Education Press.

Stoll, L. and Louis, K. (2007), *Professional Learning Communities: Divergence, depth and dilemmas*. Maidenhead: McGraw-Hill Education.

Sturgis, C. and Casey, K. (2018), *Quality Principles for Competency-Based Education*. iNACOL, www.aurora-institute.org/wp-content/uploads/Quality-Principles-Book.pdf

Syed, M. (2019), *Rebel Ideas: The power of diverse thinking*. London: John Murray Press.

Taylor, C., Davies, R., Rhys, M. and Waldron, S. (2015), 'Evaluating the foundation phase: The outcomes of foundation phase pupils up to 2011/12 (Report 2)', Welsh Government, https://orca.cardiff.ac.uk/id/eprint/88763/1/150107-outcomes-foundation-phase-pupils-2011-12-report-2-en.pdf

Taylor, D. W., Berry, P. C. and Block, C. H. (1958), 'Does group participation when using brainstorming facilitate or inhibit creative thinking?'. *Administrative Science Quarterly*, 3, (1), 23–47.

Taylor, J. L. (2012), *Think Again: A philosophical approach to teaching*. London: A&C Black.

Taylor, J. (2016), 'The examined life', Aeon, https://aeon.co/essays/can-school-today-teach-anything-more-than-how-to-pass-exams

Taylor, J. L. (2018), *Bloomsbury CPD Library: Independent learning*. London: Bloomsbury.

Taylor, T. (2016), *A Beginner's Guide to Mantle of the Expert*. Norwich: Singular Publishing.

Taylor, T. (2018), 'Introducing Mantle of the Expert', Mantle of the Expert, www.mantleoftheexpert.com/wp-content/uploads/2018/01/Intro-moe-Lit-co..pdf

The Schools, Students and Teachers Network (SSAT) (2024), 'Rethinking headship: Labouring to love headship: Overwhelming challenge and underwhelming support', www.ssatuk.co.uk/the-library/publications/labouring-to-love-headship

Thomas, K. W. and Kilmann, R. H. (200), *Thomas-Kilmann Conflict Mode Instrument*. Mountain View, CA: CPP.

Times Education Commission (2022), 'Bringing out the best: How to transform education and unleash the potential of every child', https://s3.documentcloud.org/documents/22056664/times-education-commission-final-report.pdf

Timperley, H., Kaser, L. and Halbert, J. (2014), *A Framework for Transforming Learning in Schools: Innovation and the Spiral of Inquiry*. Melbourne: Centre for Strategic Education.

Tolstoy, L. (1900), *Pamphlets: Translated from the Russian*. Christchurch, UK: The Free Age Press.

UNESCO (2021), 'Reimagining our futures together: A new social contract for education', International Commission on the Futures of Education, https://unesdoc.unesco.org/ark:/48223/pf0000379707.locale=en

UNESCO International Bureau of Education (IBE) (2023), 'The necessity to broaden assessment and how we can do it', Curriculum on the Move, thematic notes no. 18, https://unesdoc.unesco.org/ark:/48223/pf0000384874

University of Cambridge (2019), 'Classroom dialogue', Faculty of Education, www.educ.cam.ac.uk/research/programmes/classroomdialogue

van Poortvliet, M., Clarke, A. and Gross, J. (2019), 'Improving social and emotional learning in primary schools: Guidance report', Education Endowment Foundation, https://educationendowmentfoundation.org.uk/education-evidence/guidance-reports/primary-sel

Victorian Curriculum and Assessment Authority (2024), 'The Victorian Curriculum F-10: Version 2.0', https://f10.vcaa.vic.edu.au

Vincent-Lancrin, S. and van der Vlies, R. (2020), 'Trustworthy artificial intelligence (AI) in education: Promises and challenges', OECD Education Working Papers, No. 218, www.oecd.org/content/dam/oecd/en/publications/reports/2020/04/trustworthy-artificial-intelligence-ai-in-education_f1a7c415/a6c90fa9-en.pdf

Visentin, C., Pellegatti, M., Garraffa, M., Di Domenico, A. and Prodi, N. (2023), 'Effects of chatter noise on listening comprehension for primary school students', *10th Convention of the European Acoustics Association Forum Acusticum 2023*, https://dael.euracoustics.org/confs/fa2023/data/articles/000560.pdf

Vygotsky, L. S. (1967), 'Play and its role in the mental development of the child'. *Soviet Psychology*, 5, (3), 6–18.

Warin, J. and Hibbin, R. (2020), 'Embedding restorative practice in schools', Centre for Social Justice & Wellbeing in Education, https://transformingconflict.org/wp-content/uploads/2021/04/Embedding-Restorative-Practice-in-Schools.-Jo-Warin-Rebecca-Hibbin-2020-002.pdf

Wass, S. and Goldenberg, G. (2025), *Take Action on Distraction: The definitive guide to improving attention and focus in the Early Years and Key Stage One.* London: Bloomsbury Publishing.

Waters, M. (2017), 'Moving the curriculum forwards'. In: Price, M. (ed.), *Education Forward: Moving schools into the future.* Horley: Crux Publishing, pp. 45–47.

Watkins, C. (2010), 'Learning, performance and improvement'. *INSI Research Matters*, 34, 1–16.

Webber, A. (2024), 'Most think school does not prepare pupils for work', *Personnel Today*, www.personneltoday.com/hr/most-think-school-does-not-prepare-pupils-for-work/#:~:text=Two%2Dthirds%20of%20voters%20do,look%20after%20pupils%27%20mental%20health

Wenger, E., Trayner, B. and De Laat, M. (2011), 'Promoting and assessing value creation in communities and networks: A conceptual framework', Heerlen: Open Universiteit, www.betterevaluation.org/sites/default/files/Wenger_Trayner_DeLaat_Value_creation.pdf

Wilkinson, K. and Petrich, M. (2014), *The Art of Tinkering: Meet 150 makers working at the intersection of art, science & technology.* San Rafael, CA: Weldon Owen.

Williams, F. (2017), *The Nature Fix: Why nature makes us happier, healthier, and more creative.* London: W. W. Norton & Company.

Wilson, H. and Kara, B. (2022), *Diverse Educators: A manifesto.* London: University of Buckingham Press.

World Economic Forum (2023), 'Future of jobs report: 2023', https://www3.weforum.org/docs/WEF_Future_of_Jobs_2023.pdf

World Economic Forum (2025), 'Future of jobs report: 2025', https://reports.weforum.org/docs/WEF_Future_of_Jobs_Report_2025.pdf

Young, T. (2014), *Prisoners of the Blob.* London: Civitas.

Youth Sport Trust (2025), 'PE and school sport: The annual report 2025', www.youthsporttrust.org/media/qw5i5s4h/yst_pe_school_sport_report_2025_final.pdf

Index

after-school clubs 124
anchor institutions 113–15
Ardnashee School and College (ASC)'s Learning and Pastoral Pathways model 71–3
assessment 206
   competency progression 195–202
   interdisciplinary qualifications 215–20
   learner profiles 206–14
Atelier 21, founder's mindset at 106
   challenges and successes 109–10
   democratic approach 107
   Learning Mode and Performance Mode 108–9
   learnish 108–9
   project-based learning (PBL) 108
   self-directed learning (SDL) 107
Axford, N. 64

BACs *see* Bedales Assessed Courses (BACs)
banking education 91
Barthakur, A. 208
Bedales Assessed Courses (BACs) 94–6, 216
   challenges and successes 218–19
   of humanities 217
   of outdoor work 217
Bellwood, Claudia 162
Berger, Ron 84
Biesta, G. J. J. 32
Big 8 tools 14, 19
Big Education Diagnostic Tool 52–3
Billington, Michelle 110
booster clubs 124
Bowles, Katie 37
Bransby, Kath 85
Brown, C. 33

Carr Manor Community School, coaching in 63–5
Ciftci, Laura 19–20

citizenship education 114–15, 116
   challenges and successes 117
civic anchor institutions 114, 115
   Fair Fares campaign 117–18
   Radford Primary Academy park campaign 118–19
classroom environment 140–1
clubs 124
coaching 47
   in Carr Manor Community School 63–5
collaboration 45
collaborative pastoral support 67–73
collective wisdom 45
Comino Foundation 81
competency progression 195–202
considered action model 18
constructionism 151
COOL (Choose Our Own Learning) time 141
Cranleigh School, EPQ, HPQ and iPQ programmes at 224–8
creativity 150–3, 185–6
Cubitt Town Primary School, oracy at 174–5

Darwen Aldridge Community Academy, entrepreneurial mindset in 110–12
data 31–2
define phase, Double Diamond model 22–4, 28
DEIB *see* diversity, equity, inclusion and belonging (DEIB)
deliver phase, Double Diamond model 23, 25, 29
democracy 114–15
design thinking 22–3
   challenges and successes 26–7
   Double Diamond model 22–3, 26, 28–9
   Surrey Square, implementation in 24–7
   for tackling teacher workload 27–9

develop phase, Double Diamond model 23, 25, 28
dialogic teaching 167
digital learner profiles 206–11
disciplined innovation 44
discover phase, Double Diamond model 22–3, 24, 28
Divergent Association Task 153
divergent thinking 151, 153
diversity, equity, inclusion and belonging (DEIB) 97–8
  diagnostic tool 100–2, 103
  Ladybridge 102–3
  School 360 98–102
Double Diamond design thinking model 22–3, 26
  teacher workload, tackling 28–9

Edge Foundation 234
educational purpose 77–8, 89–90
Education Endowment Foundation (EEF) 32
Education Forward (Waters) 78
Education - Power - Change (Chapleau) 115
Emmerson, Tony 219
emotional health 123
English College, interdisciplinary courses in 219–20
entrepreneurial spirit (entrepreneurialism) 105–12
Everyday Trivium 80
evidence 31–2
evidence-based practice 32, 44
  challenges and successes 36–7
  classroom inquiry, conducting 34
  lesson study (LS) 37–9
  research engagement 33
  using rich data 34–5
Extended Project Qualification (EPQ) 224

family-style dining 130–1, 133
feedback 19, 25, 47, 48, 49, 53, 54, 55, 57, 62, 174
film-making project 227
founder's mindset 105–6

at Atelier 21 106–9
challenges and successes 109–10
secondary curriculum, development in 110–12
Freire, Paulo 91

Ganz, M. 114
GCSEs 84, 94–6, 215–16
Gill, K. 60
Godfrey, D. 32
Goldsmith, Will 94
Good Morning Programme (GMP) 72–3
Great Teaching Toolkit 48
guided play 140

Hallgarten, Joe 228
Hannay, Jeremy 201
Hanover Primary School, play-based learning in 145–6
Hargreaves, D. 34
health
  challenges and successes 125
  emotional 123
  importance of 121–2
  Manchester Communication Academy (MCA) strategic approach for improving 126–7
  physical 122–3
  play impact on 139–40
  Regulation and Relationships Policy 124
  science 123
  sporting activities 124
Heathcote, Dorothy 177
Hibbin, R. 64
Hiebert, J. 37
Higher Project Qualification (HPQ) 224
high-stakes inspection 51–2
hooks, bell 91

imagination
  importance of 149–50
  iOi's creativity 150–3
  at St Joseph's Primary School 154–5
ImpactEd 63
inclusive curriculum 24

indoor learning 157
    attention and engagement, impact on 158–9
    benefits of 159–60
    challenges and successes 161
    children's self-regulated behaviour 159
    strategies for maximizing 160–1
innovation 44
interdisciplinary qualifications 215–20
International Baccalaureate (IB) 219–20
International Baccalaureate Middle Years Programme (IB MYP) 108
intrinsic motivation 61, 77
iOi's creativity 150–3

Jerounds Primary School, leadership culture at 19–20
journalling 201

Kieran, Richard 182
Kierkegaard, Søren 91
King Alfred School
    assessment system 198–9
    Deeper Learning Wheel 196–9
    Explorations Programme 197, 199
    peer review at 56–7
    reporting system 198–9, 200
    rubrics, use of 198
    skills integration into curriculum 196–201
knowing-doing gap 42

Ladybridge High School, DEIB of 102–3
Ladybridge High School, PBL at 79, 82–3
    challenges and successes 83–4
    'I do, we do, you do' sequence 81
    partnerships 81–2
    'Trivium' philosophy 79–80
leadership 13–14, 113
    challenges and successes 18–19
    connecting as tool for 14–16
    contracting 16
    emotional awareness and regulation 17–18
    responding to questions with a question 17

learner behaviours 61–3
learner profiles 206–9
    challenges and successes 209–11
    at Surrey Square Primary School 211–12
    at Wapping High School 213–14
Learner Profile Starter Kit 210–11
learner's wellbeing 62–3, 67–73, 121–7
    Leuven Scale for 35
    play and *see* play-based learning
Learning and Pastoral Pathways model, ASC's 71–3
learning approaches, continuum of 78
learnish 108–9
lesson study (LS) 37–9
Leuven Scale 35
lunchtime
    allergies, management of 132
    challenges and successes 132–4
    family-style dining 130–1, 133
    food waste 133
    loose parts play approach 132
    packed lunches 132–3
    playtimes during 131, 133
    problem 129–30
    transformation of 130–2

Maker{Cycle} 186–7
    challenges and successes 189–90
    for exploring and combining materials 188–9
    for gathering and generating ideas 188
    stages 187
    St Joseph's Academy, implementation in 191–2
    time as limiting factor for 190
Malaguzzi, Louis 109
Manchester Communication Academy (MCA), health strategies of 126–7
Mantle of the Expert (MoE) 177–81
    challenges and successes 181
    definition 177
    at Woodrow First School 182–3
Mastery Transcript Consortium 206
Mccrea, Peps 50
McFarlane, Debra 191

McFeeters, R. 71
Meet Your Coach Days 64
mentoring 226
MoE see Mantle of the Expert (MoE)
Morden, Matt 211

Open Door Fortnight 48, 49
oracy 99, 130
   on academic outcomes, impact on 167
   assemblies 174–5
   challenges and successes 172–3
   continuous professional development through 171
   at Cubitt Town Primary School 174–5
   curriculum, embedding into 169–71
   definition 166
   peer review of 53, 56
   restorative practice 172
   school council 171–2
   school culture and 171–2
   at secondary school, challenges 173
   teaching and learning 167–8
outdoor learning 158
   attention and engagement, impact on 158–9
   effects of 158–61
   noise and stress level of 158
   at School 360 162–3
Outdoor Play and Learning (OPAL) project 132, 135

'pants-on-the-inside' leadership 14
'pants-on-the-outside' leadership 13
pastoral support 67–73
pastoral team meeting 68
PBL see project-based learning (PBL)
Pear, Nicky 174
peer review 52–4
   challenges and successes 54–6
   duration, reviewing 55
   evaluation and follow-up call 54
   feedback 54, 57
   at King Alfred School 56–7
   of oracy 53, 56
   reviewing by lead reviewer 53

   written summary of observations 54
PEPA see Primary Extended Project Award (PEPA)
performance management 47
physical health 122–3, 150
Pinner Wood's oracy 166
   council meetings with oracy approach 171
   dialogic teaching 167
   progression grid 169–70
   speech night progression 170
   Speech Week 170
   Talking Time poster 169
play-based learning 62
   challenges and successes 141–4
   classroom environment 140–1
   COOL (Choose Our Own Learning) time 141
   at Hanover Primary School 145–6
   outdoor play 141
   play, importance of 139–40
   professional development from 142
   TRAIL (Teachers Reflecting on Agency in Learning) materials for 142–3
   for Year 3 144
playground 134–6
playtimes 131, 133
Plutarch 90
PMMs see Provision Mapping Meetings (PMMs)
Power of Play 152
Primary Extended Project Award (PEPA) 228–9
professional development 41–2, 52, 54, 70, 141, 227
   action (practice change in classroom) 45–6
   aspects of 42
   Big Education's principles of 42–6
   breadth 43
   challenges and successes 46
   collaboration 45
   disciplined innovation 44
   evidence-based practice for see evidence-based practice

from play-based learning 142
pragmatism 43–4
Sandringham Primary School for, lesson study at 37–9
through oracy 171
at Wapping High School 47–50
Professional Development and Coaching (PDC) programme 47
professional growth 47–50
project-based learning (PBL) 62, 79, 99, 111
of Atelier 21's founder's mindset 108
challenges and successes 83–4
to EPQ, HPQ and iPQ programmes 225–8
at Ladybridge High School 79–84
Waldorf curriculum, human approach to 85–7
project model 226–7
Project Trivium 79–80
provision mapping 68–70
challenges and successes 70–1
end-of-year reports 70
eportfolio 70
Golden Week 70
Provision Mapping Meetings (PMMs) 68–9
weekly pastoral team meeting 68
Provision Mapping Meetings (PMMs) 68–9
Puch, Kathryn 134
pupil progress meetings 67
Putnam, Robert 114

randomised control trials (RCTs) 32
real-world learning 90–1, 116
Bedales Assessed Courses (BACs) 94–6
challenges and successes 93–4
horticulture curriculum 91–2
philosophical foundations 90–1
Redriff Primary School, teacher workload in 27–9
Regulation and Relationships Policy 124
research engagement 33, 36

research-informed practice 32
Rethinking Assessment 206–9, 234
Rethinking School project 234
rich data 34–5
'right answer' model 224
Roberts, Tanya 37
role-play 177–83
Rosser, Katy 27

Sanders, Serra 47, 213
Sandringham Primary School, lesson study at 37–9
Schein, E. H. 17
School 21's oracy 166
curriculum 170–1
Oracy Expectations 169
Oracy Triangle 167, 168
restorative practice 172
school council 172
School 360
loose parts play approach 132
lunchtimes in 129–34
outdoor learning in 162–3
outside spaces transformation 134
play-based learning in 139–44
playtimes 131, 133
values 59–60
School 360, DEIB of 98–100
diagnostic tool 100–2
protected characteristics 98, 101
Schools of Tomorrow 234–5
self-directed learning (SDL) 107
self-disclosure 15
Shaw, Tom 63
Shields, Polly 145
skills
importance of 195–6
integration into curriculum 196–201
spirals of enquiry 34
Stigler, J. 37
St Joseph's Academy, Maker{Cycle} implementation at 191–2
St Joseph's Primary School, imagination at 154–5
Stoll, L. 33
'strips activity' technique 33

Surrey Square Primary School 21
  demographic and socio-economic context of 68
  design thinking process of 24–7
  digital portfolio 211–12
  playground development in 134–6

teacher-designed observation tool 36
teacher workload 27–9
Three Bridges Primary, competency progression of 201–2
Timperley, H. 34
tinkering process 34
Tolstoy, L. 19
'Trivium' philosophy of education 79–80

uniform 123–4

values-led relational approach 61–3
van der Vlies, R. 150

video ethnography 201–2
Vincent-Lancrin, S. 150

Waldorf curriculum, PBL at 85–7
Wapping High School
  learner profiles at 213–14
  professional growth at 47–50
Wasielewska, Katarzyna 154
Waters, Mick 78
Watmough, Sue 126
wellbeing *see* learner's wellbeing
Well Schools 235
Wenger, E. 34
Whole Education 235
Woodrow First School, MoE at 182–3
written project 227

Yeung, Takako 56